Smoke Th

The Grand Canyon and the Creation of a New Century

by

Bob Finkbine

To Jessica —
a girl to match
the Canyon —
       Much love,
            "DAD" Fink

Atwell Publishing
Phoenix, Arizona

Smoke That Roars

Finkbine, Bob.
    Smoke that roars : the Grand Canyon and the creation
of a new century / by Bob Finkbine. — lst American ed.

        p. cm.
        Includes bibliographical references and index.
        ISBN 0-9713171-0-0

        1. Grand Canyon (Ariz.)—History. 2. Finkbine,
        Bob—Journeys–Arizona–Grand Canyon. 3. Grand
        Canyon (Ariz.)–Biography. 4. Environmental
        sciences–Philosophy. 5. Environmentalism
        I. Title

        F788.F56 2002   979.1'32
                                         QBI02-701288

The Title: *Mosi—oa—Tunya or Smoke That Roars* is a
Native-American term meaning any roaring or powerful
body of water whether waterfall or rapid that sprays mist
in the air.

The *cover design* is the creative work of artist *Pete Kersten*.
Pete and his brother Rick have run *Kersten Brothers Studio* in
Scottsdale, Arizona for over forty years.

Smoke That Roars chronicles the adventures, dangers, humor and awareness of beauty of private river rafters in the Grand Canyon. In addition, it is a call to arms in defense of an intelligent, non-toxic, recyling, biodegradable and sustainable free market capitalism guided by reverence for the earth. The book advocates a sustainable future as an alternative to continuing degradation of the planet and a holocaust of political hype, over-population, and human misery.

Dedication

Dedicated to those who love to breathe clear air, drink clean water, hike mountains, run wild rivers and know that in the celebration and preservation of wilderness lies the salvation of humanity.

To my family, my daughters Terri, Tracy, Jody and Kristi and sons Mark and Steven. This love of wild places and the earth is your legacy.

To my river sisters and brothers who have shared many wild rapids and starry nights with me. Too numerous to list, you know who you are. Without your companionship and our shared laughter and adventures this work would have never been born and brought to fruition.

To the *Sun Valley Writers' Conference* particularly director Reva Tooley, hosts John and Leslie Maksik, and writers Ridley Pearson, W.P. Kinsella, Naomi Nye, Annie Lamont, Ethan Canin, Mark Salzman, Frank McCourt, Margaret Atwood, Phil Jackson, and Mitch Albom for encouragement and inspiration.

To Karla Payne Elling and the *Arizona State University Creative Writing MBA Program*, especially Professors Jeannine and Norman Dubie, for their expertise and contributions to the evolution of my writing skills.

To Bob Kerry and Bob Rink for photographic contributions.

To Susan and Robert Marley Sr. and also Margie and Robert Marley, Jr., Cindy Gomez, Robert Henschen, Kristi Atwell, Juli Loughrey, Eric Davis, and Tom Martin for invaluable editorial commentary, layout, and proof-reading assistance.

To the memory of **Patchen Miller** and **Tom Pillsbury**.

ACKNOWLEDGMENTS

To the following writers, poets, photographers, painters, and publishers for permission for the use of quotations, photographs, pictures, statistics, poems, songs, and facts. From:

AMERICAN MODERNS: BOHEMIAN NEW YORK AND THE CREATION OF A NEW CENTURY, copyright 2000 by Christine Stansell. Reprinted by permission of Henry Holt & Co., LLC.

ANAPURNA by Maurice Herzog, copyright 1952, re-copyrighted in 1997 by Lyon Press, New York, New York.

A NATURAL HISTORY OF THE SENSES by Diane Ackerman, copyright © 1990, published by Vintage Books, a division of Random House, New York, New York.

BOBOS IN PARADISE: THE NEW UPPER CLASS AND HOW THEY GOT THERE by David Brooks, copyright 2000. A Touchstone Book published by Simon & Schuster, New York, New York.

Cahill, Tom, "A DARKNESS ON THE RIVER," from *OUTSIDE MAGAZINE,* November, 1995, Sante Fe, New Mexico.

DOWNCANYON: A NATURALIST EXPLORES THE COLORADO RIVER THROUGH THE GRAND CANYON by Ann Haymond Zwinger. Copyright © 1995 Ann Haymond Zwinger. Reprinted by permission of the University of Arizona Press.

GALILEO'S DAUGHTER: A HISTORICAL MEMOIR OF SCIENCE, DEATH, AND LOVE by Dava Sobel, copyright © 1999. Reprinted with permission from Walker and Company, 435 Hudson Street, New York, New York 10014, 1-800-289-2553. All rights reserved.

"GOD'S WORLD" by Edna St. Vincent Millay. From *COLLECTED POEMS*, Harper Collins. Copyright 1913, 1941 by Edna St. Vincent Millay.

LEAD US INTO TEMPTATION: THE TRIUMPH OF AMERICAN MATERIALISM by James B. Twitchell, copyright 1999. Published by Columbia University Press.

"MR. TAMBOURINE MAN" - Copyright © 1964, 1965 by Warner Brothers, Inc., copyright renewed 1992 by Special Rider Music.

OUR STOLEN FUTURE by Dr. Theo Colborn and Dianne Dumanoski, and Dr. John Peterson Myers, copyright © 1996 by Dr. Theo Colborn and Dianne Dumanoski, and Dr. John Peterson Myers. Used by permission of Dutton, a division of Penquin Putnam Inc.

"NATURAL CAPITALISM" by Paul Hawkens in *Mother Jones* magazine published by the Foundation for National Progress, San Francisco, California.

NEVER TURN BACK: THE LIFE OF WHITEWATER PIONEER WALT BLACKADAR by Ron Walters, ©1994, available form the Great Rift Press, Pocatello, Idaho, 1-800-585-6857.

ROUGH WATER MAN by Richard E. Westwood, copyright 1992, published by the University of Nevada Press, Reno, Nevada.

STATE OF THE WORLD 2001: A WORLD WATCH INSTITUTE REPORT PROGRESS TOWARDS A SUSTAINABLE SOCIETY, edited by Lester R. Brown, et al. Copyright © 2001 by Worldwatch Institute. Used by permission of W. W. Norton & Company, Inc.

"SUNSTONE" by Octavio Paz, translated by Eliot Weinburger, from *COLLECTED POEMS 1957-1987,* copyright ©1986 by Octavio Paz and Eliot Weinberger. Reprinted by permission of New Directions Publishing Corporation.

THE MARCH OF FOLLY by Barbara Tuchman, copyright 1979 by Barbara Tuchman. Used by permission of Alfred A. Knopf, a division of Random House, Inc.

THE MODERN MIND: AN INTELLECTUAL HISTORY OF THE 20TH CENTURY by PETER WATSON. Copyright 2001 by Peter Watson. Reprinted by permission of HarperCollins Publishers Inc.

THE SPELL OF THE SENSUOUS by David Abram, copyright 1996. Permission granted by Pantheon Books, a division of Random House.

"THE TIMES THEY ARE A CHANGIN'" --Copyright 1963, 1965 by Warner Brothers, Inc., copyright renewed 1992 by Special Rider Music.

THE TWILIGHT OF AMERICAN CULTURE by Morris Berman, copyright 2000. Published by W. W. Norton & Company.

PHOTOGRAPHS

Clarence S. Darrow. Idaho State Historical Society, Boise, Idaho. Accession number 79-2. 117.

General John Burgoyne painted by Sir Joshua Reynolds, COPYRIGHT THE FRICK COLLECTION, NEW YORK.

Lord George Germaine drawn by Dowfield Hardy, permission of the William L. Clements Library, the University of Michigan, Ann Arbor, Michigan.

Sir Douglas Haig, Dead Soldier in Trenches of WW I, Kaiser Wilhelm II from THE AMERICAN HERITAGE BOOK OF WORLD WAR I, permission courtesy of The Imperial War Museum, London.

Ku Klux Klan marching in the 1920s, courtest of Brown Brothers, Stock Photos, Sterline, Pennsylvania.

Table of Contents

Poems

Also by Bob Finkbine

Antietam
Tangled Leaves
Blue Smoke
The Fall of the Gods
Dishonoring Aristotle
Crossroads
Mademoiselle Miss
The Ancient Way
Alcatraz: Don't Follow Me
Ginnie Moon: Confederate Spy

Preface —Searching Coyote Country

I t was a drizzly Friday afternoon in December of 1967. My last American History class of the day was agonizing over their weekly exam at Arcadia High School in Scottsdale, Arizona. I gazed out the window thinking that after school I would do one of two things; get a bottle of wine and write poetry in the orange grove or gather my boys and their friends and play football. Nothing is more fun than football in the rain.

The decision was settled when I arrived home and my sons ran out of the carport clamoring to play ball. We collected the neighborhood gang and were soon hard at it, smeared with mud, on the near-by Hopi Elementary School playground we euphemistically called Hopi Coliseum. On one play, I handed the ball to my youngest son, Steve, and he dodged two bigger boys and ran right over a third at the goal line to score. He raced back out of the end zone with a victorious glint in his eyes. As we ran back up the field to kick off, throwing the ball back and forth between us, that soft,

Steve

warm December rain descending, a rainbow flashed across the sky from one side of the valley to the other. I glanced down and my boy glanced up, our eyes met and held. I could see my image mixed with the rainbow in his eyes and he could see his rainbow image in mine. Filled with unconditional love, I had the momentary sensation that he and I were one being. A surge of energy coursed through me.

Late that night when my wife and five children were asleep, I climbed Camelback Mountain. From the top, I gazed out over the lights of Phoenix and Scottsdale, then looked up at the stars and thin sliver of moon. I lay on my back staring at the Milky Way, reached up and could swear I held a star in my hand. My cells and synapses seem to fuse with atoms light-years away. The star pulsed like a heart beating. I experienced my interconnection to it and the rest of the universe. I was a part of the whole. Filled with euphoria, I was swept into an oceanic flood of unity with creation.

In the ensuing weeks, I entered a delicious insanity. Spontaneous and creative, I taught, coached and parented with tremendous joy, needing only a few hours of sleep a night. I wrote more in a few weeks than I had in the previous five years. Stopping to touch the leaves on a tree or petals of a flower, I discerned a reversibility of perception in which they were watching me at the same moment I was admiring them. Near-by sparrows chattered to me. After jogging, I put my ear against a slender eucalyptus tree in our backyard and it stethoscoped me underground. I could hear seeds burst, roots tendril and worms at work. The tree gently bathed me

Of the land

with oxygen. My senses overlapped and enlivened one another. The scent of orange blossoms, rush of wind, chill of shade, presence of ocotillo and taste of approaching rain symphonized to produce a natural high, an exuberant intensity of being. Colors exploded within me. I loved deeply as if drinking pure water from an inexhaustible spring and felt my blood pulsing in my children's veins. In this interminable cradle of life, I was of the land, fluid song dreaming in burnished notes, colors surrendering themselves, everything I was or meant to be summoned by the glance of a flower or flutter of a bird's wing at dawn.

Crazy, I thought, *I am unbelievingly screaming and stomping mad but in a glorious way.* Although my altered consciousness sang bravely through my writing, I didn't dare tell anyone about it. No one would believe me. They'd think I had gone over the edge. I might as well have told my students to run naked through the orange groves to welcome the Age of Aquarius. My school was located in Barry Goldwater's neighborhood where, even in the late 1960s, some ordinarily intelligent and affluent citizens believed sex education and Beatles music were part of the Communist conspiracy for world domination. They probably had Senator Joseph McCarthy photos on their wall at home next to those of J. Edgar Hoover.

I had some sense of why this extraordinary shift in consciousness had taken place. I loved my family and my teaching. The students at Arcadia were infused with talent. A young Stephen Spielberg made movies and showed them to his fellow students. Linda Carter appeared in numerous high school productions. When she was a Titan senior, pompon girl Margie Murphy helped lead the anti-war attack on the ROTC buildings at Arizona State University. An average class at Arcadia was like an advanced one at other schools. They were exciting and talented kids. If I could get them to visualize historic figures as real, live, paradoxical human beings rather than cardboard stereotypes—people with hemorrhoids, headaches and idiosyncratic quirks often caught in situations without viable options and plagued by vested interests—students could be drawn into the subject. Dates and facts were dogfood. The stories behind the facts were filet mignon wrapped in bacon with ice cream for dessert.

I told them, "Each time your heart beats it's beating you back into history. You know how alive you feel, the hopes and dreams you have, the challenge of a life to live. You know how deeply you can hurt and want and love. Well, they were once just like you. They had their heartaches, colds, flatulence, and indigestion; their courage and their breaking points."

In addition to the satisfaction of teaching, I had just finished a six-year grind to get my M.A. in History at nights and summers at Arizona State. I was in excellent shape. My health was superb. I had dropped beneath my high school football weight and felt I could run forever. The act of running in the dry desert heat gave me energy. I had fallen in love with words and poetry and began writing regularly, achieving insights I didn't fully understand until years later. It seemed as though all of these factors, like separate mountain streams, had come together with enough mass and force to lift me into a transcendental state beyond normal consciousness. It was a magic carpet ride.

The late modern psychologist, Dr. Abraham Maslow researched sustained transcendental consciousness. He detailed his studies of self-actualization and "peak experiences" in his monumental work, *Toward a Psychology of Being*. Later, I was sorry I read the book. Its brilliant analysis took some of the mystique out of my magical wholeness and pinned it to systematic research. Eventually, constrained and repressed by the system, emotionally suffocated by the ordinary and often petty perceptions of those around me, outraged at Vietnam and the assassinations of 1968, I was grudgingly dragged down from my enchanted plateau and was depressed for months. Emotionally wounded, I fell from grace.

I had never learned or been taught to feel myself as a part of nature in any way or interwoven with the world in any form. I had been a city kid.

Yet my unforeseen and unanticipated transcending experience changed me. I became engrossed in the discoveries of the cutting edge of modern science, quantum physics, and how it was formulating a new world view with striking similarities to beliefs held by ancient shaman, Tibetan monks and medicine men.

The shaman's powers could only be sustained by continuous exposure to wild nature, its patterns and hardships, its interweaving between human and nonhuman nature. The earth is the sustaining womb of the lifeworld. It is the encompassing ark, the root of all life. Subatomic research, through the scientific study of the particle/waves of atoms, molecules and the intricate complexity of cells, bones and brains, shows we are interwoven with all other life forms. In short, at the subatomic level, we are part and parcel to everything

The sustaining womb

else in creation. Geneticists have unraveled molecular codes revealing that microbes, salamanders and apes are our common ancestors. We share more than 98 percent of our genes with chimpanzees, sweat fluids reminiscent of seawater and crave sugar that provided our ancestors with energy three billion years before the first hominoid crouched upright. We carry our past with us. Evolution tells us a story of our emergence from the long lineage of a miraculous, convoluted, tremored, quivering life force recreating itself as it interactively adjusted to the ever-changing conditions of environmental factors.

Wisdom is the deep realization of our nature *as* nature. It is a mindfulness of our co-emergence with the elements, the sea and atmosphere, cellular life and sunlight, plants and animals within the evolutionary process. Thousands of years ago, through meditation, Buddhist monks uncovered the basic principles of subatomic physics. They believed there is no solidity anywhere, the observer cannot be separated from what is observed, phenomena seem to appear out of emptiness, everything affects everything else in a co-emergent system and nothing can be separated from anything else: wave-particle, space-time, matter-energy. Our bodies are composed of the same elements as the earth—carbon, nitrogen, oxygen, sulfur and minerals. Our bones are made of calcium phosphate, the clay of the earth molded into human shape. Our blood is also the earth's blood, the salty waters of the ocean infused with fire and pushed through our veins.

Thich Nhat Hanh, a Buddhist Monk explained, "As I look more deeply, I can see that in a former life I was a cloud. And I was a rock. This is not poetry; this is science. This is not a question of a belief in reincarnation. This is a history of life on earth."

Ghosts live inside us that are much older than our great-great-great-great grandparents. They are the ghosts of our biological past. We are inhabited by the earth itself, its cellular life, the ancestor animals that forged their haphazard way towards our own existence. As Jack Kerouac expressed it in his *Visions of Cody,* "The eye bone's connected to the air bone, the air bone's connected to the sky bone, the sky bone's connected to the angel bone, the angel bone's connected to the god bone, the god bone's connected to the bone bone."

I introduced the concept of environmental unity into my classes based on the latest findings of subatomic physics. Quoting the marvelous poet and paleontologist Loren Eiseley, I pointed out that the evolution of the angiosperm (encased seed) made possible the rise of flowering grasses and plants which, in turn, coaxed life inland from the water's edge and laid the foundation of the age of mammals. I concluded, "So in a way flowers and flowering grasses are our ancestors and modern society blinds us to this fact. Do you ever think of this when you see a field of wildflowers? Our subatomic particles are matter/energy that is indestructible. So where have our sub quantum particles been the last few million years? Is it possible that a portion of us was once part of a cliff, a tree, a patch of lichen, a weed or a mountain lion? What's going to happen to these infinitely small particles after we die? Do we have a deeper and closer relationship to nature than our society conditions us to perceive?"

Ancestor grasses

I remember the wary eyes, scratching of heads, skeptical looks when I tried to introduce adolescents to what seemed to them off-the-wall ideas before the rise of our current degree of ecological consciousness. I probably had as much success then, however, as I would now competing with Nintendo, the Simpsons, body piercing, rappers, raves, gang bangers, the Internet and the shopping mall mystique of acquisition and possession.

The author teaching at Arcadia High School in the 1960s.

It's difficult to get anyone outside their societal conditioning to the place where they will attain a perspective encouraging them to adopt a lifestyle based on radically different values. Society would rather kill their prophets than change the status quo. Through my extraordinary peak experience I had gained a glimpse of another reality. In truth, I felt schizophrenic as I shifted back and forth from conventional societal norms and my poetic oneness with existence. Each one seemed crazy from the other perspective.

One night, after taking my kids to a movie, we dropped by Farrell's for ice cream before heading home. I heard a familiar voice in the booth next to us. It was Suzie, one of my students, and she was telling her friends, "Talk about crazy! Wow! I've got this American History teacher who wants us to find a tree we like, introduce ourselves to it, taste it, feel it, commune with it for an hour, and then write a paper on our true relationship with trees. He wants us to thank it for giving us oxygen or fruit. Talk about fruits, man, they are going to come with their white coats, burst into class, ram him into a straight jacket, and drag him down to the loony bin."

On my way out, I poked my head in their booth and said, "Why, hi there, Suzie. What a surprise. Having a night out with your friends. That's great. I sure hope you did your homework first. You know I might call on you tomorrow to handle one of the answers or maybe read your tree essay."

Then there was the principal, reinforced by the two vice principals and the department chairman, faces glowering, tapping his finger on one of my study guides demanding to know what the concept of environmental unity had to do with American History. Real history was facts, dates, presidents, wars and the cherry tree, okay? Even though I knew I was right, I felt shame and fear at not fitting in, not being a *member of the team,* misunderstood, rejected and threatened. Somehow it all seemed my fault. Why didn't I perceive reality like normal people?

Even submerged in the demands of daily life, my new roots to the land had begun to tendril down inside me. More and more, I found myself

6

taking my children out into the desert, up in the mountains, down rivers, out into splendid scenery: the Sawtooth, White Cloud, High Sierra, Superstition, Chiricahua and Sierra Ancha mountains; the Middle Fork,

Idaho's Sawtooth Mountains

Main Salmon, Selway, Rio Grande, Yampa, Green and Upper Salt rivers. Loving wild places, I did nine- to 15-day solo trips in the Bighorn Crags, San Juan Mountains and Wind River Range. As the years passed, our ultimate outdoor adventure became our 18- to 24-day trips covering 225 to 279 miles on the Colorado River through the Grand Canyon.

The Grand Canyon possesses an environment unlike any other on the face of the earth. If you hike in or out from the North Rim you traverse a billion years of geological history and travel six of the seven life zones and vegetational communities of North America. You can climb from burning deserts to the sight of volcanic peaks nearly 13,000 feet high. The journey into the Canyon provides geological insight into the structure of the earth's outer shell and contains some of the oldest exposed rock, 2.2 billion-year-old Vishnu Schist. From this ancient metamorphic rock the canyon rises to 245 million-year-old Kaibab

The haunting beauty of the Grand Canyon

7

Limestone at the rim. The cutting and sculpturing of the canyon took place only five to 20 million years ago. Hell's Canyon in Idaho, Copper Canyon in Mexico, Colca Canyon in Peru or the Yarlung Tsangpo Gorge of Tibet are deeper, but none provide such a miraculous combination of depth, length, size and extent. Nowhere else can you see such an immensity and magnificent array of pyramids, temples, escarpments, monoclines, alcoves, side canyons, plateaus, pillars and distant rims with so little evidence of the presence of man.

It's difficult to imagine that the ancestral Grand Canyon was for 300 million years a flat illimitable featureless plain covered five separate times by the sea. In its striated layering can be seen white sandstone from beaches, red shale and mud from swamps, and cream and tan limestone from deeper water.

> *"The Grand Canyon is an unparalleled wonder unique thoughout the entire world."*
> . . . *Theodore Roosevelt*

This endless plain was located south of the equator and rotated 90 degrees. What now faces west once pointed north. The now separate continents were geographically joined in a super landmass called Pangea. This was at the close of the explosion of life marking the Paleozoic Era 570 to 245 million years ago. Near the end of this geological period occurred a mass extinction that destroyed 90 percent of the existing marine invertebrates and led to the rise of dinosaurs in Mesozoic time.

Continental drift rotated the area carrying it through a succession of tropical rainforests and sandy deserts to its present position. Here, the lifting up began 65 million years ago with the slow grinding of tectonic plates in the Laramide Orogeny. I stand on the rim listening to the wind sound like the waves of ancient oceans. I think how I would only be halfway out of the canyon in time past. The same erosion that has helped cut the depths of the Grand Canyon, has also stripped away younger rocks that once lay above the current rim. If those rocks had not been worn away, roughly another mile of cliffs and terraces would lie above me. They have not vanished completely. Standing on the rim facing north they can be seen as successive banks of multicolored cliffs rising behind the wall of the North Rim: the Vermilion, Chocolate, White, Gray and Pink Cliffs of the Grand Staircase. A mile above the desert in the high plateaus of southwestern Utah, the surface of the Colorado Plateau comes face to face with the present.

I especially treasure our off-season trips, after the commercial firms have closed down, when we see few other rafters or backpackers and glide gratefully into the silence and majestic solitude surrounding us. Then, more than any other time, we immerse ourselves in the seclusion of side hikes, giant rapids, inspiring scenery and explore tucked-away magical places like Elves Chasm, Thunder River, Matkatamiba or Sinyala canyons. We shed our city selves and reach to touch our roots intertwined with stone and spawned millions of years ago.

The beauty of the Grand Canyon: Thunder River

In 1903, President Theodore Roosevelt camped at the bottom of the Canyon near Bright Angel Creek at the site that later became Phantom Ranch. He left us an ecological treasure of his thoughts. After describing the Canyon as an unparalleled wonder unique throughout the world, he admonished Americans not to build in it or change it in any way, so it remained in all of its splendor for our children, grandchildren, and their children down through the ages. The President asserted, "We have gotten past the stage, my fellow citizens, when we are to be pardoned if we treat any part of our country as something to be skinned for two or three years for the use of the present generation, whether it be the forest, the water, the scenery."

I wonder what Teddy would think today of the clear cutting, pollution, toxicity and degradation of the planet for immediate profit that has taken place in the face of his well-intended advice? I wonder how he, Ronald Reagan, George Bush Jr. and James Watt would have gotten along on a 24-day rowing trip in small rafts through the extent of the Canyon? Would ketchup count as a vegetable for their lunches? Heck, if you've seen one rock formation, you've seen them all. Isn't there oil down here someplace?

I devour miles, driving north into color differentials, desolate buttes, shadowed monuments, ridges where spirits walk and curse the trail of tears. I pass hogans, ocotillo fences, road signs with bullet holes, telephone poles, future archeological finds and stratified escarpments pocked with uranium mines and pilfered ruins; the 21st century stealing pottery, exhuming bones, building warheads, intransigent, victorious. Sick of cities,

9

I watch the miles slip away listening to African chanted songs on the stereo, searching coyote country for a way to see myself through my own eyes.

I am driving north to Lees Ferry, truck loaded with rafts, frames, straps, oars, paddles, personal dry bags, rocket boxes, medical kits, packed ice chests, water purifiers, an emergency radio, old river buddies and innumerable cases of beer. Rolling along the highway, we anticipate running rapids, hiking side canyons, sipping cocktails at happy hours, telling stories, cooking outdoors and sleeping under starry skies framed by canyon walls.

The ensuing stories grew out of my love for the Grand Canyon, a tribute to its splendor, an attempt to write of a majesty that cannot be captured by words alone. Perhaps, like tiny invertebrate shells drifting down to ocean bottoms to become limestone, these thoughts will become a portion of the accruement of public resolve needed to safeguard our natural birthright for the generations that follow us through the mists of history and the repeated cycles of birth and death.

Come, come with me on a storyteller's journey through the Grand Canyon, a journey of words along a river into the temple depths of time.

Slamming whitewater at Hermit Rapids

Part I — Stories From the River

My most restless nights, outside of camping above Crystal Rapid or Lava Falls, have been those spent at Lees Ferry. Lying in an alcove of tamarisk trees above the beach strewn with equipment and partially rigged rafts, keyed with anticipation, I yearn for dawn and the start of another adventure through the Canyon.

Tamarisk or salt cedar is a deciduous tree that grew from the Mediterranean up to Northern China. It was used as off shore windbreaks and for dyes as well as its medicinal properties. The tree was brought in from Asia for erosion control and has taken over beaches and bottom lands. On a solo float through the sluggish waters of the Green River between Split Mountain and Sand Wash, I found mile after mile where I couldn't land because the invader had grown into a solid barrier. Attacked constantly by biting flies and mosquitoes housed in the trees, I rowed all night under a full moon. I was slapping insects and cursing the whole way down to meet boaters for a Gray-Desolation Canyon run.

Tamarisk

Tamarisk entered Marble Canyon about 1925. Its long taproot and ability to unleash massive amounts of tufted, airborne seeds make it an insatiable colonizer. It can withstand inundation for up to a month and low water for several years. In summertime it is home to vast colonies of insects and provides a fast food stop for migratory birds. Although in the Grand, I occasionally see beaches where we once camped covered with tamarisk, it hasn't taken over canyons with swift flowing water and rapids the way it has the slow, flat portions of other rivers.

Lees Ferry is the only place for hundreds of miles up or downstream where the Colorado can be approached without a descent into a sheer and nearly impassible canyon. It was also the only place where the river could be reached from both sides. Mormon explorer Jacob Hamblin discovered the crossing in 1860. Jacob, often called the "buckskin apostle," had two white and two Paiute wives. He learned several native dialects, was fair to the Native Americans, seldom showed fear and had a slow way of talking that appealed to the Indians. He acted as a diplomat to the tribes in times of tension.

Hamblin later told John Doyle Lee how to find the crossing. Lee, a fugitive from federal authorities for his part in the Mountain Meadows Massacre, established a small farm and ferry in the fall of 1871, using one of Major John Wesley Powell's boats that had been stored there for the winter. Lee was eventually tried and shot for his part in the massacre, a unique Mormon version of the mass paranoia that periodically strikes Americans as it did in seventeenth century Salem in the witchcraft trials, in the "Big Red Scare" of 1919-1920 and in the rabid McCarthyism of the 1950's. It is currently evident in neo-Nazi militia and other hate groups of today's lunatic fringe. Even now Lees Ferry has the only road to the river for launching boats between Glen Canyon and Diamond Creek 225 miles downstream.

Groover demonstration: No urine allowed

After morning coffee, bagels and lox, we get checked out by the ranger. Some are real sticklers. One woman would find tiny tears in some of our life jackets and rip them open declaring them inadequate for the trip. Then there are good old boys who know that we know that they know that we know what we are doing. One big-bellied fellow with a "If it flies, it dies" bumper sticker informed us, "I don't know what this fuss is about condors. They ain't nothing but extra big buzzards."

I hang out with the gear while the group takes in the orientation presentation at the trailer just down the road. No urine in the groovers and don't tease rattlesnakes plus a slide of a jackalope are the great lessons learned. The latest buzzword is *microtrash*. If you leave little bits of food waste around, here come the ants, then the scorpions, then the lizards, then the mice and then the rattlesnakes. So beware! There's the final loading and double tying down of personal bags followed by our impatient traditional total group expedition photo.

Then comes the exhilaration of those first oar strokes away from the beach and the thrill when the current catches the raft and whirls it towards the left bank and downstream.

Usually, the river is clear at the launch, an icy emerald green so translucent that it is easy to watch the bottom rocks as the craft glides over them and accelerates into the first ripples. There's a sensation of flying as the variegated

Exhilaration of those first strokes

riverbed races by beneath the raft. On the river, I feel a rising elation so familiar yet brand-new each time as we head out for the entire length of the Canyon.

This section of the trip enters Marble Canyon. Major Powell named it on his initial exploration. After mentioning cutting through sandstones and limestones, he wrote about drifting through a great bed of marble a 1000 feet in thickness. "In this," he continued, "great numbers of caves are hollowed out, and carvings are seen which suggest architectural form, though on a scale so grand that architectural terms belittle them. As this great bed forms a distinct feature of the canyon, we call it Marble Canyon."

Marble Canyon is not really marble but 245 to 400 million-year-old Paleozoic Redwall Limestone. It is the raised portion of an ancient seabed laid down before the age of dinosaurs, rock made by life itself. As microscopic organisms died, their calcium shells sifted slowly to the bottom, accumulating at the rate of one meter every 100,000 years. Five geological layers are revealed in the first 21 miles of river and it is fascinating to think that those sheer walls towering higher and higher above us used to be ocean bottoms, seashores, sand dunes, and river deltas. Even the tip of still-rising Mount Everest is marine limestone that once lay at the bottom of the Indian Ocean.

As we drift along, I think of what lies ahead. Soon we'll hit our first taste of whitewater at Badger and Soap Creek rapids. Their names came from Jacob Hamblin. He killed a badger in the first stream and hauled it down to the next drainage where he made camp and put the animal in a pot of water over a fire to make stew. When he awoke the next morning,

Upper hole at House Rock, 18,000 cfs

Hamblin found he had a kettle of soap from the mix of alkaline water and badger fat. Badger and Soap Creek rapids, like most in the Canyon, were formed by flash floods washing boulders out into the main stream.

Sixteen miles down-river we used to slam the upper hole at House Rock and take the giant lower hole almost head-on, a crash-bang warm up for larger and more difficult runs later on. There, a massive wave at the bottom twists to the right. A boatman taking the brunt of its force needs to over-compensate by turning left of center and having his passenger ready to high side left. On the beach in the eddy across the river, we have towed in and

Up and over

righted numerous capsized boats that failed to make this adjustment.

House Rock casualty

Typically, rapids change at different water levels or by rocks shifting over time. At a slightly higher cycle of 12,000 to 19,000 cubic feet per second (cfs.), the upper hole in House Rock has become enormous. It has a hidden lateral swelling from beneath the left side. After a flip, swimmers are often carried through the infamous lower hole. Stubborn, I flipped in the upper hole on three consecutive trips still trying to take it head on. On the ensuing trip, I got so far to the right, I relaxed at the oars, was swept left, and suddenly found myself facing a great wall of water in the lower hole. *Oh, my Lord,* I thought, *not a fourth straight time.* But with Dana and Kelly, the "Texas seesters," as we called them, hanging it all out in front and me bracing with every ounce of my might, we rode out a tremendous hit. Now, like most sane river runners, I skirt right on the outside of the wave train avoiding the instant shock of cold water and inconvenience of righting and re-rigging the craft.

The spunky runs and beauty of a ten-mile stretch of rapids known as the "Roaring Twenties," follows. At Mile 22 lies Indian Dick Rapid. Legend says the phallic tower of Supai sandstone at the right of the white-water was named for an Indian, Richard, who kept lonely ladies company while their boyfriends and husbands

Indian-Dicked

worked on the river. In reality, two geologists who flipped there in 1955, christened it after a turbulent swim. Looking at the raised stone tower, the name Indian Dick came to them in a moment of inspired insight. We had gathered a congenial group for our October trip in 1992. Sadly, there was one exception. Eighteen days can be an eternity when one person can't fit in and get along. As often as not the person is male, but in this case it was a woman who wheedled other boaters into carrying her gear, setting up her tent, holding her portable shower and rubbing lotion on her back. Amply endowed, she tried to substitute sex appeal for genuine interaction with the group. We nicknamed her, "Her Highness." The second day out she was sitting in the front of my 16-foot Achilles telling me how sensuous the Canyon was. She emphasized the word sensuous by thrusting forward her life-jacketed breasts and licking her lips. "Yes, the canyon is so *sensuous.* The rock forms are *sensuous* because they are feminine. The contrasting and complementary colors stimulate the *senses*. Oh, it's so *sensuous* here, don't you agree?" As she said *sensuous* for the twelfth time giving an extra special chest thrust, the phallic rock column by the rapid came into view and seemed to rise out of the center of her head. I laughed and laughed.

"What's so funny?" she asked.

"Oh, it's just that everything is so *sensuous*," I said. We finally chipped in and paid one of the boatmen to make out with "Her Highness" and, as much as possible, keep her away from the rest of the group.

A month later, I was down with another trip, four of us running an eleven-foot Aire Puma paddle raft through the rapid when the initial right side lateral roared towards us. High-siding to anticipate the impact, we leaned right to absorb the blow when the wave inexplicably died and we fell in and were washed away. Stupidly, we had Indian-dicked ourselves. If I could have re-christened the rapid at that point it would still have the same name.

Buried at Mile 24

In 1989, we were excited when the ranger, Tom Workman, told us rocks had shifted and created a new rapid at Mile 24. The first time I hit straight over the main drop, it folded the raft in two and launched it clear of the water. My youngest son was crunched between the front of the raft and the frame. Luckily, his yogic and tai 'chi limberness saved him from broken bones. One girl in another boat severely wrenched her back. We thought she would have to be evacuated, but painkillers, a massage therapist and an acupuncturist kept her on the river. It pays to have expertise woven into your group. The rocks have shifted now and that straight drop is not as formidable as it was initially. It has been renamed Georgie Rapid after the noted big rig boatwoman of the Colorado, Georgie White.

In October of 1999, I led the way into Mile 24.5 Rapid. I had the wrong perspective and discovered I was trying to pull left of the left ledge hole instead of getting to the right of it. There was nothing to do but square up and take it head on. The impact stood my 14-foot Momentum straight up. Adrenaline and elation churned together as we crashed on through. *What a wonderful life,* I thought, *even mistakes are fun.*

I allowed the bottom lateral in Mile 25 Rapid to sneak up on me in 1991. My Achilles went straight up on its left tube throwing my 21-year-old daughter, Kristi, and myself out into the chilling current. I looked up and could see the raft start to come over on top of me. It hesitated past perpendicular and bounced back right side up, avoiding by a fraction of an inch the

Up on edge and almost over

struggle to run down a flipped raft, tow it to shore, get it back over and re-tie everything before continuing on. We were lucky. That's one I owed the river. Since then, I've paid the debt a number of times.

At the end of the "Roaring Twenties" we stop at South Canyon. The center of interest is a climb up into a cave that appears to end but then crevices through to a chamber and ledge perched 400-feet above the canyon's narrow, winding floor. Crawling through the slot, I feel like I'm in an *Indiana Jones* movie. Sitting on the ledge in June of 1986, we heard donkeys braying or goats bleating. Clambering down to investigate, we found the raucous noise came from tiny frogs the size of a half-dollar. Their procreation time is limited so they have been endowed with bellowing

voices to attract mates. Although indecipherable to the human ear, each frog has a distinctive voice to tell its prospective partner what pool it is in. Their resounding cries are soon translated into strings of fertilized eggs some of which hatch in two days. The tadpoles quiver as they voraciously tug at algae, and

At the "Indiana Jones" Cave

some types even cannibalize their brethren to survive and carry the gene pool forward.

These spade-footed toads are an epitome of how creatures adjust to

17

extreme climates and they fill me with awe at the diversity and mutability of life. They have a wedge-shaped attachment on each back foot. Instinct tells them when it's time to dig down about 24 inches under a shrub and secrete a fluid that forms a cocoon around them. Protected, they hibernate through the inferno season until the rains come. Instinctively, they awake, break out of their shield, dig their way to the surface and call for mates. Life clings so tenaciously to this planet that each multiform kind is a marvel inviting reverence.

The "Indiana Jones Cave" is to the left of some Anasazi ruins. Sitting there, I attempt to get my mind around the lives of the Anasazi, the people who were in the South Canyon area a 1000 years ago. There is little evidence of permanent settlement such as ceremonial kivas or burial sites. The ruins were probably the temporary camps of hunters and gatherers inhabited when prickly pear fruit ripened or ricegrass was ready to be harvested, when Mormon tea and mallow were ripe. Fifty to 80 percent of their nourishment came from plants, a more dependable source of food than animals. Many grasses, amaranth, yucca and mesquite also grew there. Grasses were an important part of their diet, especially dropseed that has easy-to-harvest, hull-less, long-lived seeds and ricegrass with its tiny, nourishing black seeds.

Everyone shared in gathering food and divided what they had gleaned. This meant food for those too old or too young to gather. It preserved the tribal elders' knowledge of plants and animals and insured the survival of a new generation. Yucca furnished fibers for the weaving of sandals and baskets. It also gave them saponin, a steroid, from which they made soap for washing. They trapped mice, squirrels, bats, birds and various insects. Higher up towards the rim, bighorn sheep were hunted. In areas near Nankoweap and Unkar they grew beans, squash and corn. In poor years, they faced starvation. It was a high-risk lifestyle that required a great amount of mobility to survive. Their prehistoric diet with less fat, more vitamins, greater variety and without pesticides was healthier than a modern one. Today, diabetes emasculates many tribes. The ancient seeds and grains released sugar more slowly into the bloodstream than modern processed foods.

Their pharmacies grew wild. The Anasazi used plants that put them to sleep and others that increased their supply of energy. They gathered roots that induced dreams, sap for healing and items deemed sacred for prayer bundles. About a quarter of modern pharmaceuticals were derived from wild plants well known to prehistoric peoples. Willows growing along the river contain salicin, a compound chemically close to acetylsalicylic acid (aspirin) whose alleviating effects were also utilized by the ancient

Greeks and Romans.

Just downstream, 150-feet up in Redwall limestone, fronted by a vaulted symmetrical arch, is Stanton's Cave. Robert Brewster Stanton was the chief engineer for the Denver, Colorado Canyon and Pacific Railroad. In 1889, he was sent to survey a railroad route along the river. Either ignorant of the force of the rapids or trying to cut cost, the leader of the group, Frank M. Brown, neglected to bring life preservers. He conveniently blamed this oversight on a lack of warning from Major Powell. They portaged Badger and Soap Creek rapids, but when Brown tried to row backwards through the tail waves at Soap Creek, his round-bottomed, unstable boat flipped and he drowned in a whirlpool. Stanton took control and the work continued. Three days later, Peter Hansborough and Henry Richards drowned in swift water at Mile 25. That night a ferocious storm raged up Marble Canyon and, realizing the dangers of the task ahead and the incomparable fury of nature, Stanton cached his supplies in the cave now bearing his name and led the group out by way of South Canyon.

Stanton completed the survey the following year but failed to convince railroad investors that the project was feasible. It was fitting that he made the attempt. One way human progress was measured in that age was through the conquest of natural barriers by railroads, bridges, tunnels and canals. Later would come the skyscrapers and dams.

Making only the eleventh trip through the Canyon in 1934, Bus Hatch entered Stanton's Cave on July 19. He discovered split-twig figurines of deer and bighorn sheep. Radiocarbon dating places their creation around 4,000 years ago. It was the earliest evidence of human habitation in the Canyon. The figures, often seeming alive in the slant of a head or twist

Stanton's Cave

of a leg, were created by splitting a long, slender, willow twig almost to the end and, with delicate bending and winding, creating a four-legged figure. Sometimes a small, pointed stick pierces the figure. These figurines fit the pattern called ritual deposition, a ceremonial use of caves by nomadic, pre-pottery and pre-agricultural peoples. Also found in the cave were the bones of an extinct camel and those of a giant teratorn, *Teratornis merriami*, a monsterous bird with a 12-foot wingspan, thought to be the ancestor of the California condor. Condors, however, are in the vulture family, while teratorns have their own distinct grouping. Its bones lay sealed in a wood rat midden, enabling them to be carbon-dated at about 15,000-years-old. Condors were birds so large it took almost a year to incubate and fledge a single one. Prospectors supposedly shot the last one in 1881, but they have been reintroduced and sail the sheer red walls again.

In the spring of 2001, we saw them riding the thermals above Marble Canyon. Around Mile 14 we were surprised to see one perched on a rock about ten feet above us on river right. The giant creature remained immovable and paid us no heed. With its turtleneck sweater look, thick neck and grotesque beak, the bird seemed an eerie apparition from the past. As we passed by I spotted a large white "34" on the side of the creature. I said to Dana, my passenger, "Gee, I didn't know they had a team."

Immediately around the bend from the cave lies Vasey's Paradise, a breathtaking panorama of water pouring down over rock through green gardens of water crest and poison ivy. This is the only place in the Canyon where an underground limestone cave, lake and stream channel system opens directly on the river. We usually fill our water jugs here. It's easier than filtering it through a Katadyn pump. Rangers had warned us that tests

have shown that harmful organisms have been found in the normally pure underground water reservoir, a sign of the impact of man in isolated and pristine places. We remain in denial and still drink directly from Vasey's as well as use its watercress for salads. On a trip in 1996, a New Age girl named Nancy ignored our warnings and tramped all through the shrubbery at Vasey's and ended up with itchy poison ivy bumps all over her legs.

Vasey's Paradise

They drove her wild. Steve, my acupuncturist son, tried to cure her with his ancient practices and needles.

I was incredulous. "Damn it," I said, "just scrub her with strong soap, put some alcohol on it, then cover the ivy with calamine lotion. That will take care of it. It'll dry it out and she'll get rid of it." No one paid any attention to my advice. Several days later, Steve was still using needles and the bumps, some of them blistered, were still there.

One of his close friends, Joy-U, told me, "Your son has won a lot of money off of me in dominos and cribbage."

I replied, "Well, he needs to supplement his income. I mean, he can't make a living in acupuncture. Why, he can't even cure poison ivy."

Steve looked up from tending Nancy and said, "Well, Dad, there's a lot of things I can't cure with acupuncture. Like in your case—senility, vulgarity and inflation of the ego." Everyone laughed at me. I mused, *I hate it when they are too old to spank.*

The attitude we try to inculcate on our trips is exemplified by a story about a fellow river rat, Doctor Tim, a public health physician. With his Irish face squinted and jaw firm, Tim was captaining a paddle raft in Cataract Canyon through giant waves into the high water fury of Big Drop III. With its legendary rapids, Cataract was called the graveyard of the Colorado. Although only 40-miles long, its rapids drowned more boaters in the early days of river running than the 280 miles of the Grand Canyon. Dr. Tim raised up to check his run over the swollen crests and saw his raft was headed right into the boiling center of the hole located next to Satan's Gut, a narrow water bridge between two ledge drops growling like the gates of hell. Angrily, the current pulled them down like a fierce claw, too late to shift direction and avoid their fate. Paddling like mad in the front of the raft, Pat McCormick yelled, "Tim, how's our line?"

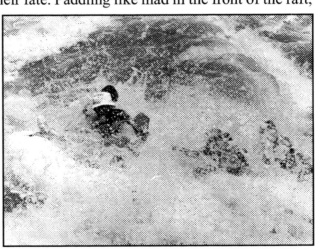

"Perfect."

Bouncing on the back of the bucking bronc Avon, staring into the eyes of oblivion, Doc screamed back, *"Perfect!"*

Five seconds later the raft flipped, breaking Dr. Tim's wrist and scattering people across the furious water like ten pins.

Freezing sleet storms, icy flips in pounding water, sand storms stinging eyes, wind blowing away tents, changes in water level leaving rafts stranded on the beach, nothing left to eat but Oreos and mayonnaise, lightning and thunder cracking down, rock falls, sitting on scorpions, sleeping with snakes. How's life on the river?

PERFECT. YOU'RE ON THE RIVER.

No whining allowed!

Drums and Smoke

Sitting cross-legged around our fire,
we have fled the city and come to the desert
to bury one year and birth another.
Blanched alkali flats stretch to the feet
of volcanic ridges. Creosote and sage
straggle across the plain.

Bones grumble in burial grounds,
marrow dried in days when buffalo grass
grew into children, when wolves,
wreathed in smoke, stalked campfiress
in the graveled voices of grandfathers.

The heart of the earth beats in our drums;
the flute trills a succession of harsh notes,
shek-shik-jaaeg, shek-shek-jaaeg,
cry of a shrike striking its prey;
pebbled gourds rattle the quick coil
and s-curve of a diamondback's neck.

Boom, boom, beat, boom, boom,
shakes the sacred ground, bones protrude,
rise and semble into forms clothed
in the flesh of memory.
Tangled in the drums and rising scale
of flute song, furious tick-tick-tack-tic
of rattles, ancient warriors stamp
and bow and arrow across moonlit flats.

We stare into smoldering coals
and see the burdens of the past,
people who were here first
and thought they would stay forever.

River People

We refer to ourselves as "River People." We were given this sobriquet on an Upper Salt Canyon trip in 1986 when Charlie, a young man in our party, fell off a boulder and cracked his head. By the time we got him immobilized and on the raft, floated down and set up camp, it was dark. He was semi conscious and we didn't want to take chances with a head injury so one of our boatmen jogged out and radioed in a rescue helicopter. Camp was a war zone. We built a huge bonfire and had orange panels out in a giant X on a landing spot to guide the pilot in. Around midnight, we heard the rotor blades throbbing down canyon and the pilot set the chopper down with wind and sand flying everywhere. A physician holding a black leather bag hopped out and hurried over to where the injured boy was lying with his head in the lap of his girlfriend. She was trim and had lovely close-cropped dark hair, her attractive face creased with worry.

The doctor had barely begun examining Charlie's eyes with a pencil-thin light when the girlfriend blurted out, sobbing and crying and trying to talk at the same time, "I was his father's mistress for five years and then we realized we were in love and we ran away together and this is our *first* trip together and *look* what *happened*."

The doctor looked up and stared at the girl. Then he turned his head and glared at all of us in obvious disgust. "River people!" he growled, shaking his head.

We accursed "River People" certainly have our rowdy, anything goes times, but we also like the quiet and mystic sites of the Canyon as much as we love happy hour or the roller coaster thrills of the rapids. After South Canyon, we enter gentler water with only one rapid in the next 40 miles.

The Malgosa Crest

Yet, anticipation remains keen. This section, among other points of

*Looking up from the base of
the Malgosa Crest*

interest, includes climbing the Malgosa Crest, a visit to Bert Loper's boat, toiling upwards to the ruins and our Meditation Cave at Nankoweap, a terrific loop hike between Nankoweap and Kwagunt canyons, looking over the cliff face straight down into Unkar Rapid and exploring Anasazi ruins scattered throughout the Unkar Delta.

In April of 2001, we pushed 20 miles each of the first three days so we could lay over at Kwagunt Canyon and tackle the Malgosa Crest. All but one of the select crew planning to go for the top had extensive technical climbing experience. Bob Kerry had written books on climbs throughout southern Arizona. He is an indefatigable and intensely curious hiker, often exploring side ledges and caves that might reveal interesting artifacts. Chris Roley and Steve Tweito had been all over the map and back again. Steve Bambina is a thin, mean, climbing machine and Mike Stamps had climbed spires and famed landmarks throughout the Canyon. You have to watch Stamps, however. Hiding behind a beneficent smile, he is the acknowledged greatest joke poacher ever to row the Grand. If participants aren't careful, they will hear all their best laughs doled out at happy hour before they get a chance to use them. Sure, now, there ought to be a law but there isn't and he's busy stealing the best stories night and day. We've tried duct tape but he's a ventriloquist.

*Mike Stamps, harmless-
looking joke poacher,*

I was the one non-technical, scramble climber in the group, the nerdy chubby boy in films who wants to tag along with the gang. Totally against their better judgment, they let me come on the climb. I had just turned 70 and had more excess flesh on my body than the rest of them put together.

The location of our camp was at an

elevation of 2,730 feet in a layer of Bright Angel Shale. Our goal was the crest at 5,313 feet, a gain of 2,583 perpendicular feet. Right from the first step, the way up through Muav into Redwall Limestone was steep, the kind of loose scree where you take one step forward and slide two back hitting a cactus or two in the process. As we toiled upward, I was continually gulping air and falling behind the others. They exhibited unbelievable patience waiting for me to catch up. From a high notch, we started into a climb through a narrow upward gap into the Supai Group consisting of layers of sandstone, shale, and conglomerate to reach the high base of dark red Hermit Shale that the crest rests on. Stopping again to suck air into my lungs, I was standing on what appeared to be a large, solid rock when it suddenly gave way. I rolled down the slope, then dropped six feet over an edge, bounced on my back on a hard rock ledge and rolled some more through cactus and loose scree. When I hit the ledge, I was slammed, in my mind, back into a college football game. All I could think of was that I had taken a hard hit and had to get up and get back in the action. Chris and Steve bandaged my lacerated, bleeding left hand, then like

Reaching the vertical gap

good shepherds, thinking they would probably have to catch me sooner or later, followed right behind me as I pushed myself on. I refused to turn back. It was the fourth quarter and we had to win the game.

Crumbly handholds and loose rock were everywhere. Someone up ahead yelled, "Rock." Chris, now standing in front of me, reached his hand up instinctively and, without seeing it, caught a rock large as a good-sized cabbage hurtling right at my head. He had robbed the river gods of a home run.

When we reached the nearly vertical climb of the Coconino Sandstone crest itself, my compatriots roped me up and guided me through narrow chimneys and out over exposed ledges. We didn't have a harness, so I had to be careful not to raise my hands too high or I could slip out of the rope. My legs had started to cramp. The effort to pull myself directly up took about every bit of energy I had left. Much of the rock was razor sharp.

I thought, *It would be easier to climb a saguaro.* We were too close to quit now. I willed myself up the sheer wall.

The time, care and encouragement the others lavished on me were selfless comradeship of the finest kind. We reached a narrow defile only 40 feet from the top where we had to squeeze through a constricted, boulder-choked slot. Only Bambina and Stamps could make it through to the summit. I could see myself stuck there for centuries in a less than dignified

Nearing the top

position so I stopped where I was. Yet, I enjoyed how high and far I had climbed. The long trek back took me until about nine-thirty that night. To atone for all the poaching he had done, Stamps stayed with me to the end. I had turned what probably would have been a seven-hour hike for the guys into a 14-hour survival trek. With a sigh of tremendous relief, I stumbled into camp and collapsed in a folding chair. Mike's wife, Cindy, still had hot food ready, a loving trip mother with fresh tortillas for all. Besides that, she doesn't poach jokes. Chris told me, "Well, Fink, you succeeded in wasting an entire day for death. It was so humiliated, it crawled back into its cave."

I had reached beyond my limits that day, transcending age and the lack of climbing skill. In doing so, I had opened a door of perception out to the wilderness and simultaneously back into myself. I realized that the exhausting effort, plus the soaring heights and surrounding beauty, touched a submerged portion of myself, a place of primal residue from countless years of man's outdoor existence. It had lain, for the most part, dormant and unrecognized in modern urban life and had been pierced and released by our adventure that day. Once again, after so many years, I felt interconnected with the land. I was at home in the Canyon. Experiencing wild places in their fullness requires hard work to penetrate into them and through them into our own psyche. It is not a sedentary occupation.

Bert Loper, the grand old man of the Colorado River, was born in 1869, the year of Major Powell's first exploration. We stop every year between Buck Farm and Bert's Canyon at Mile 41.2 to see Loper's last boat which was abandoned there in 1949. Each season, buffeted by wind and rain, more paint has peeled away and the wood has slowly pried apart and seems more submerged into the ground. It is a miniscule part of the gargantuan erosive process ever at work in the Canyon. The remains and a nearby plaque pay homage to the man.

Orphaned young, Bert Loper had worked his way west doing odd jobs and mining. By the late 1890s, he had discovered boating and began rowing the San Juan, Green and Colorado rivers prospecting gravel bars. Looking for color, he semi-hermited at Red Canyon, a side barranca that marked the beginning of Glen Canyon. In the early 1920s, the United States Geological Survey hired Loper as head boatman for their measurement of the San Juan and Green rivers. He led the boat crews by day and entertained them by night with accounts of the trap-

Bert Loper's boat

pers and prospectors of an earlier era. Later, he ran groups of Boy Scouts through Glen Canyon at every opportunity. He was a man who loved the river as men do their children; a man who grew strong, then old, riding its bucking, hump-backed tide, at home in the colossal indifference of the Canyon and its striated story of the planet.

Buzz Holmstrom was only the fifth man to run the entire length of the Green-Colorado River system from Green River, Wyoming through the Grand Canyon and the first to negotiate it *alone*. He discovered Loper penniless and living in the basement of the Masonic Temple in Salt Lake City. Loper was 69 and Holmstrom was surprised to find a strapping man who looked to be about 50. Loper filled Holmstrom with tales of the river, its history and people. Essentially loners, without adequate financial resources, each had begun by building boats and had fallen in love with the river. They found in each other reflections of themselves. Even with his legendary reputation, Loper had yet to run the Grand Canyon. Then, in the winter of 1938-1939, Don Harris of the USGS asked Bert for advice on a movie-making run of the Grand. Loper convinced Harris to take him along on the trip. The party took two boats. Bert rowed one and Harris the other. They completed the run just a few days before Loper's 70th birthday. At the end of the trip they made a pact to go down again in a decade to celebrate his 80th.

In July 1949, about a month before attaining his status as an octogenarian, Bert met Don Harris and four other men at Lees Ferry for the promised run. The heat was oppressive. Loper did not look well, but would not let anyone spell him at the oars. One day he said, if anything happened to him, that he wanted to be buried beside the river. On the afternoon of July 8, Bert led off through the big rapid at Mile 24.5 without stopping to scout. Wayne Nichols, his passenger, said Loper suddenly turned rigid. He yelled at Bert but got no response. The boat hit a big wave and capsized. Nichols grabbed hold of the lifeline on the side of the boat and hung on. Looking back, he saw Loper floating along in his life preserver, his eyes wide open, looking straight ahead.

When the current slowed before Mile 25 Rapid, Nichols climbed on the bottom of the boat, got an oar loose and poled it into an eddy. He saw Loper float by into the rapid. Nichols jumped on shore from the circling boat before it, too, plunged on downstream. The party spent the rest of the day looking for Bert. That evening they found the empty boat lodged on a bar 16 miles downstream. The next morning they hauled it well above the flood line and painted on its bow, "Bert Loper, Grand Old Man of the Colorado. Born: July 31, 1869. Died: July 8, 1949."

In 1975, a hiker found a human skeleton at Mile 71, the mouth of Cardenas Creek. The skeleton reflected advanced age and the skull had no teeth—suggesting it might be that of Loper. Forensic artists, who had never seen Loper or a picture of him, composed a face the skull structure would support, and those who knew him said it looked like Bert. The bones were shipped to Salt Lake City and buried beside his wife, Rachel.

Loper's attitude towards the river was a prototype for the self-made boaters and professional guides who followed him on the Canyon's winding, bareback tide. Looking back over years of battling mud, water rising and falling, lining and portaging rapids, running others, the weather good and bad, the placid places and scent of pines down from the rim, the towering canyon and a 400-mile trip ahead, Loper speculated that it was a wonderful world to live in when he could experience the grandiosity of the Canyon and see the sights he did. He talked about how time seemed to turn backward and he felt like a kid again on the beginning of each trip. He concluded, "Who in the hell wants to be a white-collar sissy when one can enjoy such grandeur and beauty as this?"

On one of our private trips in 1986, camping in the flats above one of the rapids, we discovered an eight-foot boulder hollowed out into what appeared to be an ancient throne. It was covered with petroglyphs and sat above what might have been a ceremonial site. Other boulders displayed similarly carved symbols and figures. I imagined prehistoric people chanting in a shuffling dance and wondered who sat in the throne chair. The Anasazi in this region lived in small bands. Who would have that much authority? Perhaps it was for an unseen god manifested through right-hemispheric ritual and belief.

The "Throne"—Queen for a day

From the granaries at Nankoweap, the view downriver is the most spectacular and photographed in the entire Canyon. The Anasazi built the granaries to protect their harvests. They were sealed so well that even rodents and insects could not get at the food.

There are two stories about the name Nankoweap. One says it comes from *weap* that means place and *nunko* meaning Indian battle. The story is that Apaches forded the river one summer night beneath the skin of the sky and crept in on a sleeping Kaibab camp. They crushed the skulls of their victims killing all but one woman who escaped to report the massacre. The other explanation says the name is Paiute for echo. On his second exploration, Major Powell heard an enormous echo in the area and called it Nankoweap.

The view at Nankoweap

Sitting 600 feet above the river, encased in the majesty of redwall and Kaibab-Toroweap-Coconino cliffs separated by the crumbling debris of Hermit Shale and the Supai group, I again call upon the lingering presence of the ones who were here first. Navajos drifting west called their predecessors the "Old Enemies." I visualize them planting corn, squash and beans in the delta below, gathering cactus fruit and seeds, carrying food to the granaries. I think of them using the slots where sunrise hit at various places along the rim to tell when it was time to plant or celebrate the solstice. I see their amazement, fear, and wonder at the sight of the Crab Nebula Supernova blazing in the daytime sky for 23 days in 1054 CE or watching Haley's Comet in 1066. Did they fear an apocalypse then or when, during summer migrations to the rim, they witnessed the ongoing volcanic eruptions of Sunset Crater from 1064 to 1067?

These early people foreshadowed the boom and bust nature of the American West. At Unkar Delta, the wet years from 1050 to 1070 fueled population growth but the area was abandoned during a subsequent ten-year drought. I wonder what will happen to our modern Sunbelt when the next ten-year drought comes along?

There is a cave I call the Meditation Cave high on one of the canyon walls. Usually I climb up early and sit in the back of the hollowed opening to watch my breath. Meditating, I relax into a dreamy peace in which I feel encompassed by untold tons of stone suspended halfway between river and rim. I am touched by my kinship to the immense cliff as if it, too, is ancestral to the rise of *homo sapiens*. The murmur of the river drifts up from below as if an ancient mother is singing softly to me. It is my favorite place in the world to sit and follow my breath.

Soon others join me. Sometimes we do a group meditation, sometimes beat drums, dance, and chant. Hoven Riley, a Texas countrified,

recovering Nature Conservancy bureaucrat, voluntarily demoted himself from white-collar status back to the field. He went from suit and tie lobbying in the Texas State capitol in Austin to Ramsey Canyon in southern Arizona where he revealed its unique qualities to everyday tourists.

Hoven played his flute as four of the girls and then the rest of us danced. His flute was the bone sound of raven wings, of buds unfolding, a lament of something gone never to return. It was an intonation coaxing stone to speak of passing seasons, a windy sigh of spear-tipped agave and enclaves of cactus claw; the sound of afternoon sun on cliffs, throaty breath that sits at the foot of the century and lifts us over upthrust land, floating us motionless and moon-nighted above our own lives. The cave is a place of memories, all of them good, some sublime.

On our way up to the granaries we dip through a grove of dead mesquite trees that I call Skid Row because their twisted arms and bent trunks remind me of homeless men living out on the streets. They look as though they all have rheumatism or arthritis or the DTs. Like tamarisk, the mesquite can sink a main taproot down as far as 60 meters to find water and sustain life in desert heat. It also bears a bean pod that can be ground into flour.

Skid Row

That reminds me of reading about a priest exploring Baja in 1742. He visited a village and was welcomed to supper. Afterwards, he asked what he had eaten. The village existed on the cusp of survival and had to use every food source available. In fact, the next tribe south, the Seris, practiced cannibalism. Each year the tribe harvested the *pitahaya*, the fruit of the organ pipe cactus. The fruit had seeds so tiny they could not be digested. So the entire village defecated at a designated spot and when the feces dried out, they sifted it to recover the undigested seeds and ground them into flour. When the priest found out where his meal had come from, he wished he hadn't asked.

The cliff across from Nankoweap is one of the most beautiful in the Canyon. Locked in strata of

> *"Who in the hell wants to be a white collar sissy when one can enjoy such grandeur and beauty as this?"*
>
> *Bert Loper*

stone where the late sun and moonlight play are the places where seas ebbed and flowed, ancient fish swam, dunes drifted, fossils formed, species developed and expired, all, in their way, a prelude and prerequisite to the rise of man. The cliff is another page of stone chronicling evolutionary progression.

After its confluence with the Little Colorado, the Canyon opens from narrow cliffs into a vast panorama; a far vista of peaks, buttes, pyramids, alcoves, side canyons, momuments, temples and cathedrals. This is an area of Dox Sandstone, a softer rock that erodes and topples the harder Tapeats, Muav, and Redwall above it. The widening space, perspective and extension of sight are magnificent and humbling.

On a trip in 1984, pugnacious, bacchanal, short-fused Matt McCorkle, a boatman, reminded me of one of my former students. The student's name was Kelly Kitchell. He was absolutely crazy about girls. He would flirt, pass notes, try to look up the dress and catch the eye of every female in class. He had a No Vacancy sign in his mind as far as history was concerned. He was an irritant in class so, finally, I put him in the middle seat of the front row where I could practically hold his head straight ahead while I lectured.

One day, we were talking about the power of new ideas and how selling by mail caught on in the mid-nineteenth century. As an example, I used Aaron Montgomery Ward who started in a 12' by 16' room over a stable in Chicago with a one-page list of items and within ten years sent out a huge catalogue every year. What spurred his rise was the fact that the Farm Grange endorsed him and that he instituted a ten-day try out period. If the item you ordered wasn't exactly what you wanted you could keep it up to ten days and send it back for a full refund. It was a no lose proposition.

People were so lonely out on the sod frontier that they often wrote letters with their orders. They would write things like, "You may be wondering why we haven't ordered for awhile but the cow done kicked my leg and broke it and my wife came down with the fits. Well, we are both healed up now and would you please send us bonnet number 78." Another couple wrote, "You are such a fine man to do business with we have named our new baby Aaron Ward Shlockheimer." A shrewd businessman, Ward had his secretaries answer every letter. One time a man wrote and asked if he could buy a wife by mail. The company wrote back and informed him they didn't deal in wives and it would be better for him to meet someone and get to know them. For the first time, Kelly was enthused about something that I said in class. "Wow, Mr. Finkbine, what a great idea, buying wives in the mail. Wow, wow, wow!"

I thought, *Ah at last I have provoked an interest in history in Mr. Kitchell.* With pride I asked, "What's so great about it, Kelly?"

He answered, "The ten-day try out period."

Anyway, the lusting McCorkle brought along a woman executive named Adrian. Matt held high expectations but his drinking and blatant need alienated his companion so she gave him the most unmagical of words, "No."

Frustrated and tight-groined, the Irishman took to fishing off the back of his raft at night. There was no way he was going to catch anything because he was jerking the rod around and angrily winding in the lure as he cursed wacko women and the mess *they* had made of *his* life. I came down, sat on the bank, drank beer, and celebrated his discomfort. It was the best show going.

Matt whipped the pole to cast and he let go of the reel too soon and the line shot straight out backwards and wrapped around a tree limb at the edge of the water. Glaring with a what-the-hell-more-can-happen stare, he threw the rod down and stomped across his boat and through a sea of profanity to disentangle the line. We heard a flip, flop, splash, splish, flip, flop, splash. The hook end of the tangled line had dropped over a limb and down into the river and a trout snapped it up. It was the only one he caught the entire trip.

I yelled out, "There's one for you. You know how to spawn, don't you?" then beat a hasty retreat with a foaming beer can aimed at my back.

The Canyon opens up

Baptism in Hance

We bounce down Unkar Rapid, miss the two bouldered pour-overs at the bottom of Nevills, and head into an ominous closing of canyon walls. This is the beginning of Granite Gorge, the most dramatic and action-packed section of the river. Here we see some of the oldest exposed rock on the surface of the earth. This is the realm of 2.2 billion-year-old Vishnu Schist and Zoroaster Granite.

Action-packed

These were early sandstones, shales and limestones crushed by enormous pressure and heat until metamorphosed into schist. Molten granite magma forced through cracks in the schist gives it a pink, cross-lined effect. Life existed when these rocks were formed as bacteria, a kind of blue-green algae. This enormously hard stone thrusting six miles deep below the Colorado resists the wearing, ceaseless abrasion of the river. With less erosion the Canyon remains narrow and the black polished schist is mysterious, sometimes fluted, creating a somber warp of sense and time. Here, too, the constricted channel forces the water deeper, squeezing it into massive hydraulics, boils, fierce side and back eddies and ferocious rapids.

> *Vishnu schist—at 2.2 billion years is some of the oldest exposed rock in the world*

The first of the giants is Hance Rapid, a sure-fire rubber wrapper at low flows, and rated a "9" out of a possible "10" at higher levels. It has a

30-foot drop in half a mile, the largest in the Canyon. This breathtaking obstacle was named after Captain John Hance, the first permanent settler on the South Rim. He built trails and a cabin where he entertained the first Canyon visitors. Reputably, Hance was a grand storyteller and claimed his index finger was shortened because he plumb wore it off pointing out all the beautiful scenery to tourists. The last 20 years of his life were spent as a historical attraction at Bright Angel Lodge telling stories to visitors as a paid bit of local color. He swore the clouds were so thick one day that he snow-shoed across to the North Rim. Hance died penniless in 1919.

My initial attempt to run Hance was a disaster. It was my first time rowing the Canyon in the high-water year of 1984. The flow was a steady 44,000 cfs. our entire trip. The rapid was the longest and most dangerous looking we had yet encountered. As we scouted, I wondered why I was rowing the Grand Canyon. *God*, I thought, *I could be home watching Wild Kingdom on television or reading National Geographic and being vicariously adventurous.*

We debated whether to run right or left of a huge pour-over rock at the top. At normal levels, it thrusts itself eight feet out of the water, but at that time had current surging over the top of its full height. We decided two of us would try the right

Running the wrong side of the rock

side while the other three boatmen watched our runs. They saw me fail to break a large reversal wave just past the boulder. My two passengers, Tammy and James, were washed out of the raft. I fought the force of the wave, caught the frame with my right hand, and pulled myself back in, but by that time my boat had been sucked back into the pulsating "keeper hole" behind the rock. Straining at the oars, I dueled the intense force of the hole until water roaring over the rock hit my left tube and slammed the raft upside down. I was caught in the maelstrom beneath the boat then, fortunately, was spit back out into the surging waves racing downstream into the heart of the rapid. One way people drown in whitewater is to be held and recirculated in a keeper until it is too late to escape alive. Out of the hole and able to breathe, I checked to see if my glasses were still attached to the cord tied to my life jacket, then started swimming left to stay out of the furi-

Life in Granite Gorge

ous holes at the bottom, center and right of the rapid. Adrenaline pumping through my body mitigated the extreme cold of the water. My craft was held and mangled, the cauldron force of the hole breaking both oars, bending the steel frame and tearing loose several D-rings before releasing it downstream.

I felt depressed thinking, *If that's the first of the big rapids and this is how I ended up, this is going to be one hell of a hard trip.* Yet, I felt elated at swimming in the gigantic waves and force of the rapid. Terrified, James had babbled like a baby, alienating Tammy. I lied and told her my back had been wrenched in the flip. She came up into my tent and massaged it. Tammy turned out to be a keeper.

Later, James told everyone, "The son-of-a-bitch almost drowned me and then he tried to steal my girlfriend." Carnage pays!

In June of 1990, a commercial group headed into Hance at low water. One of their huge "baloney boats," a 33-foot, motorized rig got too far left and breached on an exposed boulder. The rig slid right up on it and turned sideways. Pointed towards shore 60 feet away, the bow began to wrap around the rock and fill with water. Creaking and

A commercial motorized rig

36

groaning, the frame sounded like it was breaking apart. The motor and a load of gear tumbled out of the stern. The two guides and 15 passengers were trapped on the hamstrung vessel from 1:30 pm until nearly 7:30 that evening.

Some of the tourists were terror-stricken. One man was so frightened his wife had to sit in front of him face to face, make him breathe deeply and hold her until he could control himself. He promised, if they survived, he would never miss church again.

Having difficulty with the radio, the guides finally flashed a S.O.S by mirror to a passing jet that radioed in a medical helicopter. It surveyed the scene, then left and returned with a second chopper and rescue gear. Stabilizing lines were attached and a pulley system rigged up with a harness to remove the trapped people one-by-one. The lighter ones were pulled across the surface by those gathered on shore while portly passengers took a dunking being dragged to safety. All were rescued. The commercial company, a first-class operation, gave them their choice of continuing downriver on another trip just a half day behind or being flown out to safety. Interestingly, those who chose to fly out were the younger members of the expedition. There was one exception. One fellow, 54, had to leave because he was coerced by his son and daughter. He would rather have stayed.

Dr. W. W. Phillips

Dr. W. W. Phillips, a retired professor of history from ASU, said, "When we were trapped with the raft quivering and frame grinding, you could see terror in the young people's eyes. I think it was the first time they had ever faced the sobering fact of their own mortality. We older and wearing-out people were well aware of ours." Phillips and the other older passengers finished the trip.

The next rapid bears my favorite name for whitewater—Sockdolager. Rafts take some hard hits there and *sockdolager* is Swedish for a knockout blow. Powell referred to the Grand Canyon below the Little Colorado as "the Sockdolager of the World." At one time, the term sockdolager referred to a type of fishhook that wouldn't let go.

I heard another story about the name. When John Wilkes Booth planned the assassination of President Lincoln, he hung around Ford's Theater watching rehearsals of *My American Cousin*. No one thought it strange that a famous actor would drop by. Unknown to the management or cast, he drilled a hole in the door to the presidential box so he could see where everyone was sitting before making his move. In addition, Booth chipped plaster out of the walls so he could wedge a board across the hallway door leading to the entrances of the box seats. He would not be interrupted once he set his plan in motion.

The assassin selected the exact moment of the play to strike. It was a scene in the third act where there are only two people on stage, Lady Mounchessington and the comic relief character, Trenchard. As she leaves, he calls out, "Well, I guess I know enough to turn you inside out, old gal, you *sockdolagizing* old mantrap." It was a line that invariably sent a huge roar of laughter through the audience. The noise so effectively muffled Booth's derringer that Mary Todd

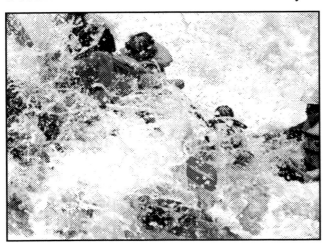

The "sock" in Sockdolager

Lincoln, seated beside the President, did not know he had been shot. She realized something was amiss when she noticed her husband slump forward and saw a figure standing above him with a drawn knife. When the killer leaped to the stage, only Trenchard was there to bar his escape. Even though the assassin broke a small leg bone above his ankle in the jump, he made his getaway. Powell came down Canyon four years later. Many people of the time were familiar with the fateful line and some say that's where the Civil War veteran got the name for the rapid.

Whatever its origin, Sockdolager is a slamming, crash-bang run as is the next rapid, Grapevine, almost a twin to Sock. Running Sockdolager at 28,000 cfs. in 1986, I braced for a tremendous head-on hit that slammed my raft around sideways. The next great mass of water rushing at me was a lateral and I was unintentionally in perfect position for it. Just plain luck got me through the rapid that day. In Grapevine, on a trip in 1969, we picked up a wet-suited, half-drowned swimmer with his gear stowed in a 55-gallon drum floating beside him. When we pulled him from the current, he coughed up water and gurgled he was attempting to swim the entire river. (He had gotten tired of sky diving.) We left him off at Phantom Ranch to hike out and find another way to live a short and happy life.

The sacred datura

On Halloween of 1991, we hiked the steep canyon at Cremation Camp. Some say prehistoric people burned the bodies of their dead and sifted the ashes over the cliff at this spot. Others say the name comes from the fact that the campsite bakes like an oven in the summer. Our hike turned into a steep climb as we struggled up 1,600 vertical feet over boulders, slides, loose rock and sheer crevices to the Tonto Platform. On our way up we came across a number of datura flowers in bloom. They have a deadly fascination, particularly the contrast between the beauty of the moon goddess white or lavender petals and their nightshade toxicity. A member of the potato family, it's perhaps better known by its name as jimsonweed, a corruption of Jamestown. Fresh datura leaves were thrown in the cooking pots and poisoned many soldiers sent there to crush Bacon's Rebellion in 1676. The plant has been used as a medicinal narcotic since before recorded time and once figured centrally in the religious ceremonies of southwestern tribes.

Smoke of the plant has bronchiole-dilating properties that relieve asthma. It can also be fatal because its concentrations of alkaloids is so unpredictable. Alkaloids are any number of hetrocyclic, colorless, crystalline, bitter organic substances such as caffeine, morphine, quinine and strychnine having alkaline properties and containing nitrogen. Ingesting datura can cause increased blood pressure and body heat, failing muscle coordination, confusion and hallucination. It demands quick treatment or can prove fatal. Eerily visible in the dark, it glows deceptively virginal in light of its toxic qualities. Its ability to kill gives it a wraithlike and phantasmal presence.

Pulling ourselves over the final edge, we stood on a mystical plateau surrounded by a sublime array of temples, pyramids, and buttes. I walked over the top of a small hill and startled a group of perhaps 15 bighorn sheep. The ground trembled as they bounded off with their powerful shoulders hunched forward and hooves thundering. We looked out at hazy reds and browns lazed in the ebbed light; at temples and spires where

Bighorns

time stirred stone to flesh. The scene so filled us with its immensity that we screamed in joy. We were coyotes of the sky breathing the ghosted day moon and exhaling stars into the dawn of night. We were lesser wolves of carving winds baying through the squawky caw of ravens to the river far below, imploring the datura to unfold and offer pollen; keening to a presence we could not see.

On the way back down I cautioned my daughter, Kristi, to watch her step. Suddenly the boulder I was standing on fell out from under me and went crashing down. Instinctively, I got enough thrust off of it to throw my chest against another rock and cling to it with all my might. I barely avoided a 25-foot fall and a long tumble afterwards.

"You better do as you say," answered Kristi. Speechless, I pulled myself up on the narrow ledge rubbing my bruises like a chastised child. I thought, *I still hate it when they are too old to spank.*

Where time stirred stone to flesh

Lucidity

Curved claws
of mesquite stand watch
over the quickening
of rock nettle and scorpionweed.
The datura raises its cobra head.

Time runs uphill
from black breast of schist
through epochal layers to Moenkopi Siltstone.
Ringtail cats, half-grown,
slip soft padded by buckhorn cholla,
fat black ravens wallow in the wind.

Water masses down drops
roaring like a wounded beast,
swift fluidity

exploding into scrubbed scent of spray.

An illimitable world,
its enclosed intricate cycles
and connective proliferation spun down
to blinking wings of butterflies clothed in pollen
on a podded prickly pear bud so pale and new
it is the center of the universe.

Old Tom

Downstream from Phantom Ranch lurk the Big Four. In relatively close order are the giant rapids Horn Creek, Granite, Hermit and Crystal. This is, without a doubt, the most exhilarating and, at the same time, the most dangerous section of the river. Beyond Crystal are "The Jewels," a chain of sock-'em rapids like Sapphire,

The Big Four—Horn Creek

Ruby and Turquoise that have plenty of kick. I had always wondered where Tuna Rapid fit into the Jewels, where its name came from. The rapid has two parts: a 9.5-foot drop in the upper end and a four-foot fall at the lower part. During the survey of 1923, the group planned to have lunch on the left side between the drops. Lewis Freeman in his boat, *The Grand,* missed the pull in and went careening down the river. Those on *The Grand* had only tuna fish available on their boat. Later, after some kidding about missing the pull in, they named the creek and the rapid Tuna.

Running this portion of the Canyon, we've hit as many as 14 stretches of whitewater in one day. The adventure can be quite a shock to those who hike in at Phantom Ranch and have never rafted the Grand Canyon before.

The Big Four—Granite

Bang! Slam! Wham! Within the first day and a half, they've been hit with the best punch the river has except for Lava Falls. In 1988, a couple of portly couch potatoes hiked in to join us. After their first rides through the convoluted maelstrom of Horn Creek and hard slams of Granite, they decided to hike the rest of the rapids. We camped above Hermit that night. In the morning I told them, "Look, the boatmen are experienced. We've all been through these rapids a number of times. By hiking you hold up the group. Hiking you could sprain an ankle, be bitten by a rattlesnake, take a nasty fall. You could get to a place where we couldn't get back to you and you couldn't get down to us. Just get in the raft and hold on tight. It's fun. You'll be fine, I guarantee you. Dave here has such a powerful forward stroke they call him "Evinrude." In fact, in all his years on the rivers, he has never flipped a raft." That last fact convinced them.

Dutifully, they climbed into Dave's lead raft. He rowed out to the wide, beautiful tongue sliding down into the immense rollers of the rapid. At certain levels the giant in the wave train can be 18 feet high. Dave made a perfect run, but at the top of the fifth awesome and exploding mound of water, it seemed like a giant hand came up, twisted the raft sideways, and dumped it over. Holy wham, David had his first, and to this writing, his last flip ever, and our porky tenderfoots were being washed downstream in icy water ahead of the entire group. They never listened to anything I said after that. It

The Big Four—Couch potatoes swim at Hermit

may have been their first and last Grand trip. Behind them, Cal Kenny and his paddle raft boys flipped also. There was something downright mean about that wave that day. Cal loved the Grand Canyon so much that he left a wife two weeks overdue with twins to make the trip. His last words to her before departing were, "Don't name them until I get back." I haven't heard from him since.

Below Hermit and Boucher rapids the river pools and quiets as we near Crystal. In that high water year of 1984, we seemed to have floated into the hush before conception, the quiet of an old tomb. Crystal was born in early December of 1966 when a storm unleashed 14 inches of rain on the North Rim within 36 hours. Crystal Creek, normally an ankle to knee-deep stream, became a roaring, 40-foot wall of water carrying 40- and 50-ton boulders. It was a 1,000-year flood washing out Anasazi ruins that had stood since the last millennium. It pushed house-sized boulders out into the main stream. Great ponderosa pine were ripped loose along the rim and carried all the way into the Canyon. Over night, what had once been a placid bend in the river became a gigantic and dangerous rapid. The rocks are still shifting and the configuration of the awesome whitewater is still in process. In 1984, the silence was broken by a thin line of sound, a nearly inaudible growl. The growl grew into a roar and carried a throbbing sense of power. We pulled our five rafts into the right bank just before the water began to accelerate and race out of sight.

Over a decade of rowing whitewater had not prepared me for the sight that overwhelmed our senses as we picked our way along what was left of the shore and scrambled over rocks to scout. It looked like a 1000 years of stored rage had been unleashed. At 44,000 cfs., tons of water raged around a bend to the right pushing everything to the left into two monstrous killer holes. Their pulsating and exploding 35-foot waves looked like the jaws of hell. Surrounding the holes was a frenzy of turbulence descending in great waves towards another gigantic hole that, at normal flows, was a rock island. At the upper right where we would try to cheat past the killer holes were a series of lateral waves and holes

The Big Four—Omar and Cal Kenny in Crystal

large enough to be labeled serious whitewater. These, too, were straining madly towards the impossible center of the river. Crystal enraged at high water was the most horrific sight I'd ever seen. Long and hazardous, it is at certain levels, one of the most dangerous rapids run on a regular basis anywhere in the United States.

A cross-section of river rats, our five boatmen looked in awe at the raging water. The most experienced boatman and trip leader, Bob, muttered, "This is the worst I've ever seen it." Scott, a lawyer, nodded in mute agreement. Next to them, Jeff, an Upper Salt River expert, wordlessly fixed his gaze on the river. A few feet away, chin thrust forward, stood Tom, a longtime Sierra Club explorer from the Bay Area. He was an enigmatic figure, hard to decipher, liberally mixing fiction with fact in our nightly conversations. Tom's white beard shot out from ruddy cheeks and, below hunched shoulders, his sunken chest sloped down to a potbelly. His arms were long and sinewy but were losing strength. He was in his late 60s. Tom talked with one eye on the sky as if addressing the universe, and if anyone else happened to hear his comments it was their incidental good fortune. He told us that in a previous run at Crystal, "The holes were so big I flipped over backwards and did a somersault and came out right side up. Now wait 'till you try that."

In the seven days and nights we had been together, I formed two vivid impressions of "Old Tom" as we called him. These may or may not have been accurate. The first was that some parts of his life were disintegrating. A second and unwanted divorce, money problems, and

Old Tom

separation from his family had plagued him through the past year. He had difficulty establishing genuine intimacy. He would talk at people rather than interact with them. In response to these deficiencies, Tom was spending more and more time in wilderness activity, scheduling one trip after another. He planned to run the Tuolumne two days after our Canyon trip ended. At Christmas he had completed a Sierra Club wilderness hike, then turned around and marched back the way he had just traveled.

The second insight about Tom was that he liked to "push the envelope." He enjoyed putting himself on the edge, that wild-all-out-no-holds-barred energy rush compensating for warmth now missing or diminished in his life. He pushed his luck farther than necessary. To row a 15-foot, patched-up raft 225 miles through the Canyon at his age and take on major rapids without a wetsuit seemed an act of defiance. The 44 to 47 degrees water was liquid ice. It could debilitate the strongest swimmer within five to ten minutes and the sinewy old boatman didn't have a lot of body heat to spare. Looking at Crystal, my own adrenaline level was building. A heady mixture of fear and nearly uncontrollable excitement raced through me. After 20 minutes of watching the exploding waves and fluid pandemonium, Bob advised, "Well, we'd better go ahead and run it before we get a bad case of boatman's nerves."

Speaking to myself as much as to the group, I said, "What do you mean before?"

With his 18-foot Avon Spirit and the most expertise, Bob ran first. Scott, Jeff, myself, and Old Tom were to follow in that order. Bob and Scott pushed off. My passengers, Ed and Kathy, friendly and enthusiastic members of the Central Arizona Mountain Rescue Team, climbed in the front of the raft. We were upstream around

> *The 44 to 47 degrees water was liquid ice. It could debilitate the strongest swimmer within five to ten minutes*

the bend clinging to the tamarisk inundated by the flood-level water. I was checking my oars when I heard Jeff yell, "Boat's over, Scott's over. He flipped right at the top." Trying to punch the first lateral backwards, Scott had mistimed his turn, hit the wave sideways, and was upside down. The two girls riding with him, Susan and Linda, were trapped under the raft, then swept into and through the jaws of the monster holes. Tumbled, terrified and tossed, they swallowed then nearly breathed water as they were sucked down and held under before being spit out downstream. I heard Jeff cry out, "Old Tom's pulled out ahead of us. My God, he's way out to the

left." The old timer was being pulled straight into the killer holes. I wondered if he was attempting a rescue and if his arms were too frail to stroke against the intense current driving everything to the center.

"Let's go!"

"Let's go," I

yelled to Kathy and Ed as we pushed off. Our eyes met with a mixture of excitement and dread. The current picked up and swept us around the bend as I worked furiously to stay close to the right bank. I pushed hard forward into the first series of drops and lateral waves, then pulled madly away from the left. We accelerated into a procession of waves so huge that half the time my oars were up in the air as the raft rocked back and forth. The good strokes I did get in kept us on the right edge of the monster holes and then I spun to face the turbulence that lifted and bounced the craft as if it were a toy. Ed and Kathy leaned far over the nose into the cascading white fury as we punched the giant waves again and again and crashed through the large hole at the bottom. We screamed, "We did it. We did it." I stood and danced on the frame, my blood on fire and surging through my body.

Our celebration was short-lived. We had two rafts, Scott's and Tom's, over and six people carried in icy water towards Tuna Rapid just downstream. We saw Linda, pale and shaken, clinging to a rock ledge and rowed over to pick her up. Bob had pulled Scott and Susan out of the water and towed the second raft into an eddy in a small rock cove. While Bob was occupied with the initial rescue, Tom floated by on the other side of the river. The old fellow waved his hand and called for help but didn't seem capable of making an effort to get himself to shore.

That's the last glimpse anyone had of Old Tom alive.

The remainder of the day became a blurred collage: straining to get Scott's raft right side up and re-rigged; the search downriver through several more rapids hoping Jeff had caught up with the others; picking up one of Tom's passengers, Polly, in the first stages of hypothermia after she swam both Crystal and Tuna; spotting Monica, the other passenger, safe in Jeff's raft, then sweeping around a bend to see a ranger patrol on the right bank kneeling over a prostrate figure.

Grand Canyon National Park rangers had discovered Tom floating immobilized over a mile below Crystal. They administered CPR to him on their raft until they reached a spot at Mile 104.5 where they could bring in a rescue helicopter. As they and people in our group continued to work on Old Tom, a medical team flew in, adding electric shock and IV stimulants to the on-going resuscitation attempts. I wondered if the aged boatman would make it but told myself, *The way he keeps staring at the sun I wouldn't bet on it.* Tom never did come around. His lips were rubbery and cold. He was flown out and pronounced dead of hypothermia at the hospital in Flagstaff. There was no water in his lungs, a "dry drowning" in which his throat had closed. Crystal had claimed its second life in less than a year and Tom was now beyond the chop of helicopter blades and the miracles of modern medicine.

Unique, cantankerous, colorful, the old boatman was his own person, weathered by time and grained by the the earth. Carrying the broken promises of youth, family and love to the bosom of his wilderness mother, he lived and died on the edge as, veins shouting with life, he pulled his battered raft into the current at Crystal, an ironic smile lighting his wind-worn and time-textured face.

Old Tom running Hance

Our group had little choice but to continue downriver with our rafts and gear for another eight days. It was a challenge to revive sagging spirits and pull people together for obstacles like Waltenberg, Deubendorff and, of course, Lava Falls. We held a beachside service the night after Tom was flown out to honor his passing and discharge emotion. Retrieving his raft 14 miles downstream at Forster Canyon, we repaired it. Two quick-learning and athletic young men who had never rowed whitewater, Mike and Howard, took it the rest of the way. At the take out at Diamond Creek, Tom's nephew, son and stepson were waiting to get a first-hand report and gather up his jeep, raft and gear. Tom was cremated and his ashes flown back to San Francisco where two well-attended ceremonies bid him a final farewell.

Old Tom was of the land,
his sinews woven of trees;
leaves cried a lonesome sound in his blood,
the dew of the grass were his tears
and the green-water lady his last love.

A brave death they say,
head on into Crystal's gargantuan rage,
its wet embrace carrying him
to that place buried deep within us all,
that oblivious copulation with starry nights
and the howling of wolves along the timberline
a thousand thousand years before our birth.

Old Tom reaching all alone
for the love that never ends
—to breathe the whole sky
and roll with rivers to the sea.

And roll with rivers to the sea

The Fawn

Mule deer spooked
by foreboding scent of man.
With a swift kick of hooves
she disappears, spindly,
stilt-legged fawn
following.

A second fawn,
trapped from its mother,
bewildered, lying still,
playing dead, quivering
in its spotted jacket of fear,
nose trembling, ribs heaving.

Through the vulnerable hush of twilight
we carefully part branches,
staring with sad eyes
(fluted call of a single wren)
at the huddled remnants
of
our
own
mortality.

"Nibble on Her Toes"

merging from the brooding presence of the Inner Gorge we enter a portion of the Canyon offering a wondrous array of hiking and climbing adventures; magical places like Elves Chasm, Thunder River, Surprise Valley, Deer Creek Falls, Matkatamiba, Sinyala and Havasu canyons.

One afternoon at Elves Chasm in 1990, amid its lush array of ferns, cardinal monkey flowers, columbines and orchids, I was with Tim, a consummate Oregon fisherman. He was telling me stories of big ones caught and big ones that got away. Then he talked about his time in Vietnam. Over there he said were giant lizards, four to six feet long, who, when they did their push ups, would cry out, "Flwawk, fwawk, flwawk, fwaeke eue-e-e-e-e-e." In addition, there were large, cumbersome birds who waddled about chirping, "Re-up, re-up, re-up, re-up." The men sat around at night and through the tangled danger of the jungle heard, "Re-up, re-up, re-up," then, "Flwawk, fwaek, flwawk, fwawk eue-e-e-e-e."

The fifth level at Elves Chasm

Tim told me with a hint of a smile, "You know, that's exactly how we felt about it."

One of my favorite names in this area is Hakatai, a Havasupai Indian word for the Grand Canyon that means any large roaring noise, whether from wind or raging whitewater. I enjoy the sound of it and the feel of my mouth shaping the name. Both a rapid and a side canyon bear the sobriquet. Asbestos fibers mined and shipped out of Hakatai Canyon were in great demand because of their unusual three- to four-inch length. That made them easier to spin than the shorter ones more commonly mined. They were used to create fireproof curtains for the grand theaters of Europe in the early portion of the twentieth century.

Drifting along Stephen and Conquistador aisles, my imagination visualizes the gargoyle countenances of deities and monarchs carved high on the magnificent walls, rulers of bygone empires. Stephen is an Anglicization of Esteban, the black, Christianized Moor who, along with Cabeza de Vaca, survived Panfilo de Narvaez's ill-fated exploration of Florida in 1528. Passing themselves off as medicine men and magicians, they were traded from tribe to tribe and made their way overland to reach Spanish settlements in Mexico. Their stories of that vast unknown area included the legendary tale of the Seven Cities of Gold. It was most likely one of the *move along stories* told by native people to get European intruders to leave their village and continue their explorations elsewhere. That myth, reinforced by the lies of Fray Marcos de Niza, generated the Coronado expedition of 1540. Out of that exploration came the "discovery"

The great obstacle to exploration

of the Grand Canyon by one of Coronado's lieutenants, Garcia Lopez de Cardenas. Disgusted, the frustrated conquistador considered it an insurmountable obstacle in his search for the cities of treasure or the fabled Northwest Passage. Honed from seven centuries of war to drive the Moors out of Spain and dedicated to pillage and treasure, the conquistadors of the Coronado expedition failed to value the beauty and potential of the land itself.

Randy's Rock sits in the river around Mile 126. In June of 1976, Randy Breckenridge, the boatmen and six passengers were napping after hiking Elves Chasm. Freddie Bendheim, a novice, was rowing and managed to wrap the 22-foot craft around the Tapeats rock on river left, dumping all but one person into the current. They salvaged gear but failed to retrieve the raft and continued on with everyone jammed in the remaining two boats. At Diamond Creek, the owner, Rob Elliott, thought the story of the lost boat was a practical joke until he angrily drove away from the takeout with only two instead of his three rafts.

Between Blacktail and Forster canyons, we hit stretches of river that appear to be running uphill. This is because of the reverse angle of the sandstone along the bank. It's a unique sensation. We drift past the spooky schist of Specter Canyon and down to my continuing duel to stay right at Bedrock Rapid. There, I think of my guiding buddy Karl. In 1992, he deliberately went left of the giant rock and sat there in the whirlpool eddy with no attempt to high side and purposely flipped his raft to plunge a disliked and obnoxious member of our group gurgling, flustering and freezing into the river. We all cheered. Karl's been my hero ever since. Even when you're 71, it's good to have a role model.

Smash mouth ride

Just downstream there's a smash mouth but forgiving ride through a large and long rapid named after the first fellow who flipped there back in 1909, a handyman out of Vernal, Utah, Sylvester "Dubie" Deubendorff. Dubie cut his head on his boat and was dragged down, mostly underwater, some 300 yards before floundering to the bank. He was happy to survive. Unfortunately, he died the following year of tick fever.

We reach Tapeats Creek, the site of a wonderful loop hike up to Thunder River, one of the highlights of our trips. Powell gave the area its name for Ta Pits, a Paiute Indian who pointed out the drainage to the explorer from the rim. Camped at Tapeats Creek in June of 1990, our group was caught up in the plight of one of our prettiest members, a young woman named Polly. We didn't know whether it was the change in diet or excitement of the rapids, but poor Polly was entering her eighth day of agonizing constipation. There at Tapeats, after a hard labor, she finally delivered. We celebrated, popped beers, named it "Pooper," claimed it was an eight-pounder, and made plans for a christening. Any excuse for a party. I told the others that Polly's husband, Ted, was jealous because it looked like one of the boatmen.

You hear a lot about scorpions and rattlesnakes in Arizona. At Tapeats in 1988, a boatman, Jeff, sat on a scorpion and was stung into blazing pain. As I watched Jeff lying on his stomach with his exposed swollen right bun being administered to by three of the women, Florence Nightingales every one, I thought even catastrophe has its flip side. Carnage does pay.

Thunder River

A punishing climb and three miles of trails along Tapeats Creek leads to Thunder River then upward to Thunder Springs. Thunder River is the shortest river in the world and perhaps the only river that flows into a creek. They get their name from the sound of water exploding into waterfalls from midway up a 1,000 feet of Redwall and Muav limestone. Over 3,000 feet of passageways and an underground lake have been explored within the cliff walls. Along the trail of pungent scents, we climb into an exhilaration of water exploding against rock, airy oasis of moss and mint, leaves spinning in blast of spray, gusting from the force of the falls. It is the Eden of the Grand Canyon, a place so beautiful it could have inspired a creation legend; a fabled story of how man first appeared on the planet.

Surprise Valley

After resting, lunch, and perhaps climbing to or into the mouth of the main falls, the group continues our trek upward over and into Surprise Valley. It is an enchanting journey. Suspended between the rim and the river far below, it seems we have climbed halfway to heaven. The valley curves down then upward again as if it were a pair of gigantic stone hands stretched out to receive us; we are cupped in a desert cradle patterned by gentle rain as distant thunder echoes over wet sage and crucifixion thorn.

We witness the everywhere seminal thrust of agave heavy with seed, spilled before its stick-stalked death. One by one, we weave our way amid clusters of red-needled barrel cactus and under the lazy sail of hawks high above the descending Deer Creek drop. Clouds swarm the top of the north ridge leading to the rim giving it the appearance of a smoking volcano with rainbow colors embedded within the dark gray folds on its shoulders. Shadows flung across its face seem like incantations of places I had never seen, trails yet to be hiked, mountains unclimbed, rivers not run. The scurry of lizards across boulders connects us to the teeming variety of life inhabiting the world. There is the tug of genuine experience in the mingled rain, vista, reflection and the exertion of hiking. There is only the moment and we are enlarged by the very act of not being able to comprehend how the earth opens like a baby's eyes into magnificent places. City talk is laid to rest by a hollowed boulder where catclaw combs the air and love is superfluous.

Slipping and sliding a bit down the steep trail, we descend to the clear waters of Deer Creek. Following the stream, we arrive at a small waterfall we called our Jacuzzi Pool. We plunge into the icy water and let the falls slam down on our head, back, and shoulders. It feels, to me, as if the pounding water is cleansing my brain, rinsing it of unnecessary thought, carrying away mental debris clung to but no longer needed, stuff that encumbers my mind like forgotten family furniture and clothing clutters an attic. By the edge of

The Jacuzzi pool

the pool there's a knotted and gnarled tree whose exposed roots curl about like writhing hardwood snakes. People keep telling me what kind of tree it is, but I say, "That's the American Bodhi Tree. That's where Buddha would have found enlightenment and escaped cyclic existence if he would have been over here instead of over there."

"What kind of tree?"

"A Bodhi tree. Siddhartha, the young prince, sat by a Bodhi tree determined not to move until he found enlightenment. There he entered Nirvana and became Buddha."

"Sure."

"He did. We could sit here with the sound of water running through our minds until they were scourged of everything but serenity."

"Go for it, Fink, we'll catch you next trip."

As we continue, we enter a narrowing and twisting of the walls on either side of Deer Creek. While the trail remains up top, the stream cuts

Deer Creek cutting deeper towards its fall to the river

deeper and deeper into a winding labyrinth leading to the top of 147-foot Deer Creek Falls. In September of 2000, I explored this area for the first time. My leader and companion was a doctor, photographer and climber named Jeff Reynolds. Jeff had a fact-filled, immediate recall, computer-like mind. No matter what topic came up he had an encyclopedic knowledge that encompassed it. He made me wonder, *How come some minds hold so much and others so little?*

When the subject of the witch trials came up, Doc told us that a pig had eaten a small child at Salem in 1647 and was put on trial and sentenced to be hanged by its rear legs until dead. He's the only person I've met outside of history professionals who have pieces of nasty trivia like that at their fingertips.

I could have never made the exploration without Doc because he set ropes so we could climb around and down past other falls leading to the main drop.

Where the striped chamber-walled streamed ran horizontal, it seemed like we were probing dungeon corridors burrowed beneath an ancient castle. The sense of investigating someplace new excited me. Even if thousands of others have been there before, when I transverse a difficult climb or hike, I get that magical sense that I am the first person to ever see it. That sense of discovery deep within the snaking passages made the day unforgettable. Finally, we reached the edge of a 50-foot falls beyond which we could see the opening where the main falls crashes down to the river.

Joseph Campbell commented on people always seeking the meaning of life. That's not really it, he maintained. What we are searching for is experience that shafts through us like a spear of sunshine and touches us so intimately we actually feel the *rapture* of being alive.

In a side canyon back up on top, I had spotted a leaf cutting bee, its wings whirring as it approached a flower. It is a small, plump, mid-sized, solitary insect that does most of the pollinating in the desert southwest. Females who collect pollen carry it beneath their abdomens on pale red brushes, not on their hind legs like honeybees. Imagine one female cutting 1,064 precise disks of leaves with which to line a nest for her eggs. She fashions a cylindrical case that looks like a tiny, flat-ended, neatly wrapped cigar, sometimes placing several end to end in whatever small hollow she has selected for their laying place. Before sealing the tube, the female bee provisions it with pollen and nectar and lays an egg inside. Many solitary bees also deposit an antibiotic in the nest cells at the time of laying. They seem to be their own drug store. Finally the female seals the cylinder with a circular piece of leaf that fits snugly because she cuts it a fraction larger than the diameter of the cell. The bee's antennae are elbowed, and the tips diverge so that they automatically calibrate openings and measure width. They are their own calipers. The young solitary bees hatch as their favorite flowers come into bloom. They may, in fact, respond to the same signs of spring such as temperature and moisture.

In the pitiless cycle of the food chain, the leaf cutting bee's greatest enemy is a chameleon-like creature that can adjust to the color of the flower in which it anchors itself to wait for the approach of the pollinator. This is the crab spider, named because they walk sideways. Secure in the flower they have color matched, a process that might take up to three days, they have the leverage to capture and feast on larger insects. After grabbing its prey, a crab spider pulls its own front legs back out of the danger of a sting or a bite and buries its jaws in the meaty head or thorax of

The church of my choice

its meal.

It is in these adaptive capabilities of life forms—cutting exactly sized pieces of leaves, injecting an antibiotic to protect eggs, color matching its hunting lair—that I discover and retain a reverence for the intricate way the fretwork of ecology has formed along the ragged coast of time. Inherent in the intricacies of evolution exists an overwhelming conviction of the tenacity and sanctity of all life. As I look around and feel the canyon walls rise on each side of me, I find a peace that a truly religious person must feel kneeling in the church of his or her most profound faith.

Downstream, we like to hit Havasu Canyon in the off-season, as guides refer to it as *Havazoo* in the summer months when it is choked with commercial trip tourists. In May of 1992, we were hiking up to Beaver Falls to jump and dive off the ledges, swim in the pools and perhaps rediscover the underwater grotto. Everywhere along the way were signs of the 1990 flash flood that sent a 14-foot wall of water down the canyon washing out travertine terraces, diminishing Mooney Falls by several feet, and flinging trees with tangled branches high up on the banks.

Rain waterfalls pour into Havasu Canyon

On our hike, the stream was running its uniquely clear and enchanting turquoise, a rare lucid tint sliding over drops, deepening in pools, and foaming over diminutive falls. Without warning, a storm blew in. Within minutes thunder shook the earth and a deluge of rain crashed down as lightning forked across the sky. Waterfalls began pouring off the rim, Havasu Creek turned a chocolate mud color, and began rising precipitously. We raced back downstream to be able to cross before it was too high to get back to our rafts. The swiftness of the storm and rapidly increasing level of water reminded us of our own vulnerability against the unleashed power of nature. It was an awe-provoking race, the stakes raised because of the cameras we carried and the possibility of being washed out into the river's main channel.

I was traveling this section in 1986 with a group that included a 15-

year-old budding boatman and kayaker named Scotty. Scott's dad, Bob, the head boatman, was absorbed in getting to know a lovely woman, Susie, whom he later would marry. Scotty was left to fend for himself so I started calling him the "Night Orphan." Staid and uninspiring, the group was mostly school-teachers, so one night a spunky oars-woman, Linda, and I streaked the campfire to try and stir things up. Our shared adventure led to days and nights of togetherness termed a "river romance."

Scotty, the night orphan

One night we were sleeping in my tent when a hard rainstorm swept in. We decided we had better go get the Night Orphan before he drowned. The three of us slept comfortably in the protective shelter for the rest of the night. In the morning drizzle I started whis-pering to Scotty that although he must think I'm a pretty old guy, I remembered what it was like to be 15 and certain urges I had at that age. I told him, as his good friend, I was going to leave him alone with Linda so he could have a good time but, just in case he wasn't sure exactly what to do, I'd sit outside the tent and whisper instructions to him. I promised not to peek. Linda went along with it because the two of us were always teasing any likely target on the trip. I positioned myself outside the tent; a butterball crouched against the sprinkling rain, and said, "Okay, you ready, Scotty?"

"I guess so," he stammered.

"Okay, lick your lips. Now the first thing you do is take her right arm and raise it high up in the air and kiss her armpit. Girls love to have their armpits kissed." I waited a moment and inquired, "How's that going?"

A wary, "I don't know," came back from inside the tent.

"Okay, Scottie, now quick, quick, down on her toes and nibble on her toes. Girls love to have their toes nibbled on. How's that going?" A sec-ond indecisive answer issued from the tent. "Now quick, don't lose momen-tum, rub her nose with your nose. Girls love to rub noses."

He replied, "I don't know, Uncle Bob. You know, I think they do it differently *these* days than since when you were *young*."

Storm at Havasu

An October squall
lashes the plateau,
grumbling prophecy
punctured by broken
sticks of lightning.
Washes hurtle off cliffs
into a hundred waterfalls,

drums bellow rim to rim.
Silted river runs seaward,
born before man raised upright
and aped his way
towards designer jeans
and microchips.

The storm calms me;
its thunder knells
no civilization has lasted
as long as this canyon.

"Wait 'til You See Lava"

For the 22 uneventful miles above the great-granddaddy of all rapids, anticipation begins to build. "Wait 'til you see Lava," Old Tom used to say. Its impassable ledge hole, steep gravitational force, laterals, V-wave and death rock have created an awe-

The fury of Lava Falls

some mystique. When on crapper duty in the days before the modern regulations, I noticed the rocket box was twice as full on Lava morning as any other day on the trip. The explosive waves, recirculating force and unmitigated fury of the rapid are notorious. Recently, debris has washed in on the left side that makes the run more difficult. Most boatmen can only look at it so long before they want to get down to the rafts and get it over with, their bodies jittered with raised levels of adrenaline.

One of my favorite rafting couples, Patty and Dave Huizingh, were on a trip in 1988 where Patty was beginning to row some of the whitewater. Finally, she did her first big one, Upset Rapid. Watching their run, I could see Dave's arms gesturing and his lips moving, yelling instructions to his wife. The next morning, Patty was smashing beer and pop cans with a huge rock, slamming them flat, bang, bang, bang, one after another.

"Do you want help or do you need to do that?" I asked.

Patty smashing cans

"I need to do this," she replied. Patty smashed another can, bang, bang, bang. Later, her anger poured out in a scolding to Dave that the entire camp couldn't help but hear. "If you trust me enough to row, then let me row. Stop yelling out every little thing I'm supposed to do! Pretty soon you'll want to blow my nose for me. For Pete's sake, let me do it on my own." Dave's mouth was anything but shut, dropped open at the normally sweet and even-keeled Patty laying down the law.

When we reached Lava, Jeff, one of the boatmen, did a quick left cheat, rowed across the river and scurried back up the right bank to get another ride. He yelled at me but I was already out in the current looking for the bubble line and pretended I didn't hear him. The bubbles lead over the first drop to a water bridge between two snarling holes you wouldn't want to hit. Jeff ran farther up the bank and asked Patty and Dave if he could ride with them. They said yes, and he jumped in. Patty was sitting in the oar seat. Jeff waited for Patty and Dave to trade places. They didn't. Jeff's eyes bugged out when the raft was pushed off with Patty still at the oars headed for the jumbled, V-wave, death-rock right side.

As they dropped over the lip and down the steep slide to oblivion, Jeff, not daring to say anything directly to Patty, announced loudly to Dave, "Don't you think we're too far right?"

Dave cringed.

Far right or not, Patty made it through. Later that night she told me she wondered what it would have been like to flip in Lava because the swim would have been exciting. It was my turn to cringe. I reached for a beer. I had run Lava right once when I should have gone left. I was right on the bubble line, dropped in and smashed through

Patty at the oars

the first waves, had a perfect and well-braced entry into the V-wave and it ate me alive. Sucked down, I have never moved through water that fast in my life. I was helpless in its force. I thought, *If I hit a rock at this speed, I'll fracture a leg, hip, arm or skull for sure.* I finally popped up and got a breath in the third wave carrying me across the tip of the Death Rock, then was washed downstream. I thought about the experience some more and opened another beer.

A registered OB\GYN nurse, Patty has a wealth of fascinating stories to share around the campfire. She told us about assisting one young doctor who decided to puncture his patient's water bag in the middle of a particularly leviathan contraction. Tests showed the baby had already pooped in the amniotic fluid. Patty started to warn the unaware physician but held back, knowing how doctors hate being corrected by nurses. The fluid exploded hitting him in the face and blanketing the wall seven feet behind him. She wiped him off as he finished the delivery. As she did, Patty noticed bits of meconium in his teeth. *I could have told you so,* she thought with a bit of a of a smile creeping across her face.

Another fascinating character on our June of 1999 trip was Alaska's legendary Dick Griffith. Dick's white hair stood straight up, and he had sharp facial features. Even at 72, his shoulders were strong and square and his body exuded inexhaustible energy. Dick rowed a 16-foot boat with a nearly effortless minimum of strokes.

Dick Griffith

He always had to be doing something, whether pumping water, cleaning the fire pan or helping in the kitchen. Dick stayed a couple of days at my house before and after our trip and did more work there than I had in the previous or ensuing six months. Griffith put in a new set of square 4x4 posts to hold up my shaky back patio cover, installed a ceiling fan, planed the front door until it closed, fixed the lawnmower and cut the grass. I asked him if he couldn't stay longer, but he had a solo wilderness race to prepare for.

In 1949, he built his own wooden boat and took a girlfriend, later his wife, from Green River, Wyoming all the way through Flaming Gorge, the Gates of Lodore, Cataract, Glen, Marble and the Grand canyons to Pierce Ferry on Lake Mead. The doctors told him to go to Arizona for his health, so he decided to float there.

On our trip, one of his favorite lead lines was, "In the old days."

"In the old days, we just threw some beans, bacon and coffee in the raft. Didn't take us an hour and a half to pack all this fancy gear."

"In the old days, Martin Litton borrowed my first rubber raft for two years to get his business started."

"In the old days, we drank right out of the river. Didn't need to pump water all the time. That pump cost more than my first raft."

"In the old days, we drank coffee right out of a tin can. Didn't need all this deluxe kitchen gear."

Dick led the loop hike up to Thunder River, then across Surprise Valley and down the Deer Creek drainage. He marched off, full of steam, with Mike Opinsky and his daughters, Bridget and Natalie, plus the Huizingh boys, Bryan and Erin. The kids were between 18 and 22 years old. When he stomped up into Thunder River, only Bridget, a college track star, was still with him. I came along and asked where everyone was.

"They couldn't keep up," Dick thundered.

"Dick, when you lead a hike, don't you think you should stop now and then and pull everybody together?" I asked.

The indomitable Alaskan roared back, "I take no prisoners. They couldn't keep up." We had four members of our group lost, thrashing around somewhere in Tapeats Canyon beyond the trail cutting up to Thunder River.

Thunder River

Then Dick and Dillweed # 1, as he nick-named Bridget, started up and over Surprise Valley. As we suspected, although the lost group never reached Thunder River, they had the smarts to follow Tapeats Creek back to camp.

One of Dick's most amazing feats has been to walk solo, dragging a sled behind him, along the entire fabled Northwest Passage. For over a decade, he did it in March and April, still winter, on Arctic ice, at the clip of approximately 200 to 300 miles each year. Alone, he faced mist-laden darkness and endless jumbled ice. Dick said, "Some nights it would hit 40 below but I had my little tent and mukluks and got along just fine."

He was disdainful of large carnivores, commenting, "Those polar bears are over-rated. Heck, I slept right on my food." One night a polar bear ripped open his tent just missing his face, but Griffith slept through it. The next morning he saw the shadow of the bear on the tent, got a ski pole, and, yelling, chased it away. After breakfast he packed his sled and saw the bear sitting and watching him about 100 yards away.

Dillweed # 1

"They can smell fish cooking 50 miles away," Dick commented. He knew it would track him all day long and, if the bear got hungry, it could become dangerous. Then he got a plan. Dick got out his little stove and cooked up some frozen fish, then mixed in 20 Tylenol plus ten Advil. He buried the bait. Sure enough, as soon as he started on his way the animal came over, dug it up and devoured the morsel. "He trailed me for about two miles then he just wasn't there no more. Must have needed a big nap about that time," Dick said.

After Lava the intensity eases, and it is usually a relaxed journey on out unless you want to challenge the hole head-on at Mile 209. We love our jumping rock on the right below Pumpkin Springs. Every trip we argue about how high it is. Guesses range from 25 to 40 feet, but it seems high enough when you are standing up on top. We say that everyone has to jump because *it's the code*. Some don't see it that way. At 8,000 cfs. and under, I've touched bottom there. If you want to try it, the higher water levels are safer.

It's the code originated with my sons, students, and football players back at Arcadia High School in the mid-1960s. We would float the Lower Salt River in inner tubes and stop just around the bend down from Stewart Mountain Dam, climb a gauge tower, then up onto the cliff above for a good 55-foot leap. It was an unwritten brotherhood code that everybody jumped. One day, my boys, third and fourth graders, brought a friend along, Hervey, who had never been to the river. We climbed up on the cliff and Hervey said, "Gee, Mr. Finkbine, it's neat up here. Look, I can see the dam and everything." When my older son, Mark, suddenly disappeared over the edge of the cliff, a startled look appeared on Hervey's face. Alarmed, he asked, "Where did he go?"

One of my football players, an 11th grade hulk named Craig, answered, "Well, Hervey, it's like this. When we all come to the river we all jump the cliff. It's tradition. It's the code."

Hervey tiptoed slowly to the edge, looked down, and said in terror, "I ain't jumping off this."

I wasn't paying much attention as others jumped but whirled at the sound of a terrible scream. Craig held the writhing Hervey above his head. He looked at me with a glint of determina-

It's the Code

tion in his eyes and bellowed, "It's tradition. It's the code. *It's the code!"* and threw poor Hervey out into the void. There was a horrifying splat and a cry of pain. Hervey never came back to the river with us again.

A few years ago, Craig and I were up at Lake Powell, climbing a ledge about 50 feet above the water. Well into my 60s and overweight, I didn't want to jump. But then I looked at Craig. Although he was 20 years younger, he had to be at least 70 pounds heavier than he ought to be. Somehow I knew it would be harder on him than me.

So I touched his shoulder and said, "Craig, *it's the code!*" and jumped. He had no choice but to follow. There were two slaps when he hit, his feet and then his stomach. He did a cannon ball without having to double up.

Food is fun. We cook and eat incredible suppers, better than at home, with Dutch oven delights such as pizza or pineapple upside down cake, not to mention home-baked biscuits.

There are steaks, stews, Mexican, Italian, Indian and Asian specialties.

One sure laugh-kicking time is talent night. Everyone has to perform, share whatever they can do. Dances, songs, poetry, stories, jokes, unusual talents or any miscellaneous kind of silliness is actively encour-

aged. Steve England, a postmaster, won one night because he could name the zip code of every city and small town in Arizona. Another night a fellow who had forgotten necessary equipment and was instantly nicknamed Moronski, won by modeling his new splash jacket and rain pants fashioned out of garbage bags.

Some nights we have river communion modeled after the talking stick councils of Native-Americans. Our talking stick is a bottle of Jack Daniels.

Andre, chef supreme

We sit in a circle, it is passed around, and the others are pledged to listen to the person who holds it. He or she must try to talk from their heart. They can address a single person, the entire group, or tell a story they feel has significance or is funny. They can take a

Talent show winners

drink out of the bottle or not before they pass it on. Some of the most meaningful things said on any trip can grow out of communion night, words that bond the group together. If the bottle goes 'round enough times, some of the most inane things can be said on communion night.

Most nights doing the Grand are spent in discussions, jokes, stories and lies around the campfire. After some strenuous hikes or days spent

Warming up for girls' arm wrestling

rowing against the wind, a few members of the group crawl into their bags early. There are other special event nights like dress-up night, birthdays, cave man night, shooters happy hour, whiskey kiss night, girls' arm wrestling and Olympics time, where we might do bag races and skip rope with the bow lines. Also, on any given night, depending on the group, an all-out, raging party might erupt in spontaneous combustion beyond the pale of what can be termed civilized.

One night we decided to have a jalapeno eating contest. It was modeled after the annual event held in the middle of the bridge between El Paso, Texas and Juarez, Mexico.

One Chicano champion there ate 114, a lethal dose for an ordinary gringo; in fact, for any kind of gringo. I was burdened by a sore throat and headache that evening, wondering if I could fight it off or was destined to be sick for a few days. Nothing is more of a downer than being sick on a river trip. I managed second place with three and a half of the hot peppers, then we had a shrimp supper heavily laced with both jalapenos and garlic. Later we sipped Jack Daniels and told stories. After that we gulped more Jack and told lies. After the heavy dosage of jalapenos, garlic, and whiskey, I woke the next morning without a germ in my body. It was the best I felt in years. It was a remarkable recovery. I wonder if the cure still works now that I'm 71?

Putting up our tents at 220-Mile Canyon reminds me of a night in 1984 when a commercial outfit pulled into a downstream camp next to ours. An excited oarsman, Jeff, came running up saying, "Did you see that boatgirl down there? Come on, we've got to meet her, she's beautiful." Her name turned out to be Debbie and she was a long-legged, gorgeous river guide. Old Sly Dog, as Jeff was known around women, was at his best, tellin' stories, crackin' jokes, spoonin' out compliments, turning on the charm, poppin' beers.

Abruptly, Miss Wonderful turned and called out, "Jimmy, come over here, guy." From the shadows stepped a Greek god with more muscles in his stomach than I had in my entire body. "Boys," she announced proudly, "meet my husband." Her husband turned out to be one of the legendary Grand Canyon guides, Jimmy Hendricks.

Jeff's jaw dropped halfway to his knees, disappointment scrunched all over his face. After an apologetic retreat he stomped back to camp kicking pebbles and pouting like a little boy who wants a lollipop and can't have it.

The next morning the commercial group had an early departure. One of their guides slapped my tent about 4:30 A.M. I got up and wandered about. I thought, *Why are you up, Finkbine? You don't have to go anywhere.* Then I saw Jeff lying asleep in his bag on the sand. I went over, lay down next to him, and whispered in his ear, "Jeff, Jeff."

Still asleep, he mumbled, "What? What?"

"Debbie wants you. Debbie wants you."

"She does? She does?"

"You bet. She says you are the most masculine hunk of man she's ever met and if you hurry down right now her husband is a real sound sleeper and you and her can have a whole lot of fun."

"We can? We can?"

"She really wants you right now."

"She does? She does?"

Old Sly dog snorted; one eye crawled open, then both popped wide. "Finkbine, what are you doing? Get the hell out of here."

I pointed at the moon and said, "Look, the sun is way up. It's time to rock and roll."

He stared at the moon for a good ten seconds, then said, "Damn you, get the hell out of here."

I scrambled off laughing at those precious seconds, maybe 25 of them when I had a believer in the twilight zone.

No Regrets

There is a part of me (sometimes difficult to find)
where the wind blows from the west
as daylight flees into hushed tones
weaving gold and subterranean reds
into strands of night. Blustering through fields,
it scatters ripe grain and seed, specks flying.
It sings full-blown through tattered skies,
laughing at lost dreams and half-used yesterdays,
a dappled smile yearning to one mysterious
echo of time, open to every leaf that falls,
lazy drone of insects, black caps dance
against sprays of untamed grass.

The mountains claim their own, earth smiling
in wayward streams swollen with spring.
I want to kiss their lips, sing, and cry
(oh, how I want to cry) not be a careful, careful cog
in the world's machine, let life touch me so deep
that I am unfit for work and become tangled branches,
leaves unshed of clothes,

a white flower swiming
in seas of green with pollen on his lips
smiling as he dies.

My Family Crest

Snug around the campfire at night there is nothing finer than a good story. Not only does it harken back to the oral tradition, but it also helps establish the individuality of the group members. Somehow, I feel our fire is linked to countless thousands of other fires through history and the stories told bind us to a lost tradition invaluable in achieving a sense of who we are and where we came from.

Grandfather Wilmer Browne Finkbine

I remember visiting my Grandfather Finkbine when I was five. By that time the farm had been sold and he lived in a Victorian house surrounded by a large veranda one block from Chesapeake Bay in Annapolis, Maryland. Dad taught me to swim while we were there. The house had two sets of stairs and I thought it magical when I told my mother I was going upstairs, then raced down the back stairs and sneaked up behind her. I loved to explore grandfather's workroom. It had a lathe turned by a pedal mechanism that I played with surrounded by a fas-

Our fire linking us to countless other campfires through history

cinating array of tools, old hand-adjusted planes and hand-turned drills. It was permeated by the smell of sanded wood, oil and leather. I loved that smell. It captured a certain industry and the skilled use of hands. Grandfather had a family crest over the fireplace mantle. On it was a knight in armor within an oval supported by two coyotes raised up on their hind legs. I asked him why the coyotes were on the crest. He pulled me up on his lap and told me this story.

His father, my great-grandfather, Amos Finkbine, was the first member of our family to come west. He carved a small ranch for himself out on the windswept plains of Wyoming. There he built a small cabin for himself and my great-grandmother, Margaret. One day a storm moved in, great billowing clouds dark and ominous in the northern sky. Great-grandfather thought, *That storm will scatter the cattle to hell and gone. I'd better saddle up Old Smokey and round them up before it's too late.* So he saddled up his horse and rode up a draw, over the ridge and down into the valley where his herd was grazing. Great-grandfather misjudged how swift the storm was moving and a furious blizzard swept in and caught him out in the

Snug at story time

open. He turned his horse back towards the cabin but the fury, the incredible might of the storm was too much. It blinded Old Smokey and great-granddad and they couldn't make much headway against it. The horse stepped into a prairie dog hole and broke his leg. They went down in a heap. Great-grandfather loved that animal but he had no choice but to put it out of its misery. He tried to forge on alone but the blizzard drove him back. He huddled against the dead horse and realized he'd likely freeze to death.

Then he had an idea. It was a slim chance but at least a chance. He drew his long hunting knife, sliced open the horse's belly, and pulled out the steaming entrails. Then he wormed his way inside, pulling the carcass shut about him, huddling in the red, wet dark.

It was cold and the temperature was dropping fast. He realized he was going to freeze to death in spite of being protected from the wind. Great-grandfather said his prayers, thanked God for the life he had been given and asked that his transgressions be forgiven. He hoped, after a due period of mourning, Margaret would remarry and have a family, maybe name a little boy after him. Then he died.

Well, you know, he thought he had died. He was really surprised when he woke in the morning and discovered he was still alive. Cold, oh, he was cold, chilled right through to the marrow of his bones, but alive.

From the silence around him he realized the storm had blown itself out and he had survived. He thanked God for his miraculous escape from death and made an effort to crawl out of the horse. His heart sank. The carcass had frozen solid and he was entombed within it. He was going to die anyway.

"You expect me to believe that?"

He scrunched up and started praying, getting ready to die all over again when he heard some sniffing and scratching going on outside the horse. He peeked out the slit in the stomach and saw two coyotes gnawing at the dead animal. He waited. He was a great hunter. He waited and waited until just the right moment and reaching his fingertips through the frozen crack in the carcass, grabbed the tails of the two coyotes and hung on with all his might. Oh, they yipped and yapped, howled and snarled and struggled to get loose. They fought so hard that they broke Old Smokey free and started to drag him. Then great-grandfather discovered that if he pulled on this tail or that one he could steer the dead horse.

Well, by gum, he steered that carcass up out of the valley, over the crest, and down the draw to the front door of the cabin. He let go of those coyotes and they went yipping and yelping away. Great-grandfather called out to Margaret. She saw his predicament at a glance, got the axe and carefully chopped him out, then fixed him up some strong, hot coffee.

Too much fun

Well, about a year later they had a little boy, my grandfather who told me the story, then he had my dad and my dad had me. So you see why those coyotes are on our family crest. If it hadn't been for them, I wouldn't be sitting here tonight telling you this story.

We were having a discussion around the fire one night on a 1996 trip about the mystic quality of the Grand Canyon. I maintained that, at times, I felt like I had entered a different plane of existence within the confines of the towering walls about us. A plane at once less complicated than the city yet one with more possibilities of magic or altered perceptions. It was a place of miracles. We batted this idea back and forth as we sipped

The place of miracles

drinks and puffed on cigars. It was one of our philosophic nights. Irish John Manning, Celtic-loving, great-hearted companion on many a wild and wondrous river trip who had spent a great deal of time helping others beat alcohol and drug abuse and put their lives back together again, leaned forward and said, "Let me tell you a story." It went like this.

In the summer of 1968, I was working as a cook at the Colonel's in Phoenix. The heat from the pressure cookers in the kitchen was intense. I was 16 and looking to party, cold beers after the hot kitchen. A fellow worker, Randy, two-years-older than myself, knew where the action was. I don't remember meeting Lyle; he just became part of our group. He was tall, loud, arrogant and smart. Everyone said he was smart and I got tired of hearing about it, but he never did.

Lyle was restless and into adventure. He dragged me into the wilderness. I am forever grateful to him for that. I picked up my hiking pace from him, from trying to keep up with his long, Abe Lincoln legs. He showed me that to see the great places of the world is worth the work, that whiskey is worth the weight in your pack and that the trail into Havasupai is fascinating on two hits of acid.

My first two river trips were put together by Lyle with whatever equipment and people he could scrounge, no experience necessary. Our first trip was on the Dolores River up in Colorado in 1980, in freezing weather with only tee shirts and shorts. Suddenly, in heavy whitewater, our crew stopped paddling to wave to people on shore taking pictures. A big fellow named Rick was sucked out into a hydraulic that kept pulling him down and spitting him back up along the raft. With a burst of adrenaline and more strength than I thought I had, I hauled him back into the raft. While the idiots continued to wave, we took control of the craft and, paddling furiously, got it through the rapid. On shore, Lyle smiled smugly.

In 1981, we ran Westwater Canyon up in Utah. We got to the put in on a Friday afternoon. Our buddy Ray came down from Grand Junction but couldn't do the trip due to a recent hernia operation. He mentioned we should come see his house sometime. Lyle and I grabbed a case of beer and headed for Grand Junction. We drove through the night, looked the house over, gave Ray's wife, Helen, a hug, turned around and headed back to the put in. We put on Frank Zappa's *Mudshark* and taped the radio mike open just sure all the truckers would appreciate it. We hit the put in just at launching time. Lyle still wore his smug smile. He pointed to a boat filled with nine people and said to me, "Okay, you're the captain." Upon reflection, I'm not sure why people thought he was so smart. Well, at least no one died.

Lyle

Lost in the ecstasy and belief in the invulnerability of youth, those were great days and wild times. We headed out into the Superstition Mountains as often as we could. We jumped the cliffs and the second bridge at Canyon Lake. I remember a perfect dive off the top span of that bridge at midnight on acid and under a full moon. Now, I wonder if it was as perfect as I thought. The older I get, the better I was.

There is a boat dock near the bridge. In those days it was much smaller than it is now. Lyle thought it would be a great idea to take one of the boats for a ride. We broke the lock holding the craft to the slip easily enough, but discovered the oars were locked up in a floating shed attached to the dock. We rattled the door and jumped as what must have been an immense guard dog growled and hurled itself against the inside of the door. We noticed that there was a garage door on the backside of the shed where a boat could pull right up to it. When we banged on that door the dog, snarling with rage, threw itself against it. Johnny Rainwater climbed up on the roof with a pole to hook the door handle. Lyle banged on the door, the dog charged, John pulled the latch and Fido went for a swim. Meanwhile, grabbing the oars, we went for a boat ride. We found a hunk of Styrofoam and took turns "water skiing" on it at least as fast as we could go with a drunken teenager rowing.

We left the stolen craft at the mouth of Tortilla Creek and hiked out to the road, stopping to swim in the pools along the way. When we got back to the car, my wallet was missing. There was a group of guys looking sort of investigative. I yelled out, "Did you see a wallet?"

They yelled back, "Did you see a boat?" I had to go down and get a new driver's license when we returned to town.

Another place we loved in the Superstitions was Reavis Ranch. When we first started backpacking there, the cabin was still intact. We loved that place and took care to clean up after ourselves. October was the best time to hike in to harvest some of the apples growing in the unattended orchard there. We were learning the tradition of using the wilds and leaving it in prime condition for the next guy. It was sad to see how each year there was more damage done and a little less cabin left. One year some Air National Guard weekend warrior types stole the pot-bellied stove out of the kitchen and hauled it away by helicopter. They got caught and had to pack it back in on their backs. It never worked right again,

Irish John Manning

smoked like hell, but by then every kitchen window was busted out anyway. We were grateful for the story and had a lot of good laughs about those guys around the fire.

Lyle had a great dog he got from our buddy Randy. By then Randy was working as a roofer, so that became the dog's name. Roofer was a redbone hound, a great trail dog who would pack in his own doggy saddlebags, food, and water. One time he found a dead cow beside the trail, dived in and rolled and rolled before Lyle could stop him. I never smelled anything worse in my life. Lyle washed him in the creek and rubbed smashed apples from the orchard on his coat. It helped some but not enough in my opinion. Another great thing to do with smashed apples was to make cider. About half-smashed apples and half Wild Turkey and we got half-smashed ourselves. We had a great time howling at the moon with the stink dog.

It was about that time that Lyle married Martha, his first wife. She had gone with my brother, Paul, for a while and even though I wondered about her taste in men, I was happy for them. They were both special people to me and they had a lot of fun together. After a while, they had a daughter, Stacy, a terrific kid. She was super intelligent and had a beautiful smile. Lyle and his family seemed to be on the top of the world. We all seemed to be getting into relationships and holding regular jobs by then and I didn't see them as often.

I don't know why or how relationships turn sour. Maybe Lyle just couldn't settle down. He got

> *One good story that is yours is worth a year of television*

involved with the Arizona Bighorn Sheep Society and started doing trips with them. He immersed himself in service work, hiking in bales of hay and salt blocks to remote areas to keep the bighorns healthy. It was quite a departure for him. I remember him telling me about those guys. He was impressed by the quality of their commitment to conservation, by their love for wilderness. It was good karma for him. I don't really know what went wrong, but he and Martha got divorced. Later, he met a girl named Vicki and married her. I only met her once. Lyle talked Rick and I into doing a walk around central Phoenix for some charity, from Encanto Park to the Biltmore and back in a big circle. We made it as far as the Gopher Club Bar. They were just opening up as we walked by so we thought that was a sign. As I vaguely recall, I think we stayed until closing time. We did give money to the charity though, God bless them all.

One day Lyle and Roofer and I got the idea to go climbing in the Superstitions. Actually, Roofer had nothing to do with the idea and wanted less to do with the project. It was mid-July and hot as hell and every time we hit a red light, Roofer would jump out of the back of Lyle's truck and trot over to the nearest shade. He found trees, gas pumps, parked cars, whatever, he wasn't picky. We made it to the mountains but the dog hadn't changed his mind. He hid behind trees, big rocks, shrubs, anything giving off shade from the merciless sun. We kept yelling and kicking at him to urge Roofer on but he wasn't happy. He found a big old saguaro, plopped down, and as good as said, "No more." He refused to move. Nothing could convince him this was anything akin to fun.

I started looking over the saguaro and noticed it was split open, possibly from a lightning strike. Some of the ribs were exposed and I reached in and pulled out the nearest one. It was as though I had ordered a customized and hand-crafted walking stick. It fit me perfectly, tapered at the bottom, flared out a bit in the middle and then tapered again at the neck for my grip. The knob at the top had a small hole in it for a wrist-thong. We decided the stick was what we had come for and went back home. As soon as we turned back, Roofer led the way to the truck.

Mooney Falls

That stick became a part of me on journeys down countless trails for the next 17 years. I saved it from carelessly becoming part of a campfire more than once. It was a totem, and as the years went by and I didn't see Lyle that much, I always thought of him when I hiked with it. Then one day, for reasons that were his own, Lyle took his own life. His brother, Bob, scattered his ashes in Havasupai Canyon. For several years, I would hike in and spend some time alone talking to him, remembering old times.

Then, one year, my wife, two of our kids, and I camped at the top of Mooney Falls and made friends with Clifford, the Indian campground host. It was his job to take care of things around camp, but he found time to hang out with us swapping stories. I told him about Lyle and we agreed his spirit was happy there in the canyon. We camped a few days and then spent our last night in the village at the lodge to get an early start out in the morning.

When I got to the village that evening I was amazed to find I had walked those few miles with my pack but without my stick. After 17 years, I had inadvertently left it behind. It was getting dark, so I didn't know if I would find the stick if I went back after it, not to mention the extra six-mile walk. We knew Clifford was still in camp when we had started out, so we called the host shack. He was just locking up. When I explained what happened, he kind of groaned and said, "Oh man, my wife is going to kill me. Already I'm late and I had a couple beers after you left." I understood but explained that it was the stick Lyle and I had found together and Clifford said okay, he'd try to find it.

It is a good half-mile from the host shack to Mooney Falls and the desert sun had slipped away fast. I figured I'd better work on letting go of that stick; that's the last I would ever see of it. We settled down and ordered something to eat. It continued to gnaw away at my mind.

About an hour later, here comes Clifford with the stick. I was overjoyed to see him and began to shower thanks upon him when he said, "Wait, I got to tell you what happened. I was walking down the trail and watched the last rays of the sun disappear. It got real dark and I started to think about turning back when I heard a voice calling to me. I wondered who it was and followed the sound right up to a

Havasu Canyon

tree next to the falls. There was no one there but I reached up in the tree and pulled your stick out. I couldn't even see it but somehow I knew it was there."

I just smiled and said, "Yeah, I bet that was Lyle. He's here, watching over things."

Clifford smiled and replied, "Yeah, I guess so."

My friends and family like to go to 'Supai in August. That's when the tribe has their annual peach festival celebration. Many of tourists are insensitive as far as the Native American people are concerned, so I try to keep in mind the fact that it's their land, their home, even their separate nation as far as sovereignty is concerned. I'm their guest and I'd better be treating them and the land with respect. I try to treat all people with that same attitude, but down in the canyon it seemed a little more important.

We came back to the same beautiful camping spot by the falls we had been at exactly one year before. We had a wonderful time and when it was time to go I arrived back at the lodge and looked. Big deja vu, no stick. I could not believe it. I panicked, but then made myself stand still, take an enormous breath, and started laughing out loud. "Okay, Lyle, she's yours now. Our bond is spiritual and forever. Think of me while you're walking with it."

A few years later, Bob Finkbine was putting together a trip through the Grand Canyon. I didn't have time to do the entire trip so I hiked in and

met the group at Phantom Ranch. Two young fellows, Corey and Jay who guided with Bob on the Salt River, were going in with me. I later nicknamed them Heinous and Gnarly. They carried Corey's kayak all the way down so early in the morning it was still dark. Jay had forgotten to bring a wetsuit for me and wanted to catch the people hiking out to make sure they left one behind. As it turned out, there wasn't much chance that any of them were toting any more uphill than they absolutely had to, so I had my pick of several when I arrived. But that's the kind of guys Jay and Corey were, young men of high integrity who wanted to take care of me.

The tunnel on the trail through Havasu Canyon

I continued to think of Jay this way until the last night when we had river communion at Mile 220 with a half-gallon of Osco Tequila, nothing but the best. It was wild staying sober and watching the rest of the group. The first clue they were drinking more than they could hold came when matter-of-fact Jay, a weight lifter, suddenly began to spout spontaneous and beautiful river poetry. No one had ever heard him mention poetry before in his life. It was his latent muse flashed to life by drink that probably would have exploded if you smoked around it. The second clue we had was when Dave Harris, an expert guide who rarely drank, was suddenly swimming out in the middle of the river. We all screamed at him and luckily he returned. The final clue was when we woke in the morning and found someone had mistaken the kitchen for the groover. Harris was huddled in the fetal position unable to get up. Finkbine scooped up the mess on a shovel and laid it right in back of Dave's head. Still fetaled, his nose began to twitch and sniff. He turned his head to find the source of the foul odor and almost jammed his face right into the pile. Harris got up. Bleary-eyed, the culprit Jay confessed and did a complete clean-up, learning greater respect for the Canyon.

Our communion night an exception, there is something intensely spiritual about a river trip. One of the most fascinating sights for me on my first trip was the Vishnu Schist, some of the oldest exposed rock in the world. We did a number of wonderful hikes and stopped one day at the mouth of Havasu Creek and Canyon.

It was a cold day, so some of our group were exploring but not stopping to swim in the beautiful turquoise water. I wanted to see if I could run the four miles up to Beaver Falls. Corey and Karl, the paddle raft captain, came along. After a bit they turned back. I was running along in my wetsuit and booties on that powder soft trail, loving it, silent as a ghost. I came around a big outcropping of rock and almost fell on top of the white butt of a bighorn ewe. I quickly sidestepped into the creek up to my chest so as not to scare her anymore than I already had. She scampered up the slope maybe 50 feet or so. Now, I don't know about you, but I've never gotten close to a bighorn before; they like to keep their distance. I was feeling pretty lucky when I noticed another ewe close by. Then out walked a big ram looking proud, almost smug. Then two babies scampered out of the shrubs and stood next to him. I couldn't believe my luck. They weren't running away. That's when I noticed the ram looking me dead in the eye. I felt a familiar stirring. Calm. Content. Smug.

"Hey, Lyle," I said, "good to see you again. Where's my stick?"

Through Bouldered Slots

Blue water plummeting
through bouldered slots

yet placid in pools
and slow bends.

Silver trout spangle in sunlight,
snaking to depths
where, in the absence of clouds,
stars swim at midnight.

Night or day,
never resting tide,
heartsward sound
of a first breath
or last exhalation.

Shaped by the Land

I was once accused of being a legend. Arriving in Pilar, New Mexico in the late spring of 1988 to work on the Racecourse and Taos Box of the Upper Rio Grande, I met Catfish, a guide left over from the sixties sporting a pony tail, ear rings, and tattoos. His lined and sagging face looked like he had slept in it. When we were introduced he said, "Wow, Finkbine, Bob Finkbine. Man you're a legend, a friggin' river legend. It sure is a pleasure, believe me, a pleasure. Very seldom I gets to come face to face with a legend." He pumped my hand. I swelled with pride.

"Thanks," I replied grinning foolishly. "Thanks a hell of a lot."

"Yeah," Catfish said not letting go of my hand, "you gott'a be a legend. Why there's a hole named after you on the

Not a legend

Upper Salt." My swollen pride deflated like a punctured balloon. I went plumb flat. The hole in question was called the Souse Hole just below the Ledges and above Walnut Creek. It was a rather benign-looking keeper near the left bank at the bottom of a minor rapid. The idea was to avoid the hole and I had gotten stuck in it so often that they started calling it Fink's Hole and later Finkbine's Hole. It got the name because I was too unskilled and dumb to stay out of it, not because I was the stuff that spawned legends.

Once I was in it for 25 minutes. The boat was twisted this way and that, shaken like an old shoe by a dog, but fortunately not flipped. When I realized we probably wouldn't go over, I said knowingly to Hattie Clarendon, my novice companion, "This is what's called a keeper hole." The other boatmen got lines to our craft from downstream but even rowing with all their might could not pull us out. Finally, they secured a line to the bank and were able to extract the boat directly sideways. The thrashing we endured popped a rocket box, and our spaghetti for that evening congealed into one gigantic lump. Camping at a terrace called the Pent House, we heated up the sauce then cut hunks of glutinous, glued-up pasta into it and called it Finkichini.

Hattie was a bit on the chubby side with heavy thighs. Two days later we hiked up Cherry Creek in shorts and her thighs rubbed together until they were raw. We were on our way back and she was walking with her legs spread as far apart as possible and walked right over a coiled bull snake with a foot on each side of the serpent. We figured had she stepped on the snake it would have bitten her and although it was non-poisonous she would have thought it was a rattlesnake and died of fright like the poor horse in *Animal House*. As much as she deprecated her plumpish thighs they had saved her life.

Not that I haven't come across a legendary river man now and again. On my first run on the Main Salmon in 1971, we stopped to see a hermit

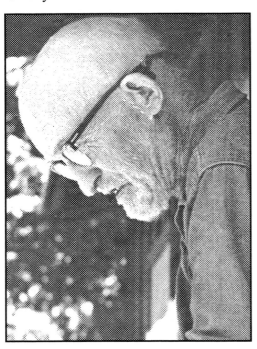

Frank Lanz

named Frank Lanz. Frank had been on the river since 1916, a *River of No Return* legendary figure. We had been warned that, at 82, he wasn't feeling good and had a feud with another hermit down the river and not to bother him. The mortal enemies, who had probably forgotten what started the whole thing, could walk by each other's cabin as long as they stayed on the trail. If they stepped off of it on to the other's property they got shot at. Worried he would send us packing, we were overjoyed when, hacking, coughing and spitting up gunk, he invited Don Petelle and me up to his porch for a beer. The rest of our crew were out picking berries for pancakes.

As the Salmon bent to the left, his cabin was on river right by a canyon with a spring, a stream, an orchard and a plethora of lodgepole pine. It was a garden spot, now named Lanz Bar. His clothes hung slack, there was spittle in his stubble beard, eyes seeing everything and nothing, clouded by memories, memories held up and examined, illuminating dimming victories and defeats in a life nearly lived out. I glanced inside his cabin at a wall I thought would hold a bear or cougar skin. Instead it was covered with chains made out of the pop tabs of Olympia beer cans. The guides coming downriver took good care of the old man.

We watched the wind ripple high grass up the hillside on the opposite side of the river. Lanz pointed a shaky hand and finger saying, "That's about as close as you'll ever get to seeing wind."

Looking out at our people searching for berries, still coughing and spitting, he started a story. "Last year I was out picking berries, I was. Well, it was so hot in July, Lord it was hot, that I sat down, leaned back against a tree, and went plumb asleep, just fast asleep." Pausing for a few moments, he suddenly waved his arms and yelled, "Whoa, agh-h-h-h-h-h, I woke and there was a huge bear and he came for me and I ran. He chased me and I ran. He chased me and I ran. He chased me and I ran. I ran right out on the ice on the river and,

you know," holding up a hand to show us just how wide it was between his thumb and fingers, "that ice was just thick enough to hold me but that bear he broke through and drownt and that *saved my life.*" Lanz sat there looking at us through watery eyes.

Finally, I said, "Come on, old man Lanz, how could there be ice on the river in July?"

Hot springs tub on the Main Salmon

He had been waiting for that. His face broke into a broad grin as he said, "Well, I just wanted you boys to know that bear chased me all the way to *January*."

What exactly is a legendary river or outdoor woman or man? A clear cut, ironclad definition does not exist. Certainly, the great masters of first ascents or descents have attained that status. Seldom do we talk about the Himalayas without mentioning, among others, Maurice Herzog, Sir Edmund Hillary, Sherpa Tenzing or Reinhold Messner. If Victoria Falls and the Zambezi come up then Dr. David Livingston and first descent leader Richard Bangs are discussed. Bangs's initial run survived both hippopotamus and crocodile attacks. Crocs often reach 15 feet in length and 1,000 pounds in weight. They consume incredible amounts of protein. The stomach of one shot in the Okavango Swamp in 1968 held the remains of a zebra, a donkey, two goats, and the still clothed body of a woman who had been missing for 17 days.

Talk of the Grand Canyon and there's Ned Galloway, Georgie White, Glen and Betsy Hyde, Buzz Holstrom and a host of others to swap stories about. Nathan Galloway had been a trapper along the river and in the 1890s he had designed a new kind of rowboat to run the Green and Colorado rivers all the way down to Needles, California. While trapping along the wild rivers of the West, Galloway often watched geese as they swam, moved, and rode choppy water. A goose's body, it seemed to him, was a good hull, stable and maneuverable. The wetted portion was basically a distended triangle with the wide breast as the base and the sides curved and flared outward as they came back to a point in the tail. Their underside was "raked," riding deeper in the water midway than at either tail or breast. The feet were the deepest and widest point where they steered the goose easily. Galloway believed a boat of the same configuration would be ideal for the rivers. He experimented, building and modifying several to see how they handled.

Another innovation that made sense to him was to drift along with the stern pointed downstream. The rower then faced the obstacles ahead and could pull away from them. Back in Ohio, Julius Stone conferred with Galloway on the design of a new river boat. Their concepts were translated into Michigan white pine. The new configuration was called the Galloway-Stone hull. It became the prototype for fast water rowboats. Facing downstream, they ran the Green River and the

*We owe our modern whitewater technique
to Ned Galloway*

Grand Canyon in 1909. Stone Canyon on river right just below Deubendorff was named after Julius.

Some legendary figures are shrouded in mystery. Talk about Canyonlands and there's Everett Reuss. Knocking about the desert with his mules, Everett had the soul of an artist. He could see in a way that transcended normal vision. His reaction to the wonders of nature went beyond normal experience, to the point where he could resonate to the light waves that struck him from all points in the landscape. His

Canyonlands

aesthetic gift set him apart. Many people can feel emotion as they gaze upon some of the more sublime vistas of canyon, desert or mountain. But Everett Reuss could sense beauty so acutely that it bordered on pain. His letters home have become treasured. Although he yearned to be an artist, he was a better writer. He represented the urge in a modern, fragmented society to cut loose from the comforts and securities of everyday existence and search for a unique destiny true to the compelling myth of the independent and individualistic Western hero. He wrote, "God, how the wild calls to me. There can be no other life for me but that of the lone wilderness wanderer. It has an irresistible fascination." His sensitivity to beauty reminds me of Edna St. Vincent Millay's ecstatic nature and her immortal lines from "God's World," circa 1915.

> *O WORLD,*
> *I cannot hold thee close enough!*
> *Thy winds, thy wide grey skies!*
> *Thy mists that roll and rise!*
> *Thy woods, this autumn day, that ache and sag*
> *And all but cry with colour! That gaunt crag*
> *To crush! To lift the lean of that black bluff!*
> *World, World, I cannot get thee close enough!*
>
> *Long have I known a glory in it all,*
> *But never knew I this;*
> *Here such a passion is*
> *As stretcheth me apart. Lord, I do fear*
> *Thou'st made the world too beautiful this year.*

My soul is all but out of me,-let fall
No burning leaf; prithee, let no bird call.

These all are famous individuals, but I champion a broader definition for people of the land. Mrs. Annie Peaches, an 80-year-old Apache,
said, "The land is always stalking people. The land makes people live right.
The land looks after us. The land looks after people."

A true person of the land, sea, mountains or rivers is someone
whose lifestyle has been shaped by an intimacy with the earth. Their metamorphosis represents the land's power to alter human values crucial to our
survival as a species. Its transformational singularity is a tool to shape ecological convictions necessary to assure an adequate quality of life for all
people. I include within this paradigm those who write, belong to organizations and use their individual resources to expose others to the experience
necessary for their own growth into responsible proponents of global sustainability.

If values change and the earth is restored, perhaps future historians
will write about the populist rising of the *Archetypical Earth Eco Warriors*
of the early 21st century. Already one of the most significant forces for
desirable change is non-governmental volunteer organizations, some working on local problems, others tackling national and world-wide environmental despoliation. They are formed, operated and supported by ordinary
people who care about the world in which their great- and great-great-

Twelve stories to the beer

grandchildren will live. The ranks of
those new collective heroes, the
Archetypical Earth Eco Warriors, is
growing. They live and work in every
town and city. They are our hope for
the future.

For an example of a fellow
Arizonian, there's Jerry Van Gasse.
Son of slickrock, snort buck of western rivers, twelve stories to the beer,
guffawin' boatman, he's a rambling
man hauling rivers and canyons and
deserts around inside of himself, set
jaw and outdoor face worn by rain,
snow, and passing seasons. His hair is
wiry, unruly, and curled. It bends
combs. Below hazel-green-blue eyes
lies a battered Will Rogers-Wallace

88

Berry grin and grizzled chin. His thick shoulders and veined wrists create a sense of power in his bearing. The last thing we hear as we settle in for the night is Van Gasse telling stories and laughing and the first thing to greet our ears as we wake in the morning is Van Gasse telling stories and laughing. We shrug, figure he's been up all night talking to the mountains, the river and his two river dogs, Bart and Ole. The Geeze, a river buddy who spends half the night pumping up his deluxe outdoor mattress, turned to square-shouldered boatman Keith Miller and asked, "Why does Jerry laugh so much?"

Keith scratched his nose, his form of contemplation, and replied, "Hell, Geeze, everyday is a holiday to a madman."

Indestructible, Van Gasse wraps himself in a single frayed Army blanket on bare ground, a rock for a pillow and the stars his tent. While others shiver inside their bags and tents he snores lustily in oblivious sleep. On really cold nights he's often sandwiched by Ole and Bart. He's fussin' up a fire at first hint of dawn, boiling coffee, Chock Full O'Nuts, in his dented black pot, charred and stained, spitting grounds at the lid, pervasive aroma shaking others from their dreams, enticing them from crumpled sleeping

Bart and Ole—River Guides

bags into the morning chill. Pouring out mud thick coffee, he's telling the half-frozen arrivals to the fire's warmth, "I was camping up in the Ute Tribal Park in southwestern Colorado and asked the chief, old Art, where he ever got a last name like Cuthair. He said, 'Jerry, you white men don't want to know.' A French tourist asked Art, 'Where are the wild Indians?' From the westerns that were popular in Europe, he expected to see warriors galloping about in war paint with bows and arrows and brandishing scalping knives.

"Art chuckled again and replied, 'Wild Indians? Oh, I think you find them down in the bars in Gallup.'"

Jerry got his river nickname in the land of dinosaur bones and tiger-striped walls on the Yampa River in 1984. On a bluff overlooking Teepee Rapid, we lanced up our tents and pulled out sleeping bags in the comfortable ritual of setting up camp. After happy hour and supper, Jerry, an engineer named Dirk, and myself were the last three awake still sharing stories and popping beers around a small fire. Jerry slumped over and went to

Land of tiger-striped walls

sleep in his folding camp chair.

"What are we going to do with him?" asked Dirk.

"All hell, it's a nice warm night, he's in the middle of the campground, let's just leave him. He'll be okay where he is," I replied with beer-fed certainty.

It was morning and my blonde sunshine daughter, Tracy, was shaking me. "Dad, wake up, wake up," she said.

"What is it, honey?"

"You've got to come see what's happened to Jerry." Grudgingly, I rose and stretched then walked over to the kitchen area. There was Van Gasse with a splint on his left wrist, an aspirin taped to his forehead and a beer in his good hand. He had awakened in the middle of the night and walked over to the bluff to relieve himself. In the dark he took one step too many and fell 20 feet bouncing off rocks into the river. Instinctively, before being pulled into the rapid, he fought his way to shore, crawled back up into

The cliff diver

camp and lay there like a wounded dog. When Jerry was discovered in the morning, Dr. Tim Flood splinted his broken wrist. Now Jerry was self-medicating. He was drinking beers and popping aspirin. When I found out what happened I nicknamed him the *Cliff Diver.*

"Hell," he exclaimed with a winced grin, "I was just warming up for Acapulco."

On that Yampa-Green trip, Jerry, my daughter Tracy and I had stopped at Jones Hole and hiked up to see the petroglyphs and pictographs. The other rafts were ahead of us. Back on the river, we came to our designated campsite and no one was there. Van

90

Gasse erupted, "How did those morons miss this site? It's as plain as the nose on your face. What a bunch of ding-a-lings." I landed and stepped out of the raft and something crunched under my foot. I jumped back up on the frame. We looked out and as far as we could see the ground was completely covered with plump, purple-dung-colored Mormon beetles. Millions of them were migrating, immediate feedback on why we weren't camping there that night. As we hurriedly pulled back out, we hit a wide swath of the insects swimming across the river. Before long some of them were marching across our oars towards the land and as I swung the raft around they instantly turned direction. Whatever instinctual gyroscope they had was honed eastward bound. Not knowing how much farther down our group had gone, we immediately opted for a floating happy hour.

The position

By the time we located our people we were well-oiled. Our compadres, waiting for our arrival, also had a prolonged happy hour. It was Dirk's birthday but the crew was too lubricated to bake a cake so we opened a can of frosting and passed it around with a spoon accompanied by a ragged rendition of "Happy Birthday." John, an engineer who rarely drank, was sitting on a rocket box longways with his knees locked together, hands inside his thighs, and head slumped down. Someone would tell a joke and a minute or two later John would start to chuckle then lean to one side until he toppled over lying on his side in exactly the same position he had been sitting. He lay there immobilized until we lifted him back into his upright position. It happened over and over, again and again. He was more entertainment than the jokes and stories. He was our new toy.

Jerry and Dirk stumbled off, picked up John's tent, and put it a good 100 yards from its original spot. When the inebriated engineer finally pried himself out of his fixed position and tried to go to bed he came back with a confused expression on his face and immediately sat back on the rocket box and assumed his slumped posture. Then, at the first joke, he toppled over. We put him back upright. He stumbled off to bed again and again returned in a dazed condition mumbling about how he was sure he knew where he had pitched his tent. Jerry and Dirk snuck off and put his tent back in its original location. John trudged off and we heard a slurred shout of triumph and, "I knew it was right here someplace." The next day our hangovers were so bad that we all taped aspirin to our foreheads.

Certain characteristics of Jerry had to be taken with a grain of salt. He has a buoyant optimism about any outdoor adventure that if taken literally could lead to disaster. With that cocksure grin he was forever throwing out phrases like, "Don't worry about it, we'll find water," or, "hell, no sweat, we'll cross that bridge when we come to it."

My daughter Jody and I drove up to meet Van Gasse and a crew he had recruited to explore the Cibique and Canyon Creek area above the Upper Salt Canyon searching for Native American ruins. The high bed International we were going to use was already full so Jerry asked for another driver saying we had good roads all the way. My daughter was about to volunteer her vehicle when I grabbed her arm and whispered, "When Van Gasse says the roads are good you've got to exercise caution. Let someone else volunteer." Sure enough a fellow named Rick and his girlfriend Maureen, a firebrand from Louisiana, volunteered to drive his small Mazda. Jody and I rode with them. The road was fine from Highway 60 to Cibique, a village of nearly 1,100 people that had been inhabited by Apaches for centuries.

The tribe, even after decades of confrontation, confinement and forced assimilation, had retained many of its distinct lifeways and linguistic practices. One was the use of place-names. Many elders seem to take great pleasure in simply saying the native names of various locations within the Cibique Valley. One aged individual remarked, "Those names are good to say. I ride in my mind that way." The names often took the shape of entire descriptive sentences such as, "Where water flows down on top of the white rock," or "where the ledges cross the river." There is a sensory bond between Apaches and the names of certain places, as if by repeating the names they can envision themselves there and draw power from those locations.

Ever the optimist

Place-name stories known as 'agodzaahi or "that which happened" have traditionally been used to encourage right behavior within the tribe. The stories mention where the event talked about took place. One goes, "At the place where whiteness spreads out descending to water, a young brave went hunting one day." This famous

92

story goes on to tell about how the warrior shot a deer but was so far down in a steep part of the canyon that he failed to carry out all of the meat. Because of such waste, ill health and poor luck haunted him until he began to hunt the ancient way. In this manner, various individual places about them remind the people of tribal mores and the traditional Apache way to live. The land retains its power to teach.

After leaving Cibique and crossing Canyon Creek the road grew rougher as it wound its way up into the hills. Soon it became a jeep trail and the Mazda was grinding over rocks that the International could clear easily. At several places three of us got out and helped push the car over spots where it had ground out. The screech-ing of metal on rock made us wince. Further up, the car rose up on a

The people who were here before

rock and crashed down hard. We got out and saw a pool of oil spreading out under the vehicle like blood from a fallen pioneer. Rick had a split in his oil pan. The group from the other car joined us to shove the Mazda clear. Smiling, Van Gasse informed Rick, "Not to worry, partner, we can fix that." From the back of the International he extracted a bar of soap and a case of oil. Grinding the soap into the crack, Jerry filled the car with oil. "Here, keep this case with you and just fill it up as you need to."

The day was bright and beautiful and the sense of height above the canyons ecstatic. Meadows brimming with blooming brittlebrush were framed by red cliffs. After steep bush-whacking we reached the base of the cliff and examined a number of Indian ruins, careful not to take or disturb anything. I believed I would be cursed if I took a piece of pottery or an arti-fact and felt that intriguing sensibility of the elasticity of time, the presence of the past, a feeling of home, of having been there before.

The cattle grazing in the meadows had just calved. Spindly little creatures with wobbly legs worked to stay near their mothers. Back in the leaking and battered car as we slowed to pass the animals, Jody called out,

"Rick, stop the car. One of the calves has bonded to it and you'll run the little guy to death." Rick immediately stopped the car and got out. The trembling little calf looked at him woefully as if to say, "Momma?"

Ever the Good Samaritan, Rick gently picked up the calf to take it back to its mother. A broad stream of yellow coursed down the front of his clothes followed by a muddy green one. As the waste products sunk in, Rick manfully carted the newborn back and set it down. He was a mess and walked slowly back brushing himself off and shaking out his hands with a disgusted look on his face. It wasn't turning out to be a good day. After bottoming out three more times, chewing one tire to pieces and replacing it, and losing the tail pipe, we finally reached the road along the Upper Salt River.

We stopped to say hello to Wilbur, the Apache Ranger. When Wilbur found out that we had dragged a small, non four wheel drive car over 80 miles of jeep road, he chuckled to himself. Smiling, he told Van Gasse, "Good idea, Jerry. Maybe next year we all get Mazdas," then turned away trying not to laugh out loud.

Back at our separate cars, Jody said to me, "It's lucky you knew how bad that road was."

"I've never been on that road before. I had no idea how it would be."

"Then why did you warn me about taking my car?"

"It's just that I know Van Gasse. When he describes what a hike, river trip or adventure will be like, I just take the agony factor and multiply it by ten. Then I decide if I want to go."

"Amazing," Jody said.

"Sure is," I answered.

On one Gates of Lodore trip, Jerry enthused people by telling them we would spend a night at Ken Sleight's ranch outside of Moab. Sleight, one of the initial commercial canyon river runners and a lover of outdoor adventure, was among the first to realize the incredible marvels of Glen Canyon before it eventually disappeared under Lake Powell. A beer-drinking Jack Mormon, he was at home away from home, leading people down rivers and out on horsepack trips. He was the prototype for Ed Abbey's Seldom Seen Smith in Ed's classic, *The Monkey Wrench Gang*. We were upset after being at the ranch for an afternoon, evening, and morning without meeting Sleight. When we voiced our displeasure, Van Gasse said, "Why do you think they call him Seldom Seen?"

Jerry is a true *Archetypical Earth Eco Warrior*. Along with his irascible and matchless personality are the battles he has fought for free running wild rivers and the number of people he has introduced to the splendor of wild places. He helped lead the battle to have the Upper Verde declared a wild and scenic river. Jerry butted heads with the Forest Service over their early failures to provide a coherent plan for the Upper Salt River. He took many, including myself, on our first Upper Salt trips. Van Gasse introduced Gail Peters to river running and later she became the fiery leader of the local chapter of the American Rivers Coalition. He took the ailing environmental fighter Moe Udall on his last outdoor trip, a journey down the Verde River, a reminder of the innumerable hours the legislator had spent in the incomparable wilds

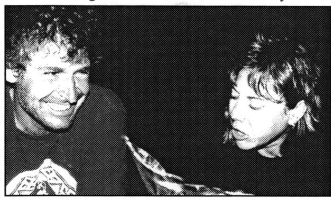

Jerry and his wife Melinda

of Arizona. Jerry's lovely daughter, nine-year-old Katrina has seen more of outdoor Arizona than most old timers. When she was little, Katrina loved to gather firewood on our camping trips. I asked her, "What's the main firewood rule, Katrina?"

She would answer, "If I pick up a stick and it wiggles or rattles, drop it."

Jerry will remain an undying symbol of the thrill of whitewater, beauty of the canyons and the willingness and iron determination to fight for them. His unconventional and uncontrollable laughter around campfires is a fitting monument to any man.

The Yampa

Crow Shadow

Crow shadow flitting across the cliff,
rising, descending, dark image bisected
on cracked rock where the river,
without tributary rains,
runs green.

Bulky wings
battling air,
shadow shifting
in and out
of crevices,
feathered over water
where colors garble.

The time I let go your waist
and slippery wrists,
turned,
and you were gone.

Pursued by memory,
crow-shadowed,

I drift the miles.
I ask for nothing.

Guardian Warriors

One night a group of teenagers were out "gooning," as they termed it, by throwing grapefruit at passing motorists. Gil had an M-80. They stuck it in a grapefruit and Kite readied to wing the sphere. Garland stood by to light it while Stiles was on point.

"Get ready, guys. Here comes a car," Stiles said. Kite leaned back and Garland lit the fuse. As Kite's arm whipped forward, Stiles yelled, "Oh, my God, it's a cop."

Gil Gillenwater

"Holy shit!" The yellow sphere, trailing smoke, was on its way. Somehow they all knew it would be a perfect throw before it even happened. They were in freeze frame, mesmerized, watching the car and grapefruit on a collision course. It hit the hood of the car, bounced up and exploded. They saw the faces of the two patrolmen filled with horror, thinking hand grenade. Then the policemen turned livid. The guys jumped a fence and ran. Hell, this was their turf and they were all athletes. The fuzz would never catch them.

Meet Gil Gillenwater, hell raiser and All State halfback at Scottsdale, Arizona's Arcadia High School. "Gooning" might not seem funny today, but that was 1970.

Then Troy, Gil's younger brother, came along. Seven years later up in the Bradshaw Mountains, a range northwest of Phoenix, the three boys finally reached the grave. A quartz slab gleamed in moonlight. Chiseled into it was a name, O.E. Perry, and a date, 1874.

"I wonder who he really was?" Mike said as he put down the case of beer he had lugged in from the ghost town of Columbia.

"Maybe he was murdered," Troy, the ringleader, said.

"I wonder if they buried his tools or guns with him?" John asked. "Maybe his ghost is still around here."

"I wonder what life was like back in the old days out here?" Troy thought out loud. "Think he was ever attacked by Yavapai?"

"Maybe he's buried without his scalp."

Near midnight they surrounded the grave with lighted candles, drank a few beers, and cut holes for eyes in the bed sheets they had hooked from the Six Belles Motel at the junction of I-17 and Bell Road. Clad as ghosts they started digging at the stroke of midnight. It was a hard exhumation through rock-filled dirt but they kept at it with grim determination. At three-and-a-half feet they unearthed a blanket. Then they heard footsteps. Spooked, the boys ran away and hid in the shrubs beyond the candlelight. They were sitting there hearing footsteps all around. Then Troy thought, *Wait a minute, if I were out walking around and came across three guys in white robes digging up a grave at midnight, I'd probably be running the other way, not us.* So he prodded the others to stand up and walk back out. The footsteps that had frightened them turned out to be a group of wild burros.

Back to work, they finally freed the blanket, pulled it out, opened it up and found it filled with decomposed bone matter. A light powder. That's all that was there: no clothing, no weapons, and no skeleton, just this ghostly powder. While his two compadres turned away and popped more beers

Troy Gillenwater

grumbling about not finding weapons, a full-out skeleton or a cache of gold, Troy, down in the pit, reached out and touched the white powder. It was the closest thing to nothing he had ever held. It felt invisible. A tremor shivered through his body. The apparent emptiness of the fine chalk-like dust was infused by his imagination into a ribbon of time binding him to the previous century. He felt connected to the life Perry had lived, perhaps one of hard work underground, danger, rot gut whiskey and love between a whore's legs. He felt riveted by the sacred dust to the disparate components of a previous existence, a once living, breathing, human being now mating with earth in a nearly forgotten grave.

Meet Troy Gillenwater. Since those adventurous teenage days, he has learned it is best not to disturb historical landmarks.

When Gil and Troy Gillenwater were young, their father, Powell, took them into the outdoors every chance he got. He put his first two boys in the truck and drove them off to Lake Pleasant or Bartlett to fish. They would sit in a little battered fishing boat armed with a small, eggbeater motor with their lines in the water. At times the boys were bored to tears but Powell would keep telling them how great it was, how beautiful the sunset was, how good it was to not talk, to be sitting on the boat not talking. The youngest, Troy, would cast into rocks, hook Powell a couple of times, but nothing could shake his father's patience or desire to be out there with him.

At other times, Powell would take them hunting. As a little guy, Troy wasn't interested in the quest for prey but he loved spending time in the outdoors either hiking with his dad or on family camping trips. Neither boy realized then how difficult it was for their father to carve space out of a busy law practice to be able to spend so much time with them. Powell pointed out how the sun glinted and danced like diamonds across the water, back-lighted the needles of jumping cholla or the splashing flow of water around rock. "Look how beautiful that is, boys. All you have to do is see something like that once a day to be happy." Without his sons knowing it, the seeds that shaped the course of their lives were being planted.

"All you have to do is to see something like that once a day to be happy"

The Gillenwaters have barely survived a series of harrowing wilderness experiences. They have rafted most major rivers in the West including the Grand Canyon, hiked the Pacific Crest Trail, walked with two burros from Mexico through the mountains of Arizona to Kanab, Utah and floated the length of the Green River.

In addition, Troy spent three winters living with a hermit named Curly up in the Bradshaws and Gil once buried himself alive for three days to enhance his budding Buddhist consciousness. These adventures climaxed in three explorations of isolated areas in Tibet including an aborted first descent of the Po Tsangpo River and exploration of the Yarlung Tsangpo Gorge, the deepest canyon in the world at 16,650 feet. In 1997, they and their companions were the first to peer into the depths of the gorge and see the fabled lost falls of the Bramaputra sought by explorers for a century and a half. Along with their younger brother Todd, they almost died of exposure and illness on their 1995 expedition crossing the 14,000-foot high Adretang Mud Bog.

On one of their raft trips down the technical Upper Salt River during a high spring run off, the three brothers were in a paddleboat with a friend named Eric. Coming out of Lower Corral Rapid into Pinball, they flipped the boat. Troy came up sputtering and immediately looked for his brothers. He spotted Gil on the other side of the raft then Todd exploded out of the water. He couldn't find Eric. Just then a dead beaver came floating by. *Wow, a dead beaver! I didn't know there were any beaver left in the Salt Canyon.* Then a stranger came swimming up to Troy. *Wow, a stranger! He*

must have seen we were in trouble and swam out from the shore to help. What a great guy. Troy yelled to the swimmer, "We've got to find Eric. I think he's trapped under the raft." The stranger stared at him. Troy thought, *Wow, imagine a*

The Salt Banks--where the Salt River gets its name

dead beaver in the midst of all this confusion. Troy yelled again, "I said we've got to find Eric. Can you help me look under the raft?" The stare became intense. Just then Troy realized that he had known the guy for nearly two years and this was the first time he realized Eric wore a toupee.

During their expedition on the Green River in 1987, they had arranged for two friends, Ethan Bindelglas and Ken Ludecke, to make a cheeseburger air drop to them just above the town of Green River, Utah near Gunnison Butte.

When they reached the drop site, Gil and Troy rowed over to the bank to wait. Two old fishermen were sitting there with poles in the water. "How long you boys been on the river?" one asked.

"Nearly two months now," Gil said.

"That's quite a spell. How far you come?"

"All the way from the headwaters in the Wind River Range."

"That a fair piece. Isn't that a fair piece of rowing, Evan?"

"Yeah, that's a fair piece all right," Evan said.

"What you stopping here for?" the first man asked.

Gil answered, "We ain't had anything to eat for nearly a week now and the Lord told us to stop here and pray for cheeseburgers."

"Pray for cheeseburgers? Now I done heard it all. Did you hear that, Evan? They are going to pray for cheeseburgers. God told 'em to do it right here."

"Pray for cheeseburgers, eh," the second old fellow laughed.

"I been a bishop in the LDS Church for over 20 years and I never done hear anything like praying for cheeseburgers. What do you think, Evan?"

"Well, Ephraim, I didn't know God was a short order cook." Both men laughed uproariously.

Gil spread his arms upward and

Gates of Lodore on the Green River

intoned, "Oh, dear Lord God, sustain us. We will starve on this river without your cheeseburger bounty, your cheeseburger goodness."

The two old fishermen shook their heads at each other. They were having a good time. Just then the far away drone of a plane could be heard and the brothers pushed off and rowed to midstream. They sat there with their arms raised imploringly in the air.

Ken's Cessna banked gracefully. They heard him cut back on the throttle, saw the wing flaps extend. Floating from the sky his plane silently dropped nearer and nearer to the river, then they heard the engine fire up and the plane would climb a little, then silence and drift back down, lower and lower, coming directly towards them. It was frightening to watch this mass of machinery in the air, knowing Ludecke was at the controls, coming towards them with tremendous speed. They could hear the air rushing beneath the plane's flaps, now 100 feet above the river, now 75, now 50, closer and closer. They saw the door pop open, watched the propeller flutter, and eyed a plastic bag hurtle from the plane and splash in the river. Then the big engine roared pulling the Cessna up and out of the canyon, making a final farewell pass, and suddenly the brothers found themselves engulfed by the ensuing silence. As they retrieved the precious supply drop, whack, the sound of a beaver tail against the water broke the silence. They watched the beaver slowly swim upstream, a V-shaped wake in the water trailing behind, as they bit into the juicy too-good-to-be-true-on-the-river burgers. They held them up for the anglers

> *Those who give, get much in return. The Guardian Warriors feel that by easing the material desperation of those in poverty, the volunteers feed a spiritual hunger that is evident in American life. It is a step towards balance in our world of vast inequalities and desperate needs.*

to see. The fishermen scratched their heads and stared in amazement.

"I bet they are ready to convert," Troy said.

"I would be," Gil added.

From repeated immersion in wilderness the Gillenwaters have acquired an expanded awareness of their interdependence and interconnection with the earth and all life. They have become *Guardian Warriors* dedicated to fighting misery and poverty. Particularly, under Gil's leadership, the brothers have established the *Rancho Feliz Charitable Foundation,* which has built an elderly care center and dormitories at *La Divina Providencia Orphanage* and organized a food program in the near third-world poverty of border town Aqua Prieta,

La Divina Orphanage

Mexico. There, women work in the *malaquidora* factory making seat belts at subsistence wages. In addition, people from the south crowding the border to illegally migrate into the United States exacerbate the high rate of unemployment. Aqua Prieta's *barrio* is a cauldron of human poverty and misery. Rancho Feliz also supports the *Naco Orphanage* in another border town 60 miles west. Besides its other activities, the charitable foundation has distributed warm clothing and sleeping bags in the barrio.

Gil has designed a series of creative events to raise money for the project. These colorful events have included an 820-mile bike ride, a 400-mile run accompanied by Tarahumara Indians, famed long distance runners from the Copper Canyon area of Mexico, joyous dance fandangos both in Scottsdale and at the historic Gadsden

Mural in the children's dorm

Hotel in border town Douglas, Arizona and auctioning off a Harley-Davidson motorcycle and a Guardian Warrior bust sculpted by Ron Sodenberg, valued at $12,000. All of these charitable endeavors entail the cooperation of the entire Gillenwater family and their close friends, many who are lifelong companions. As their sister, Elizabeth, explained, "Gil brings us all together and makes the event fun and meaningful for the entire group, even those working in support roles for the runners or bikers."

In addition, an *Exchange Program* has been initiated. Through contribu-

Crossing the border after 820 miles

tions, an exchange dormitory has been built at the orphanage for volunteers who come down to contribute their unique skills to the project. One weekend, a group of artists arrived and painted beautiful murals decorating the

walls of the children's dorm. Recently, David, a skilled plastic surgeon from San Diego, had planned a cruise for his wife's birthday. Discovering the compassionate work of Rancho

Programs at La Divina (see below)

Feliz, they donated the $4,000 for their trip to the organization, and then showed up with a crew of 20 for a service weekend. One of the members was Steve, a noted builder of million-dollar homes. With his background it was decided that their service project would be the building of a home for an impoverished barrio family. The mother had her first baby when she was 13-years-old. Their three children had been shipped out to the orphanage while the husband and wife lived in a flimsy house made of shipping pallets and cardboard. They had no running water or electricity. Queta, the mother, ached to have her children back and walked several miles to visit them. A social worker told her she could regain them if she had more stability in her life.

The result was a block home with electricity and running water built in three days. As Gil explained, "What a treat it was to see high-powered Los Angeles and San Diego executives covered head to toe

104

in cement, dirt, and sawdust. It was a tremendous experience as they worked side-by-side with their own children to improve the lives of a Mexican family. Three days later, there wasn't a dry eye among us as we waved goodbye to this reunited family standing in front of a dream home they never imagined possible." Steve looked over at Gil and said, "I have built a lot of very expensive homes in San Diego and I have never, ever had the feeling I do now. We literally changed these peoples' lives forever."

Gil and Troy feel strongly that these exchange efforts are not a one-way street. Those who give, get much in return. The *Guardian Warriors* feel that by easing the material desperation of those in poverty, the volunteers feed a spiritual hunger that is evident in American life. It is a step towards balance in our world of vast inequalities and desperate needs.

Where the spirit of the Guardian Warrior dwells

Be a Guardian Warrior

*A **Guardian Warrior** is a human being who, realizing the interconnectedness of all people and existence, subordinates his or her ego to use their energy and skills to help others. Please send donations or inquiries about service weekends to:*

The ancient Tibetan *Knot of Eternity* symbolizes the interweaving, interdependence and non-separation of all things. It has been chosen to represent the philosophy behind **Rancho Feliz.**

Rancho Feliz Charitable Foundation
6910 East Fifth Avenue
Scottsdale, Arizona 85251
Phone: (480) 946-3000   Fax: (480) 946-9000
www.ranchofeliz.org

Fences

First, the land, windswept, rainswept, free.
Then, man
   —indian, fierce brother to the soil
   —white, building fences, few and far between.
Then a town and more fences,
closer, row-on-row

and the paved road,
gas station, drive-in

PROGRESS

shopping center, subdivision
and as people walk to the pharmacy,
heels tapping pavement
a soft moaning in their soul,
wistful yearning in their bones,
they think if they could pay all the bills,
stop drinking and lose fifteen pounds,
see Alice through college
and nicely married,
it would go away.

     They have forgotten.
     First was the land.

Immersion in Wilderness

Maurice Herzog, in his triumphant ascent of Anapurna in 1950, the first ascent of a mountain over 8,000 meters, felt an enormous gulf between himself and the world he had entered. It was an alien universe, one frozen, deserted and lifeless; an ethereal universe of altitude, rock, ice, and avalanches for which man had not been designed. The climbers were stepping into a new land, entering a kingdom hostile to their presence, yet had no fear as they continued upward.

The courageous French climber believed that every person can choose from endless possibilities where he or she sets their standards. One does not have to climb Mount Everest in order to know how limited are our

The mountains of our dreams

human abilities or how inspiring is the webwork of nature's configurations. Herzog said, "Adventure is also about caring. It is important that all areas visited are left as pristine as before climbers traverse them. Then the next generation can find what was sought there—a medium. Deserts and mountains are a catalyst for our humanity. On them we can discover our human abilities and limitations. Nature, in the form of rugged scenery, is the best mirror of our souls."

Once home from the Anapurna Expedition, Herzog suffered severe depression as the mask of toughness necessary to reach the summit and endure the consequences dissolved. Yet, if he could, the trip leader would not have traded his triumph to avoid his agony. In spite of his losses and suffering, he was convinced he had entered into something new and quite abnormal. The renown climber had the strangest and most vivid impressions, such as he had never before known in the mountains. There was something unnatural in the way he saw everything around him. The diaphanous landscape, the quintessence of purity—these were not the mountains he had known, they were the mountains of his dreams. Sprinkled over every rock and gleaming in the sun, the snow held a radiant beauty that touched Herzog to the heart. He had never encountered such complete transcendence. He was living in a world of crystal. Sounds were indistinct, the atmosphere like cotton wool. An astonishing joy had welled up inside him, but he could not define it. Reflecting, he said, "Everything was so new, so unprecedented. This was quite different. We were on top of Anapurna, 8,075 meters, 26,493 feet. Our hearts overflowed with an unspeakable happiness. Above us there was nothing."

On August 25, 1971, Idaho surgeon Walt Blackadar decided to make a solo attempt on Alaska's ferocious Alsek River. Almost 50, he had learned to kayak only five years before, but had already made a name for himself by making high-risk runs that 20-year-old hotdog paddlers avoided. His first descent of the infamous Turn-Back Canyon on the Alsek became his most famous run. There, the Tweedsmuir Glacier squeezes the wide river into a gap of fatal chaos 30 feet wide with a 20 degree downgrade. Because of surges in the glacier, the river is thrown up against the walls of the canyon. It is a nine-mile stretch of hell now portaged by helicopter. The acceleration of water there is so swift it prevents salmon from swimming further upriver to spawn. Not a dam, but the water itself turns them back.

Grit-filled, glacial water rumbled against the worn walls of the gorge. The towering ice-coated mountains of the Saint Elias Range rose endlessly above. From them moved great masses of glacial ice groaning and cracking. As Blackadar, an insignificant spot in the midst of this stupendous accumulation of proportion and space, neared the canyon, a house-size slab of ice broke off and rocked his kayak. The river narrowed sharply for its entry and the floating ice crowded

Watery chaos

his run. Blackadar looked at the watery chaos ahead and felt it was an invitation to certain death. For him there was no turning back. He was going in, one man against monumental odds.

The waves were gargantuan, much larger than they had looked from the scout plane a few days before. The kayak rocked up and down as he struggled to stay upright. "I was in a frothy mess that was far worse than anything I've seen," he wrote. "It was like trying to run down a coiled rattler's back, the rattler striking me from all sides . . . I skidded and swirled and turned down this narrow line." In trying to stay on the snake's back he hit two icebergs and had to roll twice, knocked over by the water's fury. Ahead was a huge 45-degree drop of 30 feet into a boiling hell. He thought it best to portage but failed to escape the torrent. Just as he entered the drop an iceberg crowded him and he turned upstream and paddled with all his might. He entered the drop backward, flipped and hung upside down through the violent boils before rolling up.

Ahead was a 20-foot reversal wave, a keeper of terrific force. Trying to run the right side, Blackadar was trapped. The left side of his kayak deck ripped. The craft filled with water. He tried a roll and missed. While upside down he realized he had partially slipped out of his boat. "I forced myself not to swim for the surface," he later explained. "I knew it would be all over if I did. So I climbed back into that kayak even though my nerves were screaming to head for the surface." Caught in a hole below the giant keeper, he tried to roll five times and, jamming his knees hard against the side of the boat, finally popped upright on the sixth effort. He managed to get the swamped craft to the bank, where, despite a drizzling rain, he began to patch the tear. While waiting for the repair to dry he wrote, "I'm not coming back. Not for $50,000, not for all the tea in China. Read my words well and don't be a fool. It's unpaddleable." The next day, after being rammed into a cliff and executing his seventh successful roll, he paddled out of the canyon humbled yet triumphant, elated, and alive. It was the Everest of river running. He had run the impossible run.

It was June of 2000. In my damaged 14-foot Momentum self-bailer, the current swept Richard and me into Alsek Lake towards a dangerous wall of ice. I thought, *With a current this strong there must be a way through.* However, I decided the prudent thing to do was to row out and land on shore. Our second raft behind us had seen our predicament and had already pulled over. For 20 minutes I battled the current, making headway until we seemed to be almost out of the onrushing tide. I rowed with my back arched, pulling with every ounce of muscle and energy I had. Near the edge, the current was so swift it kept forcing us back in. Finally, exhausted, I dropped the oars and we drifted down against the barrier. Within five minutes other icebergs and floating chunks of ice of various sizes had closed in and we were trapped in an ice jam.

Richard and I looked at each other with concern in our eyes, not fear but more of a *what the hell do we do now* perplexity.

There was a living, stalking feeling in the ice surrounding us. Huge glaciers calving into the lake quivered the air like rolling thunder. Nearby, an iceberg turned over with a tremendous crash and the ice and water undulated. There was a constant grinding and grumbling like the empty stomach of some horrific beast. One iceberg, large as an ocean liner, came smashing through the rest. Using narrow lanes choked with smaller pieces of floating ice we worked our way away from the path of the giant. Richard pushed 15-foot chunks of ice out of our path and I rowed or shoved past them. Unexpectedly, two cyclopean icebergs closed in and began to crush the raft. It buckled, then the left tube shot up in the air. Richard leaped onto the ice. I stayed with the raft hoping it would not turn over or be obliterated by the pressure. I thought, *Christ, can we survive a full night on one of these hunks of ice? We could still die of exposure even if it didn't split in two or turn over.* We were at the mercy of ice and fate, when one berg shifted away and the raft plopped down right side up. Richard jumped back in, and we fought our way out between the behemoths.

After another hour of slow going and intense effort to stay clear of being crushed, Rich suggested that we unload the raft and drag it across the ice. Now and then we sighted open water and it seemed tantalizingly close. I

Ice Jam

said, "Rich, even if we have enough energy left to unload this thing and drag it, the ice is shifting and closing in. By the time we got it to where we see salvation there would be more ice ahead. I don't care how exhausted we feel, we are going to continue to struggle just as we have been doing. We can sit here and die or try to fight our way out." Rich stared at me, his dark eyes rimmed with fatigue. He slumped as if everything had gone out of him and just sat there. Then he inhaled a great breath, squared up his shoulders

and said,

"Okay, captain, let's get to work."

With fierce effort and agonizing slowness we fought our way down

A vast expanse of wilderness

one channel after another for three more interminable hours. Finally, we broke through to open water with a shout that our compatriots could hear all the way back across the ice flow.

That was one of the brushes with death we had on our trip down the Tatshenshini River into the heart of the vast Tatshenshini-Alsek Wilderness Preserve. It is an expanse of the Yukon, British Columbia, and Alaska crowned with range after range of snow-peaked mountains, immense snowfields and glacial corridors; with endless forests and impenetrable underbrush, a lush green mantle thick and tangled as jungle. It is the domain of grizzly and black bears, moose, elk,

A curious grizzly

beaver and eagles. It is the domain of wind, rain and ice. A roadless area, its two penetrable highways are the glacial Tatshenshini and Alsek Rivers. Innumerable side-streams feed them. It is a kingdom of perpetual snow and 15,000-year-old ice, a great white silence that could swallow lives as it almost did ours. This was the scene of the greatest out-door adventure of our lives. Just two years before an attempt to build a road through the heart of this paradise to mine copper was defeated.

My companions were John Manning, Bob Kerry, Dan Bekins and Richard Hill. These were men who had seen a lot of life, good and bad. They have built productive lives out of the torn remnants of the Sixties. They are independent, self-responsible, direct, tell it as it is, no bullshit kind of men who operate well in crisis situations. Dan, a tattooed giant who teaches people how to disarm armed men when they have no weapon of their own, once raised a bear until it was bigger than him. They wrestled together. We told him that when we came face to face with a grizzly, he would be our contact man.

Part of our trouble came from inaccurate information. We were told the rapids tended to be minor Class III's and standard gear was hip waders or heavy boots, thick jackets and multiple layers to stay warm. This outfit was not designed for swimming in near freezing water. It was garb made for the air tem-perature and could sink us in glacial silt. Of course, no one ever flips a raft on the Tat.

Our two rafts, heavily loaded, pushed out into the river from Dalton Post, a spot that you need a detective or GPS to locate. I thought it was an Indian village but, no, it was a space down a

Magnificent scenery of the Tatshenshini-Alsek Wilderness

long, steep, muddy road just wide enough to push a boat through. It was marked on the highway by an arrow painted across the surface of the road, no signs. A local policeman gave me wrong directions. If I had listened to him, we would still be looking for it. It was like maybe they don't want us to know anything about the river; maybe they don't even want us up here.

As we began our odyssey, Bob was riding with John in the

113

Bob Kerry—armed for bear

lead raft and my passengers were Big Dan and Richard. After drifting an hour with upstream wind and rain obscuring visibility, we entered a narrow canyon of continuous Class IV rapids. *Where did these class fours come from,* I wondered? My raft was overburdened so I looked downstream as far as possible to anticipate the maneuvers I had to make. We slammed a number of huge, roaring holes but, with the weight we carried, they were no problem. The danger was that many of the rocks were the same slate color of the river and difficult to see in the driving rain. Twice we went up on nearly invisible boulders and almost turned over but instantaneous high-siding prevented a flip. John had two similar close calls.

That night around our fire we speculated that if both rafts had flipped in continuous icy rapids with the gear we were wearing, there would have been fatalities, maybe five of them. Even if one of us reached shore, we would have died from exposure. We cooked and ate our T-bone steaks, glad we were there to enjoy them. Then we lit up cigars. Mosquitoes were no problem because we camped out on a flat where the strong winds blew them away. We put up a mobile shelter and wrapped a tarp about the windward side so we were snug with our stove and campfire.

The next day we were pulling away from strainers along the curves

Small raft, big river

where the current had eaten away the bank causing giant firs, still rooted to the soil, to fall into the river. To be swept underneath one was death. Clearing a downed giant fir in super swift current, John caught sight of a stick jammed into the bottom, bouncing up and down

114

directly in his path. He had no time to react. Thick as a man's biceps, the pole impacted the raft just below John's frame, above the tube, thrust under his seat and hit a rocket box. The current forced the raft deeper and deeper into the water and would have sunk the Riken but the branch snapped just in time. With its constant up and down motion, had it hit lower it would have punctured his tube; had it been higher it would have broken John's ribs. Had it held and not snapped, John and Bob would have been swimming with the raft jammed underwater behind them. Another close call.

After a layover and hike day, I was again pulling away from strainers with Bob and Richard in my Momentum. Ahead was an ominous bulge in the water. John had pulled clear of it but I had coasted a bit and found I was being sucked right over it. Squaring the raft, I took the hole head-on. We ran it successfully but then the current twisted sharply to the right and flung us against a rock wall along the edge of the river. The impact ripped open the front right tube and pushed it up the low cliff. The three of us automatically hopped up on the rising tube to force it down and allow the Momentum to spin free, but the current was still crushing us into the wall. The combined weight of three full-grown men could not keep the tube from being forced upward. My last words were, "We can't flip on the Tatshenshini," then over we went, plunged into liquid ice. It made the Colorado River in the Grand Canyon feel like a hot springs. I couldn't breathe as my heavy clothing and Sorrel boots dragged me down. Then the adrenaline kicked in. Forget that sink in glacial silt stuff. I fought my way up, broke the surface and

The endless peaks

looked like Tarzan heading for shore, Sorrels or no Sorrels. Bob climbed on the upside-down raft and floated off downriver. Richard was struggling in his hip waders but making progress. I helped him ashore. We were freezing and a stiff breeze added a wind chill factor to our growing discomfort.

I had to pee and wasn't about to take off any clothing. I just let loose in my pants. The warmth was delicious. I smiled. Richard thought, *If Fink can smile at a time like this I bet we're going to make it.* Grabbing him, I said, "We've got to get moving. I don't care if we walk all day and all night, we're going to survive. Let's get going."

"I can't walk."

"What do you mean you can't walk?"

"My hip waders are filled with water, maybe 60 pounds of it." Richard then flopped on the ground and I pulled his legs up one by one and let the torrent run out. Then he forced his way back to his feet and we started out.

The crucial factor was that John Manning was downriver ahead of us. We had no idea of how far. If he were beyond the two miles of flats we would have to try to fight through impenetrable underbrush. That would have been next to impossible. Had John gone after Bob ridding on my flipped raft or was he waiting for us? It was a life and death decision.

John, on top of the situation, was waiting about a mile downstream. Rich and I were numb and shivering as we climbed into his raft and continued downriver. We found Bob on an island and picked him up. Down farther the crippled Momentum lay in an eddy, a deflated and winded runaway. We managed to get it turned back over. I re-rigged and then tied the ripped tube back up over the boat.

Nursing the torn Momentum down to a campsite, we got a roaring fire going for Rich, Bob, and I were in the initial stages of hypothermia. We changed into warm clothes, got our tents and the shelter up and ate a large spaghetti supper. Again we celebrated our survival with coffee and cigars from John's unflipped raft.

Glacier country

The next morning we looked at the fresh bear tracks all around camp, a daily occurrence, then set to work on the Momentum, not an apt name at the time. The rip was too large to patch effectively in damp weather so we stuffed our extra life jackets and three large, empty, sealed water containers into the tube and sewed it up. Just as we finished and were congratulating ourselves on a creative patching job, there was an explosion. The baffle had blown between the front tubes. We cut the other front tube open, then with a surgeon's skill, Big Dan sliced out the thwarts with a scalpel-sharp hunting knife. We inflated the two thwarts, stuffed them into the second deflated tube and sewed it up. Now I didn't dare pump up the back tubes too far or their baffles would also blow. With one passenger and less weight and the back chambers now in front we were able to limp downstream. I now had a low rider raft. I had been seeking a name for the raft for five years and now she had one. She was now christened *The Endurance II.*

Our next adventure came when we hit the confluence of the Tatshenshini and the Alsek that quadrupled the amount of water in the river. We took a layover day to hike the Walker Glacier. From a distance, a glacier looks like a solid mass of ice and snow. It's not. In summer, it is a slow moving river of ice, groaning, creaking, splitting open crevasses and rumbling with cave-ins created by underground water. I decided to reach a promontory up on the glacier and advanced into an area where I could hear water running under me, had to jump across narrow 100-foot-deep crevasses, and cross an ice bridge. As I walked out on it I heard a rock drop under me and splash into water. I crossed a line I had never violated before, deciding to reach my goal no matter what happened instead of turning back. I had a kind of glacial summit fever. It was a long and exhaustingly glorious day in a world of mountains, ice and snow.

In every life-threatening situation we were calm and thought rationally. We felt no fear and discovered the will to face the challenge. I'm not sure why this was because it isn't always the case. But the magnificent isolation and nearness to death was exhilarating; the trip was, no doubt, the greatest outdoor adventure any of us had undertaken. I would trade a year in the city for an adventure like that. The experience will be a treasured part of our lives forevermore.

The Walker Glacier—close up

In 1989-90, the immortal moun-

"I'd trade a year in the city for an adventure like that"

taineer, Reinhold Messner walked across Antarctica. There he found he was under way, always under way. Time fell away because day and night, spring and autumn were suspended. He passed into a frozen eternity. The sense of time dissolved and space grew as one endless horizon stretched after another. Except for his breathing and the pulse in Messner's neck, all was silent. This all-embracing silence brought with it the thought, *Peace is possible when the world is not parceled out amongst people with national and territorial claims. Non-desire, the cessation of pain, the third of the Four Noble Truths of Buddhism, is transcendental for silence, peace, infinity as we experience* it in the wilds.

A frozen eternity

Blood in the Stone

Mountains let slip
their tributaries,
blue ribbons sliding over smooth stone,
over mossy browns, snaking in and out
of pools, cascading over rock,

sharpening their knives
for the carving of flamed walls
far below. The west wind
blows fine grains of sand
stirring ghosts who will not speak.
Sun-leathered lines on our faces,
we hike Matkatamiba,
follow the unclocked thread,
climbing through raised passageways,
clambering back, back, back
beyond Auschwitz, Bunker Hill, Carthage
and patriarchs sacrificing sons; back
to where we strip off our skin
and touch our blood
to the blood in the stone,
to the beating heart
of deceased centuries,
back to where our roots
lie in a shallow
excommunicated sea.

As Seconds Tick Away

Earthskin winnowed,
abraded down to rise
and walk as men.
Shaded echoes of
river sound
crawling into
the grave and out again.

I sit as seconds tick away
crouched by the skeletal ruins
of an outlaw hide boat
tucked under a ledge
in an unknown canyon.
I handle worn wood,

hand-carved paddles
and ribs, run reverent
fingers over bailing wire and nails
fastening upright bow and stern posts.
Through these wan grained bones
touch the tremors of hooves of stolen horses
run south over a century ago, nostrils flared,
wide-eyed, crashing down bouldered arroyos
through clouds of dust,
driven by rustlers
home free, cursing the heat,
laughing at the roll of the dice,
now dust in uncoffined graves.

The Price Paid

On our fall trip in 1992, my daughter Kristi brought along a friend she had met while doing a documentary study of migrant broccoli pickers in Maine. Patchen Miller was handsome, clear-eyed and vital. His body was compact and muscular, his mind alert and inquiring. Patchen radiated good-natured energy. The boy seemed an old soul, a kind of diaper guru. He had been named after the iconoclast poet Kenneth Patchen, a critic of American society in the 1930s and 40s. Patchen possessed an innate thrust towards adventure and, for a young man, an extraordinary ability to tell stories. He could spin a yarn as though he were a bent-back, cantankerous hermit or scarred veteran of life. Possessed by a deep interest and compassion for third-world peoples, he had spent two semesters at Friends World College in Huntington, New York that required students to live in two cultures other than their own. With his father, Paul Dix, a photographer and human rights activist, he had driven trucks down to the Sandinistas in Nicaragua during the Contra War. Patchen had also visited Nepal and Thailand and was sensitive to whatever environment he was in. As on our trip, people inherently liked him.

Patchen Miller

In his second grade year, with his mother Sandra, a naturalist, he collected specimens and built a sand table. Sculptured with sand islands, it held rocks, plants and the inhabitants—fish, frogs, newts and the like collected from nearby wetlands. The inhabitants got to know the Millers so well that mother and son could stroke the backs of the toads and frogs. Later they switched their collection to transportable tanks taken to grade schools in Enfield and Canaan and to the Montshire Museum of Science—all in New Hampshire. It gave the children the opportunity to observe an ecology in action. The tanks were dismantled when school was over. Once at the Montshire, Sandra was talking to one of the frogs. She bent over close to the amphibian so her voice could be soothing and low. A group of people led by the museum director came in behind her. The female bullfrog was so glad to see her that it hopped up

Patchen riding the thrill

into her mouth. Everyone was astonished. A new way for self-embarrassment had been discovered. In the fifth grade, Patchen wrote an autobiography, "Growing Up in the Woods." In it, he enthusiastically pointed out that their bird feeder had the most action around and that chickadees, flying squirrels, and chipmunks ate from his hands.

On our Grand Canyon trip we stopped at Blacktail Canyon at Mile 120 and hiked the stream into its lower confines to a ribbed chamber with a narrow slot of sky overhead. About head-high there is a seam of conglomerate nearly a foot wide. This is known as the Great Unconformity. When the area was lifted above water between 820 and 545 million years ago, erosion removed 15,000 feet of Precambrian rock. Then Cambrian

Pointing out the Great Unconformity

seas advanced and laid down a layer of conglomerate. It resisted total subsequent erosion before further inundations laid the strata that remain today. It's incredible to put one hand above the line of conglomerate and one below; the lower hand on Vishnu Schist and the upper on Tapeats Sandstone and realize that your hands span 1.2 billion years of missing geological history, nearly one-fourth of the earth's age.

Further back in Blacktail there is a small waterfall softly dropping off a smooth rockslide. It has a soothing rush water whisper. The chamber has wonderful acoustics. Patchen beat bail buckets for drums and Walt Carr whirled his flexible pipe diggeredoo with its primitive wail. The chamber magnified the sound. We danced, sang, prayed to the four directions and brought white light down upon ourselves. We shuffled to the reverberating drums and sound of a primitive musical instrument developed by the Aborigines of Australia, the primal sounds of nature—howl of wind in the trees, rush of water over rock, caw of ravens, stealthy movement of preda-tor towards prey. It was our celebration of the moment, of the fact of being, a spontaneous rite of life.

The diggeredoo in Blacktail Canyon

The marvels of the Canyon were enhanced and enlarged by sharing them with Patchen who with inno-cent wonder immersed himself in experiencing the colorful wings of butterflies, seeps trick-ling over green moss, goats clambering on sheer ledges, the soaring sheerness of cliffs and the thrill of riding treacherous rapids. Patchen's agility of mind, sense of humor and stories sparked our huddled exchanges around the winter fires. He was the epitome of the art of living, mindfulness, sheer energy, youthful ideal-ism and the promise of a new ecological and global consciousness for the future.

A year later, we were heartbroken to hear that Patchen had been murdered while he floated the Maranon River in the jungles of Peru. The Maranon drops out of the mountains and is one of the source rivers of the Amazon. With a close friend, Josh Silver, Patchen had performed volunteer work in an orphanage in Ecuador over Christmas, then hitchhiked south into Peru, bought provisions and built a raft at Muyo, a small town just upstream from their put in point. Made of balsa wood and supported by six 55-gallon oil drums, their craft was a bulky ten by 15 feet, had a roof and was powered by a pair of ten-foot oars. The 26-year-old young men planned to Huck Finn 500 miles downstream to the Amazon then continue on, using commercial craft. It would be the adventure of a lifetime.

Even though both boys believed in Indian rights and traditional ways, they knew they were undertaking a hazardous venture. Several Europeans had been killed on the Maranon a few years back. Whites and mestizos told them that the Aguaruna, whose lands they would be floating through, were a dangerous people. They were warned to stay out of the villages, stay on the river and keep going. The Aguaruna had been great warriors. They had successfully resisted attempts of the Incas, Spanish and the nation of Peru to defeat them. They were confident and unconquerable. Up until about 50 years ago they had been head hunters. Border conflict between Ecuadorian and Peruvian troops had increased tension, and a series of military checkpoints had been built along the Maranon. The Indian people were suspicious of strangers. Their fear of outsiders was symbolized by their belief in a gruesome night creature known as the *pishtaco*. Not every white man was a *pishtaco* but many were. These invaders kill in the night and suck out the life force of their victim in the form of body fat. This "grease" is used to lubricate the white man's machines explaining their advanced technology. It had been suspected that this embedded myth was behind some of the random killing of whites in the region.

The river itself was dangerous. It hit the jungle plain as a swift-moving current 300 feet wide. There were some rapids, but its major obstacles were huge whirlpools or *pongos* located where the swelling tide came out of curves and hit the bank as it straightened out, creating a twisting effect. When the banks narrowed, compressing the current around the curve, the whirlpools were as large as 40 feet across and could suck down a raft without ever releasing it again.

On their third day out, the river had risen six feet from afternoon tropical rains and the unwieldy raft was proving hard to handle. Caught in the edge of a *pongo,* Patchen struggled for 15 minutes to escape being drawn into the vortex. Minutes later the current swept them past an apparently uninhabited island perhaps a quarter of a mile long and 100 yards across at its widest point. It held patches of forest mixed with fields of sugarcane. They eddied out on its downstream edge feeling they had found a viable compromise between respecting inhabited Aguaruna land and their need to tie up, rest, let the river subside, wash clothes and do some repair work on the raft.

Although warned against contact with the Aguaruna, Patchen hailed a young native paddling by in a dugout. Seemingly shy, the Indian talked with them at a distance in Spanish, then paddled over and climbed upon the raft. He seemed about 20, his dark hair short in front and long in back and he possessed a twisted, flattened prizefighter's nose. They gave him some small gifts and drank coffee together. After dark another dugout came by with two Aguarunas. They held a conversation in their native tongue with the young man who had come aboard the raft. The two appeared to be drunk but nevertheless friendly. Eventually, they paddled away. Soon after, a rainstorm hit. When it was over their visitor showed no inclination to leave and displayed an avid interest in their gear. He wanted to see everything.

About 9:30 P.M., the two men in the dugout came back. Their previous friendliness had disappeared and they seemed curt, even belligerent. After a brief conversation with their friend they paddled on. Soon, Patchen and Josh heard some rustling in the brush near the tip of the island.

"What's that?" Josh asked in Spanish.

"It's my father. He's an evangelical minister. He wants to meet you," their visitor answered.

The Indian yelled into the brush in his own language. Patchen got up and walked to the back of the raft with his headlamp. He wanted to light the way for the father. Then a shotgun roared blasting Patchen off the raft. Josh reached for him but grabbed only water flowing through his fingers. Another shell was fired and Josh felt steel pellets tear into his left thigh. The young Indian on the raft wasn't shouting or surprised. He had set them up. As the assailant reloaded, Josh dove into the dark waters of the Maranon. Downstream, he crawled out of the river. Discovering a vine, he tied it above his wounds. He saw flashlights coming along the path and knew they were looking for him. They didn't want to leave any witnesses. Then the killings could remain a mystery. Maybe the two foolish whites could have disappeared into a *pongo*. Who would ever know?

Rubbing mud on himself to hide his white skin, he tried going up river along the bank but eventually decided to take his chances in the water. Floating along half freezing, Josh got out of the water every half-hour and, despite his injured leg, did sit-ups and push-ups to warm himself. In the morning, nearly nine hours after he dove off the raft, he saw an Indian working on his boat's small outboard motor. Risking further danger, he talked to the man, who put him in the boat and took him across the river to Oracuza, the next military checkpoint. With medical aid he survived the ordeal,

An incomprehensible loss

but Patchen had disappeared forever into the unfathomable reaches of the Maranon.

The Aguaruna are a people attempting to cope with the pressures of encroaching civilization. An oil pipeline road, built in the 1970s, slices through traditional hunting grounds. It induced settlers to come down out of the mountains to the lush, more easily farmed jungle and opened the way for those greedy for timber and gold. A government relocation program pushed more Peruvians into the area to thwart Ecuadorian border claims. These forces hit like a hammer against the indigenous people, polluting their lands and threatening their ancient way of life. Local leaders are trying to find a way to deal with these overwhelming problems.

The natives were appalled at the murder. To say the inebriated young man who pulled the trigger on an American boy represented the Aguarunas would be like saying that Charles Manson represents the average American male. The irony, of course, is the sympathy Patchen and Josh felt for the continuation of the Indians' traditional lifestyle and values. The repetitive invasion and conquest cycle played out in the American West of yesteryear is still at work in South America. It is far more at the heart of the matter than the individuals involved.

The March following his demise, a close-knit group of us returned to Blacktail Canyon and paid tribute to Patchen's memory. In that same chamber, again the drum beat thundered; the bellowing of an authentic diggeredoo bounced from the walls; songs, prayers, a poem and stories were offered as we honored him and tried to invoke his presence. It was tribute paid to a true man of the river, the son of smoke that roars. It mourned an inarticulate, incomprehensible loss. His magnificence as a human being and his unique genetic inheritance extinguished, the potential greatness never fully emerged, his humanitarian promise left undone, the future cheated. Memory is a pallid substitute for being. His is a resurrection without flesh due to the indelicate way we rot, melt like dung into the voracious earth, are scattered and torn by a thousand hungry mouths and defecations, only to rise in a coyote's lope, the burst berry, a spider's web catching silken sun. From shal-

Blacktail Canyon ceremony

126

low sea to upright rock, wind's stalking whisper, he shall walk this earth forever.

In the Eyes of a Doe

A pale golden dawn. Trees stretch tangled bodies
in shafts of sunlight and daughter flowers
are the eyes of a new day. Streams
pour themselves seaward to tie,
in thin blue ribbons, the earth together.

I look to the mountains, touch the wind
as we spin through space and time and lives.

I wish I might see through the inquisitive gaze of a deer
unseparated from dark soil and monkey flowers
by philosophy and freeways,
incessant bleat of advertising,
monolithic cities erected
to twenty-first century gods.

Yes, I would go into the eyes of a doe
to find the quiet within compassion,
to know that stranger called my soul.

The Patchen Miller Fund

Patchen's parents and friends have established the Patchen Miller Fund as a supplemental program aiding the

Upper Valley Land Trust

in New Hampshire. The Land Trust protects reserved areas, their ecology, and animal life. The fund in Patchen's name furnishes an intern each year to aid the trust and to learn and grow as a future environmentalist with his/her own unique combination of personality and skill. The Community Foundation sends contributions to the Land Trust. All donations are tax deductible.

The Patchen Miller Fund
Upper Valley Community Foundation
37 Pleasant Street
Concord, New Hampshire 03301

The Cost of Triumph

As Herzog climbed the slopes of Anapurna above 25,000 feet he entered what is referred to as the Death Zone. Here, even with bottled oxygen, the body feeds upon itself, debilitation sets in, and a climber's time is limited. Twenty-nine thousand feet with oxygen is like climbing at 26,000 feet without oxygen. Climbers have fallen prey to thrombophlebitis, an altitude-induced blood clot, heart attacks and exhaustion. Mental fatigue can become so great that it becomes pleasant doing nothing or taking an hour to put on a pair of boots.

Himalayan explorers in the Death Zone are in a race against hypothermia, frostbite, cerebral and, more commonly, pulmonary edema, the swelling produced by the collection of fluids in the lungs that hampers breathing. Edema of the brain impairs judgment with coma not far away. The slopes of Everest are littered with corpses as the discovery of the frozen body of George

The land above the sky

Mallory in May of 1999 attests. It had lain there since the mystery-shrouded British expedition of 1924.

Above 26,000 feet, the line between determination and reckless summit fever becomes perilously thin. Sleep becomes illusive, cuts and abrasions refuse to heal, appetite diminishes and the body begins to consume itself. Headaches feel like a nail is being driven between the eyes. Snow blindness stalks the burdened climbers as they plod or draw themselves slowly upward. Oxygen-starved brain cells die. Hallucination is common. In his first oxygen-less solo ascent of Everest in 1980, Reinhold Messner imagined an invisible companion with him. Exhausted, the great climber wished his phantom friend would do the cooking. On Everest in 1934, the British climber Frank Smith shared his biscuits with an imaginary partner.

Resultant suffering can be intense. Snow blind and with his feet and hands partially frozen, Herzog had to be carried off Anapurna by Sherpas where one misstep could mean a fall of thousands of feet. Doctor Jacques Oudot had difficulty finding the climber's femoral and brachial arteries for Novocain and acetylcholine injections. Acetylcholine is found in many body tissues and acts as a nerve impulse transmitter. At times, the syringe was clogged with mud-thick blood. At others, the arteries rolled away from the point. Herzog screamed and sobbed with pain. As the injections took effect they became intolerable and his feet felt like they had been plunged into boiling oil. The injections were repeated to save as much tissue as possible.

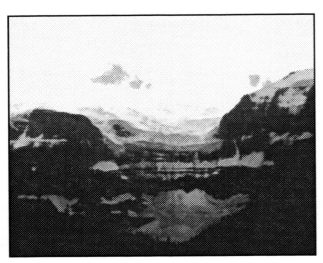

Land of ice and rock

As they continued their retreat off the mountain, Oudot began to amputate without anesthetic. Herzog braced and clenched his teeth. The doctor gave a great snip with his scissors. Herzog felt a shock tremble through his entire body. Oudet announced, "The first amputation. The little finger." Every day one or two joints from Herzog's hands and feet were removed.

On the train to India, the doctor operated whenever the engine stopped. The stench was terrible. One day his compadres opened the door and pushed everything out with a broom made of twigs. In the heap of trash a number of various-sized toes rolled at the feet of surprised natives.

One of Maurice's feet nested wriggling maggots. They withdrew into their holes at the approach of surgical tweezers. By the time the group reached Paris, the maggots had grown huge. There was more than half a pound of them. Oudot patiently assured Herzog again and again that maggots clean wounds more effectively than modern chemicals. This was the price the climber paid for his triumph at the crest of Anapurna.

Reinhold Messner attempted the Rupal Face of Nanga Parbat in 1970-71. The face was a sheer 5,000 meters, three times as high as the North Face of the Eiger. He summited with his brother Gunther. On the way down they bivouacked without blankets, sleeping bags or bivy sacks at minus 54 degrees F. After a second bivouac on the Mummery Spur, Reinhold descended first thinking his brother was right behind him. Actually, Gunther had been caught in a fresh ice avalanche. Nearly insane with grief, Reinhold searched all night in vain. His feet were so swollen he could no longer stand. He crawled and then was carried into camp. The front parts of his feet were black and blood oozed from his toes. He lost the first to the fourth left toes and the first and second toes on his right foot. His fingers were saved. His brother's death weighed heavily upon him, for Gunther would not have joined the expedition without Reinhold's encouragement. Yet, through his pain, he reasoned, *It will not help my brother if I give up climbing.*

By 1977, his wife Uschi, tired of the worry and sense of abandonment created by his climbing, left him. In 1985, another brother, Siegfried, was struck by lightning on the Stabler Tower in the Dolomites, fell, and was fatally injured. Despite these heartbreaking losses, true to his own nature and convictions, Reinhold continued to climb.

Most kayakers will tell you they are not going to drown. World class kayaker Walt Blackadar once said, "I will tell you I will never drown. I know I could paddle Niagara Falls and not drown. I just can't drown." Sadly, after surviving Alaska's two most deadly runs, less than two years later, Blackadar was trapped in a partially hidden strainer on the South Fork of the Payette River and did drown. Several shoulder operations had

decreased his paddling strength. A close friend, Julie Wilson, died on one of his trips down the West Fork of the Bruneau. Feeling responsible, her death haunted him. Blackadar was slowly deteriorating as a boatman. On the Payette, friends who had pulled over and expected him to stop were surprised to see him complacently continue over the drop without scouting

Out on the edge

the obstacle. He may have not recognized it for what it was, a death trap. That place in the river is now known as "Walt's Drop" or "Walt's

Rapid."

More recently, expert kayaker Doug Gordon, a former U.S. Team medallist in World Cup competition, perished in his attempt at a first descent of Tibet's Tsangpo Gorge. The gorge has long been identified as one of Tibet's most sacred *bayuls*, or Hidden Lands where the pious find reward and others find trouble. If the journey is taken for self-advancement, the sacred nature of the land will never be revealed and Pemako's innermost regions will remain forever out of reach.

A prep school buddy of Bill Gates, Doug was an intellectual who left behind a wife and two small children. Looking at the incredible high water turbulence ahead where the river enters the inner gorge and drops 65 feet per mile, eight times that of the Colorado through the Grand Canyon, the kayakers planned to stay in the relatively calmer water along the shore. As they alternatively paddled and portaged downstream, on one run, Gordon inexplicably swerved out over an eight-foot drop that endoed his craft. During his third attempt to roll and right the kayak, he was swept out into the thrashing mainstream current and never seen again. Afterwards, his friend and fellow boater David Halpern remarked, "I suppose we all wish he would've said, 'Yeah, I can do this, but I've got kids and a wife and maybe it's time to tone it down.' He wasn't able to say that."

In their attempt to cross the Adretang Mud Bog, Gil, the oldest of the Gillenwaters, was shivering violently. Six feet tall, with brown-blond hair and an athlete's compact build, his normally piercing green eyes were clouded with fatigue. A nearly imperceptible military squareness to his head and natural charisma gave him an air of command. Todd, the youngest, had the same hair coloring and head shape but was 6'2". The little brother had outgrown his older siblings. He was suffering stomach cramps and had been vomiting intermittently throughout the morning. Troy, the middle brother, was 5'10" and 140 pounds. He had finer, more delicate facial features but possessed the same intensity of eye contact and dogged determination as his brothers. All the Gillenwater men had a straight-to-the-point clipped way of talking, similar inflections and voice patterns.

Rain drenched down endlessly on the Tibetan plateau. Icy, unabated, it had a maddening quality. The altitude, over 14,000 feet, was taking its toll. The three brothers knew they were in peril. They didn't talk about it for fear of disheartening one another.

They had passed through gorges plunging into jungle where free-roaming tigers depleted herds of Dzos, a cross between a cow and a yak, and carried off an occasional villager. Bamboo jammed the trails. The elevation was 8,090 feet. At one point, Gil counted 22 leeches sucking blood from his body. A friend awoke one morning to find a tiger leech in his mouth. Troy discovered a monster leech on his groin. Swollen with blood, the leech rolled out of his pants and dropped to the ground. Troy would have stomped on it but was self-restrained for two reasons: to kill leeches in Pemako encourages the rain deity's wrath; secondly, if he stomped on it he would have splattered his own blood over the trail. He couldn't stand to see that. The bleeding didn't stop for nearly two hours. Leeches, when they bite, inject an anticoagulant to keep the blood flowing. They also inject an anesthetic so a person doesn't feel them attach themselves.

Lurking in the brush were some of the most deadly snakes in the world, particularly cobras and Russell's Vipers. A large snake slithered between Todd's legs across the trail one day and disappeared. He was too startled to know what kind it was.

They were close to the Indian border, a volatile area. Five years before, Indian police had stormed into the mountain valleys to subjugate the tribesmen and open the area to Indian logging interests. A tribesman was shot and killed. The next day all 35 Indian policemen were discovered beheaded. Maps of the region labeled it "unexplored territory." The physical exertion necessary to transverse this uncharted universe and its countless dangers frayed them raw. It enabled them to understand both the preciousness and possible briefness of life.

After a 4,000-foot climb, in front of them lay seven nearly impassable miles of the Adretang Mud Bog.

Gil in Pemako, Tibet

Entering the marsh, the brothers sank into knee-deep muck, their feet sloshing inside their boots. Troy bent over and threw up. Todd thought, *That's the first time I've ever seen what somebody threw up crawl around* as he watched the expelled wriggling mass of worms. Gil vomited. Now they were all sick. They had to rest or throw up every few steps. The brothers were now hopelessly behind their group of friends, pilgrims, porters and Sherpas. The severity of conditions, the altitude and incessant rain had turned the normally close-marched group into a free-for-all to reach camp.

133

It was every man for himself with survival at stake.

How much farther did the mud bog stretch? There seemed to be no end in sight. They reached a small knoll with wind-whipped prayer flags. The wind spooked the brothers. Their shivering would not stop. They were all going hypothermic. They realized they were in a menacing self-rescue situation. Shivering, exhausted, without food all day, they couldn't depend upon anyone but themselves.

The land of roaring water

Finally, at the end of the mud bog, the trail dropped off a steep boulder field. It was difficult to follow. The boulders, huge and jumbled, were angular and knife-edged. To fall would mean serious injury. The clouds thickened, the rain continued, the trail grew slick. They noticed the sky was darkening. The trail grew so steep they had to hang on to branches in their descent. They, literally, half-walked, half-fell downward. The trail moved from the boulder field to a creek, which plunged down a narrow chute. There was no way to avoid sloshing through the water or having the water up to their elbows when negotiating tricky footings where they needed their hands for additional support. They barely made it across a side stream. One slip on the wet log and they would be swept away. The rain grew even harder, the sky yet darker. It was a Dantesque scene.

Though they didn't have time to talk about it, they separately wondered why they were the only three members of the expedition who had gotten sick. Two days before they were out ahead of the main party and came to a beautiful lake, an Eden-like setting. It was fantastic. All about were towering 25,000 snow-capped mountains and this perfectly clear body of water reflecting both mountains and sky like a marriage of water and the heavens above. The brothers had stripped down naked and jumped in the lake and were swimming around. When the Sherpas and the local tribesmen came up, they waved their hands and yelled. They were horrified. The lake was sacred. Foreigners defiling it could bring down divine wrath and destroy the entire expedition. Now, not long afterwards, the Gillenwaters were deathly ill. Nobody else was. Somehow, such beliefs seemed terribly real in that mysterious land.

Or, because of defiling the lake, they could have been poisoned. After dinner one evening, Tibetan veteran Ian Baker told a harrowing tale of Tibetan sorcery. The Monpas had migrated into the region 500 years before believing a Buddhist prophecy that it was a "lost Eden." Some of them engaged in a diabolical rite. A *Dugma*, or witch, on the full moon would paint half their face black and braid their hair to one side and vow to poison someone using a lethal concoction of mushroom, snake and frog toxins. They must use the deadly mixture within 30 days or turn the poison on themselves, one of their children or their spouse. The three young men figured their sorcerer might have been Louis, the most frightening of the Monpa porters. He had made them tea on the afternoon they swam in the lake and could have poisoned them at that time.

The most rational scenario was that the brothers had picked up a bug with an incubation period at the last of the military towns. Yet, other compatriots had eaten the same things in the same places and were not ill. That left them with the two previous appalling hypotheses. And where did the worms come from?

Troy and Gil sat huddled together in a futile attempt to get warm. They were surprised when Todd said he'd go ahead. Both still thought of him as their little brother. The first to get sick, he seemed to be the first to begin recovering some of his strength. As Troy and Gil sat there, Todd said, "I think I can go for help."

Troy asked, "Are you sure?"

"Yeah, I think so," Todd replied. He turned and started up the trail. Gil and Troy continued to sit, unable to move. Troy thought, *If we were this sick in the States we'd be in a hospital.* Their muscles felt leaden and they continued to shiver violently.

"We've got to keep moving, Gil."

"You're right, We've got to move." Huddling closer the brothers continued to sit there. In the rain, they could not even attempt to build a fire.

Todd tried to run as the trail turned back uphill. He had to find camp and send help. The altitude and his sickness soon slowed him to a walk. Tortured, he pictured his brothers just sitting there. By morning they would be dead. Todd mentally flailed himself for not being able to run farther and wondered if, in the dark, he was on the right trail. If he got lost they would all die; what an ungodly country. They hadn't seen another person in the past ten days. You sure as hell didn't stand there and stick out your thumb. Even with everyone's lives depending on him, he had to stop to get his breath. In some dreams, he could not run or break away, but this was real, a living nightmare, and he could barely move. The rain continued to pour down. He reached an area where a way had been cut through bamboo by machetes. The cutting left about a foot of razor sharp shoots protruding. Todd was attempting to climb across a log when he slipped. As he fell towards the bamboo skewers he put a hand down and managed to plant a foot. A sharpened point jabbed him in the thigh but made little penetration. He scrambled back up on the log and made it across. There the trail split. Which one lead to camp? In the cold, dark, damp, rain-soaked tangle of jungle he felt the presence of death. Tilting his head back, closing his eyes, and praying, he chose one of the trails. Fifteen minutes later he was in camp and sent rested Sherpas off with a hot thermos for his brothers.

Back where he had left them, unaware that rescue was on the way, again Troy urged, "Gil, we've got to move."

"I don't know if I can stand up."

"Come on, let's give it a try. We can't just sit here."

"I know. I know." The brothers struggled to their feet and, leaning against each other, pressed on. Soon exhausted, they again slipped down to a sitting position. In a land where heaven and earth meet, where individual life seems insignificant and faith illimitable, they faced their own demise. Troy thought, *No better place to die. No better person to die with.*

We have mentioned the aesthetic receptivity of the lone wilderness wanderer, Everett Reuss. Prophetically, he wrote, "And when the time comes to die, I'll find the wildest, loneliest, most desolate spot there is." In 1934, at 20-years-of-age, he vanished. His mules were found three miles up in Davis Gulch, a side tributary of Escalante Canyon. At a small Anasazi

Sublime landscape—canyonlands

ruin above LaGorce Arch, searchers discovered where he had written *NEMO* on the ledge and carved the date *Nov 1934.* His remains have never been found. The area is now inundated by the Glen Canyon Dam and Lake Powell. One theory is that cattle rustlers may have murdered him. He lived out his last years as he wished among the sublime landscape of the plateau country and eerily predicted his own demise. The mystery haunts

136

everyone who loves and visits that region.

In early 2000, down off the Belizian barrier reef, I was out one day helping Crazy and Kent, a pair of divers and fishermen, pull up lobster traps. In one, instead of a large antennaed crustacean, was a rounded non descript fish. Kent said, "Ya mon, that's a puffer, you bet. Don't want to be eating him, mon, bad poison, sure, sure."

As Crazy threw the fish back with his gloved hand, Charlie Leslie, the proprietor of the boat and owner of the business, said, "Over in Japan, you bet, mon, they eat those damned things, ya, ya. Crazy people, crazy, sure, sure."

Intrigued, I investigated and found that licensed Japanese chefs prepare the white flesh of the puffer fish, served raw and arranged in intricate floral patterns. Gourmets pay big money for the meticulously prepared dish, which has a light, faintly sweet taste. Yet the puffer fish is horrifically poisonous. Its skin, liver and intestines contain tetrodotoxin, one of the most poisonous chemicals in the world, hundreds of times more lethal than strychnine or cyanide.

Kent in Belize

The poison produces dizziness, numbness of the mouth and lips, breathing trouble, cramps, blue lips, an agony of itchiness as of insects crawling all over one's body, vomiting, dilated pupils and then a zombie-like sleep, a neurological paralysis during which the victims are often aware of what is going on around them. Then they die. But sometimes they wake. One woman sat upright in the middle of her own funeral causing her grandfather to faint and her mother to scream amid the tears of the mourners.

Why would anyone deliberately risk such poisoning? Unless the lethal tissues are completely removed by a skilled chef, the diner will die before dessert. The greatest fugu chefs are those who leave in the barest touch of poison, just enough for the diner's lips to tingle from the nearness of the great beyond but not enough to actually kill him. The ultimate fugu epicure orders chiri, puffer flesh lightly cooked in a broth made of the poisonous livers and intestines. If a Japanese man or woman dies of fugu poison, the family waits a week before burial in case they rise from their zombielike state.

That's the appeal of the dish: eating the possibility of death, feeling the void rise within you as you chew and swallow, courting the Hemingwayian awareness of being fully alive when death whispers to you, brushes your shoulder, enhancing existence with its presence.

When we tremble on the shoulder of Crystal gazing into the maelstrom confronting us, I invariably think of Old Tom and the cold, rubbery taste to his lips as we administered CPR with his open eyes gazing into the sun. Yet, I am drawn back to the Canyon and that rapid again and

> *No better place to die. No better person to die with.*

again, occasionally attempting the more difficult left run slicing between a pour- over of tremendous magnitude and the now larger second hole, its guttural maw seeking rubberized and fiberglass prey. This route can take you into waves pounding the left wall that have flipped innumerable rafts. Crystal will always seem inimitable for me because of my first -hand experience of death at that spot. Yet, instead of the right cheat, we often choose the more difficult left run. Are we adrenaline junkies or attempting our highest level of skill in the face of danger?

Why do people flirt with death, desire to walk side by side with the grim reaper? Is it an over-sated onslaught of electronic stimuli substituted for life experience that makes us yawn and yearn for something real? Is it mundane

The fury of whitewater

routine that dulls the senses and whets the desire to be wakened by danger blowing like a raw, cold wind from the Arctic? The desire to push the envelope seems to be related to the current paradigm rooted in the production-consumption ethic.

There exists within many people an intuitive voice telling them they are missing something in their lives. They have been partially disemboweled by an inner emptiness. Power, wealth, elegant homes, $80,000 cars, travel, fast-paced work and social lives blot it out but do they offer lasting inner fulfillment? Are we capable of lasting fulfillment? Or, is our current malaise related to Nietzsche's concept of the void and man's drive to fill his vacuity with the acquisition of power—political, personal, and economic? Why do we suck in so much sex, drugs, and alcohol? Do we, in a modern technological society, lack a spiritual component necessary to human existence? Is wilderness adventure, bonding to the land, and physical-psychological risk one path to meaning?

Years ago in school, I taught the concept of the *Bourgeoisie Box*. It represented the flip side of the *Protestant Work Ethic* and the *Gospel of Success* that together created bedrock American values. On the blackboard I drew a person in a box. The box represented the attributes that lead to success. They included efficiency, moral integrity, the ability to follow instructions, punctuality, determination, a capacity for hard work, intelligence, conformity and ingenuity. Add the Boy Scout pledge and that would about wrap it up.

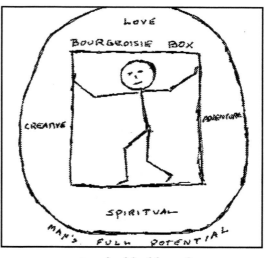

On the blackboard

Then I drew a large circle around the box and told my students, "This circle represents our full capacity to be a human being. It represents how spiritual people can be, how deeply they can love, their interconnectedness to the earth and their potential for forgiveness, understanding, tolerance and unconditional acceptance. If we remain in the *box* chances are we'll end up with a big house, luxury, comfort and adulation from our community but we may not have the opportunity to fully explore our potentialities for inner peace or a higher consciousness unconstrained by the narrow walls of dogma." Gary Snyder, the Pulitzer Prize winning Beat poet and Zen monk asked what alternatives might people have explored in the time they took to climb the ladder of opportunity. Could they have spent more time with their family, their spouse, outdoors or in meditation? Could they have lived a more significant life? Could they have found an inner peace beneath their ego-driven anxieties and ambitions?

Life within the Bourgeoisie Box can suppress, even deaden feelings. In it, media sensationalism and titillating pap are substituted for reality and genuine experience.

On the edge

People risk their lives on mountains and on wild rivers because it makes them know they are alive, truly alive and not just sleepwalking through the years. Adventure, the desire to climb, float and hike the most dangerous places on the face of the earth is a desire to strip away civilization and confront the raw and cleansing force of nature, to scour the sensibilities back to a primal state. It is a thrust to reach beyond physical discomfort and immediate danger for a new sense of being, overriding the damage done by a dysfunctional society.

Maurice Herzog wrote, "In our youth we had not been misled by fantasies, nor by the bloody battles of modern warfare which feed the imagination of the young. For us the mountains had been a natural field of activity where, playing on the frontiers of life and death, we had found the freedom for which we were blindly groping and which was as necessary to us as bread. The mountains had bestowed on us their beauties, and we adored them with a child's simplicity and revered them with a monk's veneration of the divine. Anapurna, to which we had gone empty-handed, was a treasure on which we should live the rest of our days. With this realization we turn a new page: a new life begins."

Into That Silence

Breath of frost
along the edge of night.

Flesh in sap rising,
leaves washing their
hands in the wind,
hidden penetrations of earth
bursting in quiet passion
to bear the birth of spring.

When night flies
into the eyes of another dawn,
I'll be gone into that silence

between the bud and the leaf,
where the love I feel
is earth's food
and another April morn.

Part II—The Making of a New Century

The first part of this book was inspired by 30 years of rowing, guiding, and leading trips on wild water rivers. The second half of the manuscript has grown out of the impact of that unparalleled wilderness on my sensibilities and values. That exposure has bequeathed to me a closer relationship to the earth than I imagined possible and changed the way in which I perceive the world.

In addition, over 40 years of my life have been dedicated to the study and teaching of history. I was lucky to spend my days teaching a subject I loved to students I cared about. This next portion of the book is a reflection of my evolving convictions about the land buttressed by historical events and what modern science is revealing to us about our planet.

What happened in history is fascinating if you know the behind-the-scenes stories but the truly intriguing question is *why* things happened. In 1985, teaching college at night, I created a course called *The Value of Wilderness in a Technological Age*. I was trying to figure out why human beings do so much damage to the world in which they live, why they foul their own nest. In building the course, I tried to pick situations and theories that were insightful, interesting and provocative.

The second section of **Smoke That Roars** is an examination of the historical background and causative forces that have propelled us into an era of environmental crisis. The nature of our plight is also analyzed. It shows why we have not yet fully addressed the problem and illustrates the promise of retaining open market capitalism while solving the limitations of the current system that straightjackets and imperils us. The information is factual, yet open-ended and subject to differing interpretations. I do not claim to be an all-knowing expert who is going to reveal to you eternal verities but, as with my students, encourage you to examine various historical incidents and new perspectives and think for yourselves. These insights are derived from the labor of reputable scientists, historians, sociologists and environmentalists. They establish jumping-off places for further study and analysis. This process is important because our common dilemma is as pertinent to you and me as the beating of our own hearts.

An initial fact to look at is the growing disparity of wealth on the planet. Take, for example, the impact of the Typhoon Kai-Tak on the Philippine Islands. The rain had pounded down incessantly for two days as the wind tore at Manila. In contrast to the modernized, prospering, high-tech part of the city, a neighborhood called "the Promised Land" was a combination garbage dump and shantytown, home to 50,000 people who made their living by scavenging food and materials discarded by the middle class. Garbage was piled into a huge mountain. There was no reliable source of clean water. Screams rang out as the foul-smelling debris came avalanching down, crushing hundreds of make-do homes. Electric lines were snapped, igniting fires. The screams intensified as people tried to dig for relatives and as others, trapped in the flames, were burned alive. Some of the urban poor staggered about, hands to their throats, choking on toxic chemicals released in the fire. Two hundred human beings perished.

This extreme dualism of wealth and poverty is a characteristic of the modern world. Even though the annual output of the world economy has grown from $6.3 trillion in 1950, to $31 trillion in 1990, to $42 trillion in 2000, over one billion human beings are malnourished. More than 1.2 billion do not have access to clean water. Nearly half of the world's population, 2.8 billion people, survive on less than two dollars per day.

When the Russian icebreaker *Yamal* reached the North Pole in July 2000, the scientists were confronted by an expanse of open water. The last time the polar region was ice free was 50 million years ago. Submarine sonar measurements indicate a 40 percent decline in the average thickness of polar ice since the 1950s. Atmospheric concentrations of carbon dioxide have reached their highest levels in 20 million years. Coral reefs are a marine version of the early-warning canary in coal mines. Marine biologists

Island along the Belize coral reef

estimate that one quarter of the coral reefs are sick or dying. Coral polyps are temperature sensitive and often sicken or die when ocean surface temperatures rise even slightly. Further burdens are added by urban sewage, agricultural runoff and the sedimentation that comes from deforestation. The single greatest factor in environmental degradation is human overpopulation. There has been a greater gain in population since 1950 than in all the preceding centuries of existence. But all these corrosive forces are synergistic; they are interconnected and feed one another, multiplying their impact on the land, atmosphere, and oceans.

There exists a need to develop the study of *econology*, a synthesis of history, ecology, sociology and economics to create economies that are both socially and ecologically sustainable. This is the central challenge in the new millennium. We stand at a crossroads in history when there is still time but the window is rapidly closing. By mid-century we will have nine billion people burdening the earth, pushing beyond its capacity to sustain lives that are worth living. There will be wars over water and food as well as resources. We are adding over 219,000 babies every day and 80 million human beings a year to the exponentially expanding total. The world needs leaders of vision to seize the opportunity to eliminate the ecological damage of the industrial revolution and create a new eco-economy. It will mimic nature, be closed-looped, wasteless, and powered on a clean wind, solar and hydrogen foundation. Come, explore what has happened and what can be done.

Isn't it wonderful that we still have wilderness and protected areas where we can make discoveries like this. Think of Anasazi fingers shaping and painting this pot nine hundred years ago. Then, being reverent and non acquisitive towards the earth, we leave it as we found it—hidden where others may someday know the joy of discovery

Nature and Madness

How did human beings get so separated from nature that they willingly damage the habitat that supports all life on earth; that they sacrifice future generations for short-term profit? In Paul Shepard's provocative work, *Nature and Madness*, he sets forth the proposition that in hunting and gathering tribal units a child's first bonding was to its mother. A baby was nurtured by protracted physical intimacy. People live and thrive on touch. Children living in dysfunctional homes sometimes suffer from psychological dwarfism. They simply stop growing. Touch reassures an infant that it is safe; it seems to give the body a go-ahead to grow normally, and develop cognitive abilities later. When deprived, children avoid one another. When they do come in contact with other children, they become aggressive—violent loners who do not form good relationships.

Touch is ten times stronger than verbal or emotional contact. Tribal infants were touched by others about 90 percent of the time. We believe in exiling babies to cribs, carriages or travel seats, keeping them at arm's length and out of the way. Native babies slept in womb-like bindings, a primal memory of being loved and a sustaining force in their lives.

In primitive cultures, a second bonding occurred about the age of six or seven. It was with the surrounding land, its beauty, vastness, dangers, storms; whispers of wind through leaves or murmur of water across rocks. Clues to the meaning of life were embodied in natural phenomenon. The earth herself contained magic, divine beings and numinous presences. The ontogeny or coming into being of the child was

Bonding to the beauty of the land

nurtured through ritual coming-of-age experiences and ceremonies. Their mastery of weapons, hunting and tracking skills, reverence for prey, ability to withstand hunger and pain were tested. Vision quests summoned a personal spirit guide. Boys and girls lived with a strong sense of identity in a natural setting.

In the shift to an agrarian society with its resultant rise of early civilizations, the land itself became a tool to amass individual wealth, *a possession to be utilized.* In the new system, the wild world had reduced significance in the individual's sense of self and it was often perceived as chaotic and dangerous. Ideal places were fenced in and possessed organized, garden-like qualities. Daily labor tended to become dull and repetitive. The person's relationship with his contemporaries was based on an exchange of goods and the accumulation of possessions was a measure of personal achievement. An extension of personal ego perceived the nonhuman world as a substance to be shaped by man, to be owned and exploited rather than encountered as a living presence.

History is a western invention whose central theme is rejection of habitat. It formulates experience outside of nature and conceives the past mainly in terms of biography and nations. It finds causality in the conscious ambitions of men and memorializes them in writing. The bonding ties by which men acknowledge kinship with the earth, the ancient notion of the multiplicity of truth, of hidden spirits in all things, the mystic simultaneity of past, present, and future, credence in spoken, sung, carved, drawn or danced affirmation of the cohesion of all things, the reading of nature as the divine language, the sense of the actual presence of the gods in ceremonial rites—all of these were gradually displaced by the rise of nomadic desert-born monotheism and an increased emphasis on herds, crops, and possessions.

The monotheistic search for a single sense of identity, of being a chosen people in a plural universe ignited the duality of us and them, the Cain and Abel concept, and the gap between individual and environment. Man's belief in dominion over and separation from the land and animal life stunted his ontological process. Without the intermediary experience of belonging to the Earth Mother, the individual has been condemned to an us vs. them dualism without a connecting ground to wholeness. It leaves a void to be placated with dabbling pursuits of entertainment, the need for mastery over others, accumulation of wealth and power or the drive for conquest. It engenders submerged self-hatred that is projected out on others so the Nazi needs his Jew, the Klansman his Black and the Aryan Nation its hallucinatory conspiracy of black helicopters, bankers and a UN invading force infiltrating the nation. It has resulted in Holocaust and ethnic cleansing. Possibly the whole of mankind has become neurotic. In the last two centuries man has killed 160,000,000 of his fellow men.

146

The presence of the void coupled with rise of industrial technology has resulted in clear cutting, poisoning air, land, and water, destruction of rain forest, thinning of the ozone layer, toxic poisoning, over grazing, aquifer depletion and global warming—an insane depredation of our mothering planet exacerbated by the swollen thrust of overpopulation. We could not do this if we experienced ourselves as part of the earth rather than it as a separate entity created for exploitation. It's like believing our legs alien from ourselves and cutting them off to sell the meat.

Since Rachel Carson's *Silent Spring*, a growing ecological consciousness is heartening and there is promise in new innovations such as hybrid cars and the use of plant substitutes for paper production, but the production-consumption-corporate juggernaut has momentum and is now multinational in size and impact. It is imperative that environmental values be factored in to ascertain the true cost of continuing to use the carbon-based fuels paradigm. A carbon tax would reflect the *hidden cost* of the widespread pollution, soil erosion, release of toxic substances, dangers of global warming, depletion of water resources, loss of topsoil, damage to the ozone layer and harm to human health imposed by the existing system.

Lord George Germaine

In my 31 years of teaching history it has often occurred to me that the subject has a narcissistic and almost infantile quality about it.

Lord George Germaine, the first Viscount Sackville was Britain's Minister of War in 1777. His noble upbringing did not condition him to governmental responsibility. He was born a Sackville and brought up at Knole, a family domain so vast that it looked like an entire town. He and men like him were the ego-swollen sons of aristocracy. One nobleman had an entire village moved because, from his estate, it obstructed his view of the countryside.

The Aristocracy, that glittering hub of empire, was caught in an endless whirl of societal balls and banquets, exclusive clubs, gambling, mistresses and lovers, eating heavy meals and drinking sweet wines, maintaining elegant houses in London as well as their gigantic estates with racehorses, hunting hounds and armies of servants—grooms, gamekeepers, gardeners, field laborers, and artisans. Why did they enter government? As the elite, they thought it their province and responsibility although they had little time to devote to it. Because estates were inherited by the eldest son through the law of primogeniture, political power and patronage allowed Lords to place other members of their family in positions that gave them opportunity and a means to make their way in the world regardless of their capabilities.

General John Burgoyne

For the Campaign of 1777, Lieutenant General John Burgoyne had created a tripartite plan to crush New England, the hotbed of colonial rebellion. Gentlemen Johnny, as he was called for his appreciation of the arts and female beauty, would descend along the Hudson River from the north. Colonel Barry St. Leger would penetrate the Mohawk Valley and Sir William Howe would march north from New York. The three forces would unite at Albany and crush whatever opposition was left. It would be a knockout blow to the revolution.

On his way to his country estate, Minister of War Germaine stopped at his office to sign dispatches. His Under-Secretary William Knox pointed out that no letter had been written to Howe advising him of the new plan and what was expected of him. Germaine tapped his foot impatiently. He was running late for a social gathering at which he was the host. Lord George abruptly refused to write the letter. He commanded a clerk, D'Oyley, to pen it for him complaining, "My poor horses must stand in the hot sun on the street and I shan't be on my time anywhere." He was like a spoiled child who didn't feel like finishing his homework because he was ready to go out and play. Labored over by the clerk, the war instructions to General Howe did not make ship with the regular dispatches already signed.

Whether Howe received the orders or not, the general acted as though he had never seen them. Enamored and entangled with the wife of his Commissary General, Mrs. Joshua Loring, Howe ended his campaign of 1776 short of complete victory over General Washington's beleaguered and battered forces. With Major Loring sent off on a long and dangerous mission far into Canada, Howe settled in New York in splendid comfort. The general began to receive anonymous poetry from his troops.

> Sir William, he, as snug as a flea,
> Lay all the time a-snoring,
> Nor dreamed of harm
> As he lay warm
> In bed with Mrs. Loring.

The spring of 1777 arrived bringing with it the hopes of finishing the campaign against the colonials and returning home. But March, then April, May, June and July passed with no inclination on the part of the commanding general to leave the comfort beneath his covers and move into the field. Again mysterious poetry appeared:

> Awake! Arouse, Sir Billy,
> There's forage in the plain.
> Ah, leave your little filly
> And open the campaign.
>
> Heed not a woman's prattle
> Which tickles in the ear
> But give the word for battle
> And grasp the warlike spear!

Finally, in early September, Howe moved into action defeating Washington at Brandywine and Germantown, occupying Philadelphia, and scattering the Continental Congress. Howe and Loring snuggled in for a second winter together while his adversaries shivered at Valley Forge. His bored soldiers made do. After all he was the general.

With two-thirds of his plan gone awry as Howe ended up in Philadelphia instead of Albany and St. Leger was turned back by Nicholas Herkimer's valiant stand at Oriskany, Burgoyne was in trouble. Trying to force heavy guns and wagons loaded with finery and luxuries for himself and the wives of his officers through heavy forest, his progress was stalled. Colonists chopped trees down across his path and flooded other areas of his march.

Led by John Stark, they swarmed in behind him. Surrounded, brought to bay, he failed to break through the colonial lines in the two battles at Freeman's Farm and surrendered at Saratoga, a complete disaster for British arms. The victory reignited the colonial cause and convinced the

French to support the rebellion. Without French aid the fledging colonies would have never won their bid for freedom.

It is a tale of aristocratic arrogance and human folly. That a minister of war would be more concerned about his horses standing in the sun or being late for a party than the conduct of the war, if not infantile, is at best adolescent.

With the recent historical record of environmental degradation, McCarthyism, the nuclear arms race, Vietnam, Watergate, Iran-Contra, U.S. support for death squads in Latin and South America, sex scandals in the White House, the rich getting richer, ethnic cleansing and me-first politics, *less-than-adult* human economic, military and political folly shows no sign of slackening. The bedrock American value of individualistic endeavor coupled with property rights and the desire for profit has become a thrust for instant gratification and unparalleled greed without adequate consideration of long run consequences.

In sum, man's task today is no less than to mend his broken relationship with the land; to garner from contact with its restorative power the resolve to bring sanity into the battle to preserve the environment—the earth that sustains and nourishes us all. Invading trapper, hunter, soldier, missionary, prospector, miner, cowboy, herder, raider, farmer, shopkeeper, developer, shopping mall architect, Internet wizard, junk bond manipulator, software magnate, politician and president are eroded, creviced, cracked, felled, crumbled and winnowed by the breath that lasts a million years. In the mind of space, life was flung through the universe to root on a tiny orb; mother, nurturer, procreator, defender against the unthinkable night. Her sands that silt so dry yet slick through our fingers are more holy than the cross, more portentous than church spires. They are the quiet within the clamor of the bells.

Morn's Mist

Above birds flight
Bitterroots cleft thin air.
Snowblind peaks
cradle all that lies below.

Slaked by the Selway,
pine ghost morn's mist,
row-on-row, speared arrows of the clouds.

Unseen, seedlings glade
where rows of rocks
protrude like the
buried backs of dinosaurs.

Deer nibble warily
in the presence of bear.
Each blade of grass,
misletoed tree, leaf, and fern
shade baneberry and purple loco,
roots clutching earth, grow
the silence
of disappearing America.

SLIPPERY WITH SANITY

Boundaries gone,
slippery with sanity,
we are summer leaves of light
dripping through the trees,

diamonds dancing,
fine and intricate manners of the night
selling maidens in the streets,
weeping willows crying to be weaned,
reaching roots of earth
groping for the sky.

We are high hymns
of granite facing cliffs,
wind blown souls, eyes of eagles,
prairie fires and newborn dawns,
slow stones angered by the sun,
riders of the river's
westward rhyme.

The Fatal Gap

On the eve of World War I, Sir Douglas Haig, stiff-backed and mustached commanding general of British forces told the cadets at Sandhurst, "Machine guns have very little stopping power against a good horse charge."

Aging Emperor Franz Joseph was born in 1830 when Andrew Jackson was President of the United States and ruled Austro-Hungary for 68 years. He detested new-fangled telephones and sent messages by courier. The monarch enjoyed dripping wax on the folded paper and embossing it with the seal of the empire, a tradition that went back hundreds of years.

After the assassination of Archduke Franz Ferdinand in 1914, Marish Szogyeni, the Austrian ambassador to Germany, arranged a lunch with Kaiser Wilhelm II at his summer residence in Potsdam Palace. Szogyeni's task was to negotiate German support for an Austrian invasion of Serbia. With Germany standing behind them, the Austrian generals believed that Russia, mother and protector of the Slavic nations, would not intervene. It would be a short war, Serbia

Sir Douglas Haig

would be gobbled up, the tottering Austro-Hungarian Empire strengthened and the agitation for Serbian unification that instigated the assassination of the Archduke laid to rest. Before lunch, the Kaiser informed Szogyeni that he could

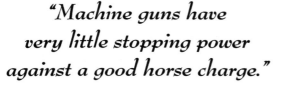

"Machine guns have very little stopping power against a good horse charge."

not give him a definitive answer until he had discussed the issue with his Foreign Minister Bethmann Holliveg. The consequences of such a move had to be carefully weighed.

They sat down to the Kaiser's favorite lunch, a meal of warm beer, chilled hock or pig's feet and clear turtle soup. Afterwards, they took a walk in Wilhelm's favorite gardens and sat on his favorite bench. There, comfortable with his meal and the beer swirling in his guts, on his favorite bench in his favorite part of the gardens, the Kaiser felt an expansive flood of well-being. Spontaneously, he turned to Szogyeni and said, "Are we not all Germans? We will be loyal to our Austrian allies even to the point of war with Russia." This was the infamous *blank check* that opened the gates to World War I. On a beer-fed whim, without consulting his Foreign Minister or due deliberation of possible consequences, he pledged the lives of ten million of his subjects to Austrio-Hungarian war aims. He tried not to think of what subsequent events might be created by an invasion of a free and independent Serbia

Kaiser Wilhelm II

as he left for his three-weeks' annual summer cruise and was gone as the crisis gathered momentum. This is the ruler who declared, "I regard myself as an instrument of heaven. I go my way without regard to the events or opinions of the day." The Kaiser also bragged that he had never read the German constitution. Yet, deep down, he did not want a full-scale war.

General V. A. Sukhomlinov, the Haig of Russia, was a pleasure-loving officer in his sixties who sold passes for Russian maneuvers to potential enemies so he could buy gifts for his 23-year-old fourth wife. His military theory dated from the 1870s and the general boasted he had not read a new military manual in 25 years. In 1913, he fired three military instructors for teaching the superiority of artillery and firepower over the use of the frontal assault. The key weapons, Sukhomlinov asserted, were still the bayonet, saber, and lance. Nothing could withstand a determined Cossack charge.

Fifty-one years *before*, General James Longstreet, a consummate poker player, had figured the odds at Gettysburg and tried to dissuade Robert Edward Lee from his disastrous frontal assault known as Pickett's Charge. Longstreet already saw that increased firepower extracted prohibitive costs from massed assaults and that the advantage had shifted to the defense. Half a century *later*, the generals of the Great War faced even greater firepower in machine guns and the rapid firing 75mm field piece plus long range heavy artillery, yet clung to the doctrine of the attack.

Wasp-waisted and monoculed, Count Alfred von Schlieffen was

Chief of the German General Staff from 1891 to 1906. He believed, in the advent of a two-front war, Germany must swiftly crush her strongest opponent. The preponderance of her armed might would be thrown forward in a gigantic envelopment of France. His motto was, "Be bold, be bold," and his awesome third wing of 700,000 assault troops, the one nearest the coast, would knock France from the war in 39 days.

French War College Director, Ferdinand Foch, declared, "A battle won is a battle in which one will not confess oneself beaten." Plan 17 was formulated committing French troops to a headlong assault against the German Center. Fired by an undefeatable spirit, *élan,* they would be in Berlin in 42 days. It would be a short war. Into the wooded hills of German

Lorraine and the Ardennes marched French infantry with bayonets fixed on their cumbersome Lebel rifles. They were dressed in baggy red trousers and red caps that had remained unchanged since 1870. Young officers from St. Cyr, the French military academy, arrayed in white gloves and waving plumes, led the French infantry. They ran headlong into massed German field artillery and entrenched machine guns. Courage and human flesh were pitted against flying steel. The fields before Morhange ran red with blood. At Virton, Tintigny, Rossignol and Neufchateau, guns roared and, in front of unbroken German lines, the dead piled up. After four days of fighting, the rain fell in an

"To those who died, thinking it not in vain."

eerie silence. Plan 17 lay dismembered on a field in Lorraine where, at the end of the day, nothing was visible but soldiers strewn in rows and sprawled in the awkward postures of sudden death. At St. Cyr, a single tablet was erected to mourn the entire class of 1914.

Against the massive wing of German might, Frenchmen stood and died rather than fall back any further. Soldiers who had retreated for ten days and who slept on the ground and were staggered with fatigue, took up their rifles and punished the German attack. In 18 days of continuous battle, the men of Castelnau and Dubail slammed shut the coastal door. The short war promise of the Von Schlieffen Plan had failed.

Defense was king; the trench, machine gun and field piece triumphant. Battle areas sank into the attrition-marred deadlock of trench warfare. By the time winter closed down, the opposing armies were deadlocked from Switzerland to the North Sea. Like a great wound scarring the land, the trenches stretched across France and Belgium. The murderous insanity, the unbreakable stalemate known as the Western Front had begun.

Thorstein Veblen, the noted American economist and social critic is renowned for his classic work, *The Theory of the Leisure Class,* published in 1899 in which he coined the term *conspicuous consumption.* Veblen was also the father of *The Differential Theory of Social Change.* In this hypothesis, he contended that pure science and its resultant technology tended to outstrip cultural institutions such as government, law, the military and religion, which, because of the anchor of tradition and vested interests, resisted change. The result was a *cultural lag* or gap between the new reality science and technology were unveiling and the way society functioned.

Cultural lag provides a major insight into the coming of the Great War. Aged generals whose concepts were shaped when they were young had little realization of the massive way in which modern technology would alter the shape, duration and impact of war. The manner of the Kaiser's decision to back Austria was that of an absolute king in the 1200s deciding, on a whim, to send 30 knights and a 1,000 foot soldiers to capture a small duchy. It was a form of decision making archaic to the realities of the twentieth century.

Generals who had spent thousands of hours developing war plans, were eager to try them out and become the Bismarcks of their age. They hid messages and plans from their rulers. In all their accumulated knowledge, still they discounted the role modern firepower would play in their schemes. Their dreams of a brief victorious war died in the barbed wire, shell holes and twisted remains of men in *No Man's Land.* Stagnated, the war would grind on destroying a generation of European youth, toppling empires and unleashing the rise of Soviet Communism—all unintended results of the decision makers who chose the path to combat. From the ashes grew the seeds of a second greater war and the Cold War that followed. The gap between reality and the consciousness and policies of the leaders proved fatal.

In 1601, an English sea captain named James Lancaster commanded four ships sailing from England to India. He decided to experiment. On one of the vessels he served the crew lemon juice every day. Most of the group remained healthy. On the other three ships 110 of the 278 sailors died from scurvy. The experiment was of exceptional importance to seafarers of the seventeenth century. Scurvy killed more sailors than any other cause including battles and accidents. Incredibly, the Royal Navy ignored his findings. The Navy conducted its own experiments in 1747 (146 years later) and did not stock citrus fruit on its ships until 1795. The British merchant marine followed suit in 1865, some two-and-a-half centuries after the first experiments with lemons. In the meantime sailors continued to die unnecessarily.

In the United States, it took 46 years for a quarter of the population to adopt electricity early in the twentieth century. But as the century unfolded, 35 years were needed for a similar proportion to adopt the telephone, 26 years were needed for television, 16 years for the computer, 13 years for the mobile phone and only seven years for the Internet. With the pace of change increasing and an entrenched corporate global conglomerate impacting the environment, the *lag* between scientific fact and our profit as usual policies is endangering the well-being of countless millions of future lives.

Lemons—a 250-year example of cultural lag

Ancient Smoke

Driving the road along the Wind River Range,
lightning to the east freezing black-backed birds
in flight, moon bareback on the surge of sunset,
I glance over at a log-fenced farm,
house disappearing into mist,
spectral horse in the corral.
Mind tuned to high tundra
and half-hidden lakes,
I'm driving into ancient smoke,
soliloquy of the past when prehistoric men speared elephants
and Goodale's Cut-off sent pioneers across snagged black lava;
when French trappers traveling with the first white woman
west of the mountains, smoked the pipe with Snake Indians
and went off together to hunt buffalo.

I cross sunken ruts,
twin traces of the wagon way west to Oregon
sorrowed with early graves.
Tranquil light in the farmhouse window
beneath snowbound peaks,

metamorphosis mixed with fog
through which trumpet and snarl
great-tusked and sabertooth ghosts
as I hurtle uphill and around a curve blown clear
trying to comprehend
why people cling to overcrowded cities
when out here the wind cracks cold
and space holds the stars apart.

Resistance to Change

An important factor limiting the pace of necessary change is the intractability of established and revered doctrine. This exacerbates the ever present danger of *cultural lag*. Galileo Galilei contributed to the transformation of man's view of the heavens by grinding powerful lenses to build the first effective telescope. In an age lacking standardized measures even of time itself, he quantified the rate of dropping bodies, the parabolic flight of cannon balls and solved inexplicable mechanical problems. Consulted on shipbuilding at the Venetian Arsenal, granted a patent on a new irrigation device, he worked on the first pendulum clock as well as being an inspirational private tutor and electrifying lecturer at the University of Padua. Unlike earlier investigators of the universe, he did not seek philosophic causes, but concentrated on objective observation and measurement. His seminal studies on the properties of motion made him one of the essential founders of the modern scientific method.

Galileo

During the Counter-Reformation, the Council of Trent, meeting periodically from 1545 to 1563, rejected Martin Luther's insistence on the right to a personal reading of the Bible. The council declared, "No one, relying on his own judgment and distorting the Sacred Scriptures according to his own conceptions, shall dare to interpret them." Its decrees became Church doctrine through a series of Papal bulls (so named for the bulla or round lead seal affixed to pronouncements from the pope).

The Roman Inquisition, after its reorganization in 1542, assumed supervision of printing projects in Italy, and in 1559 disseminated the first worldwide *Index of Prohibited Books*. Authors and publishers could be excommunicated, imprisoned, and tortured for publishing works judged as heretical. Booksellers also had to beware, subject to unannounced inspections.

One of the set truths of the church was that the earth was the center of the cosmos, man the focus of its existence. In his pivotal work, *Dialogue*, published in 1632, Galileo debated the pros and cons of the Aristotelian vs. Copernican worldviews and concluded that such debate was subordinate to Holy Scripture. However, in the three-man discussion format of the book, Galileo could not restrain himself from making Salviati, his own alter ego more clever and persuasive than Simplicio, the voice of the church-held position. The presented arguments belied the inoffensive conclusion and brought the work under papal condemnation. Adding to Urban VIII's displeasure, an astrological forecast in the spring of 1630 prophesied his own early demise. The pontiff retaliated by casting the astrologer into prison and issuing a ferocious edict prohibiting predictions of a pope's death or the death of papal family members.

The trial of Galileo seemed to represent so many other trials that followed through the next three centuries. Involved in Galileo's plight was the suppression of science by religion, the defense of individualism against authority, the clash between revolutionary and establishment factions, the challenge of radical new discoveries conflicting ancient beliefs and the struggle against intolerance for freedom of thought and freedom of speech.

As Dava Sobel wrote in her magnificent *Galileo's Daughter*, "No other process in the annals of canon or common law has ricocheted through history with more meanings, more consequences, more conjecture, more regrets."

The tribunal's verdict declared, "We say, pronounce, sentence, and declare that you, Galileo, by reason of the matters which have been detailed in the trial have rendered yourself in the judgment of this Holy Office vehemently suspected of heresy, namely of having held and believed the doctrine which is false and contrary to the Sacred and Divine Scriptures, that the Sun is the center of the world and does not move from east to west and that the Earth moves and is not the center of the world; and that one may hold and defend as probable after it has been declared and defined contrary to Holy Scripture."

To avoid prison and perhaps torture, Galileo recanted the implications of his discoveries. He swore, "I abjure with a sincere heart and unfeigned faith, I curse and detest the said errors and heresies, and generally all and every error and sect contrary to the Holy Catholic Church."

Dialogue duly appeared on the next published *Index of Prohibited Books* in 1664, where it would remain for nearly two hundred years, long after scientists had proved the earth and the other planets of the solar system rotated around the sun. Galileo was subjected to a form of house arrest during which time he continued to experiment and smuggle writings out to the Protestant scientific community in other countries. His *Two New Sciences* was published by Louis Elzevir in Leiden, Holland in 1638. He died on January 8, 1642, two weeks after the birth of Isaac Newton in England.

The Holy Office permitted the publication of books teaching the Earth's motion in 1822 and removed *Dialogue* from the list of prohibited books in 1835, a *cultural lag* of two hundred years. But similar battles would rage on through history.

Following a bitter debate in the decades after Darwin's *Origin of the Species* was published in 1859, most intelligent Christians had come to the conclusion that there was no fundamental contradiction between science and religion. The Bible was a book of parables and stories designed to help mankind live a moral and spiritual existence. Certainly, the faith it engendered was an important part of human life. The various books of the Bible did not have to be taken literally word for word. But with the rise of Christian fundamentalism in the 1920s, the conflict erupted anew in the form of Bible Belt state laws prohibiting the teaching of evolution in the public schools. Partially as a lark, partially as a chamber of commerce effort "to put Dayton on the map" and partially to test the constitutionality of the law, John Thomas Scopes, a popular coach and science teacher in Dayton, Tennessee, allowed himself to be "caught" teaching Darwinism in his classroom.

The resultant Scopes Trial became the sensation of 1925. The town prepared for the event by repainting many of its main buildings and beseeched Representative Cordell Hull to send down army tents to handle the anticipated overflow. As the event neared, the town was jammed with curious spectators and reporters. Eventually, 22 million words describing the trial would be sent out to the world.

It became even more of a media event when two celebrated men, three-time presidential candidate William Jennings Bryan and the most adept trial lawyer of his time and champion of liberal causes, Clarence Darrow, threw themselves into the fray. Among the reporters was the intellectual cynic H. L. Mencken of *The Baltimore Sun*, who referred to his fellow

> *"The Bible and the Farmer's Almanac are the only two books a man needs to read to know all he needs to know."*

Americans as *homo boobiens,* a dubious tribute to the intelligence of the

161

average citizen. This was high drama and became the first trial whose results were broadcast by radio. The town had a festive, county fair atmosphere as people jammed the streets between booths offering hot dogs, Bibles and stuffed monkeys. A reporter asked one of the local bystanders what he thought of the case of evolution that was at issue.

Clarence Darrow

The Daytonian exclaimed, "Case of evolution? Land's sakes, who's got it?"

Darrow asked one prospective juror, Jim Riley, if he had ever talked to anybody about evolution. Riley said no.

Darrow asked, "Ever heard any sermons about it?"

"No."

"Did you ever hear Mr. Bryan speak about it?"

"No, sir."

"Ever read anything he wrote about it?"

Riley replied, "No, sir. I can't read."

Darrow retorted, "Well, you are fortunate."

Nine of the selected all-male jurors were farmers and five had lived in Rhea County since their birth. Besides the illiterate Riley, three testified they had never read any book except the Bible. These were men who compensated for the narrowness of their own lives by ignoring the knowledge of others.

Linguistics expert Rabbi Herman Rosenwasser of San Francisco had readied the most telling indictment of a literal interpretation of the Bible. He could speak fluently in English, German, Yiddish, Hungarian and Hebrew. In addition, he could read or translate Latin, Greek, Chaldaic, French and Italian. To understand the Bible, the Rabbi pointed out, one must know Hebrew. The King James Version of the Bible was published in 1611 but the scientific study of Hebrew did not begin until 1753. Therefore, there were inaccuracies in the earlier translation. For example, the word *virgin* in ancient Hebrew meant *any young girl*. She could be married and have children but as long as she was still young was termed a *virgin*. The word *bara* rendered as *create,* should be *to set in motion.* Even more striking, the word *Adam* means *any living organism containing blood.* The statement that we are descended from Adam could mean we are descended from lower orders of animals. Wherever the Hebrew Bible refers to the spiritual or intellectual side of man, it uses *Gever* or *Ish,* not *Adam.* Thus natural science in the form of evolution perhaps has discovered the way by which God brought the human body into being. It does not deal with or deny the spiritual dimensions of the force within the evolutionary process.

William Jennings Bryan

The judge, John Raulston, had grown up in the mountain town of Gizzards Cove, Tennessee, and lived in the region all of his life. He was a lay preacher in the Methodist Episcopal Church. Raulston saw in the trial an opportunity for fame and votes. He blocked the introduction of much of the scientific evidence Darrow had gathered for his defense of Scopes. This induced the brilliant lawyer to turn the trial upside down and put Bryan on the stand to defend the literal truth of the Bible. Although he didn't have to, Bryan accepted the challenge. Their exchanges have become famous, as perhaps the greatest lawyer of his time twisted the renown orator into a pathetic and confused figure. Raulston had moved the trial outdoors in the sweltering summer heat and humidity. Bryan quoted a biblical scholar, Bishop Usher, who from the times of the prophets had concluded that the date of creation was 4004 B.C.

Darrow:	"Could you be more precise?"
Bryan:	"I think it was on October 23."
Darrow:	"Have you figured what time of day it was?"
Bryan:	"About 9:00 A.M."
Voice from the audience:	"Was that Eastern Standard Time?"
Darrow:	"How was the estimate arrived at?"
Bryan:	"I never made a calculation."
Darrow:	"A calculation from what?"
Bryan:	"I could not say."
Darrow:	"From the generations of man?"
Bryan:	"I would not want to say that."
Darrow:	"What do you think?"
Bryan:	"I do not think about things I don't think about."
Darrow:	"Do you think about things you do think about?"
Bryan:	"Well, sometimes."

A roar of laughter humiliating the Great Commoner. The rout was on. From the heat, the ridicule and years of gluttonous eating, Bryan died within a week of the end of the trial. Although Scopes was found guilty, dismissed from his teaching position and fined $100, the impact of the trial tended to discredit Fundamentalism and the Doctrine of Literal Interpretation. Yet, in 1929, a teacher was fired in a small Kentucky community for teaching that the earth was round. This was in an area where the people accepted as truth a statement in the Bible about the flat earth. The *cultural lag* on the issue of Darwinism continues to stretch out as Kansas circumscribed the teaching of evolution in 1999.

Such laws are designed to erect a wall of ignorance protecting *a priori* dogmatic beliefs. They defy the factual discoveries of impartial scientific inquiry. They limit access of students, in a nation falling behind in science education, to the most significant body of scientific information derived in the last 150 years.

The intricacies of its tenacious, clawing, torturous climb to complexity create a reverence for life beyond that of blind dogma. The adherents of restrictive views trample the constitution and its separation of church and state. It is difficult to understand the demand for a literal interpretation of a varied compilation of events from different eras that contain contradictions within themselves. They poignantly illustrate how modern science outstrips the church and society's ability to incorporate and utilize new information. It is another way of denying the creative and sustaining presence of the earth *within* all life forms including man.

The rise of fundamentalism in the 1920's

To view the difficulty of change from a different perspective, slip back into our history to a grungy section of New York City and its cultural transformation from 1890 to 1920. There, Greenwich Village became a place glowing with a sense of the contemporary and visions of a freer, more creative society. One night an inebriated crowd of the party prone climbed to the top of the arch in Washington Square to declare Greenwich Village an independent nation. As Christine Stansell writes in her fascinating book, **American Moderns**, "Everyone is always dancing wildly, discoursing eloquently, flirting, making friends or making love; rents are low, apartments charming and restaurants cheap."

Bohemia was originally the name of a Central European kingdom (today a region of the Czech Republic) from where the Gypsies supposedly originated, and thus it implied a loose and vagabond nature that flourished outside of society with an anti-bourgeois bias. By the mid-1800s, the word had acquired a more contemporary meaning as a den of rebels and impoverished artists, following the popular success of Henri Murger's melodrama *La Vie de Boheme*, staged in Paris in 1849.

The cast of characters was eclectic, brilliant, and idiosyncratic. They included Sherwood Anderson, Louise Bryant, Joseph Conrad, Mabel Dodge, Theodore Dreiser, Max Eastman, Elizabeth Gurley Flynn, Big Bill Haywood, Walter Lippmann, Eugene O'Neill, Edna St. Vincent Millay, John Reed and Margaret Higgins Sanger, an inflammable conglomerate of anarchists, intelligentsia, writers, women activists, intellectual Jews, labor advocates, pacifists and Ivy League graduates.

For brevity, one person can be utilized to illustrate the characteristics of the group. Emma Goldman was an English-speaking, immigrant Russian Jew who could switch to Yiddish when she chose. She was an exuberant bohemian, a daring New Woman and a brilliant cosmopolitan lover of literature. Goldman's life came to revolve around two poles of activity. She spent half the year in New York, editing the journal *Mother Earth* and living in an intense cooperative housekeeping arrangement that bound together a *Mother Earth* family of friends, lovers, ex-lovers, would-be lovers and relatives. For the other six months, she crisscrossed the nation piling up thousands of miles of railroad travel, lecturing two to three times a week, staying in cheap hotels and attending honorary dinners.

Speaking tours were a major form of popular entertainment in an age before movies were available. Goldman owed much of her success to her incredible energy and theatricality; she was a great performer. Her lectures were associative and free flowing. Part of the excitement she generated was a woman exercising male rhetorical power. So intense was her charm and impact, Emma Goldman, it was said, could change your life. Henry Miller, the future novelist, claimed, "She opened up the whole world of European culture for me and gave a new impetus to my life, as well as direction." Christine Ell, a prostitute in Denver, heard Emma speak and followed her back to New York. Christine became a cook for Greenwich Village restaurants and a bit player in the Provincetown Theater.

The supreme anti-Victorian, Emma was the woman who broke all the rules and offered instruction to those who would do the same. She championed modern drama, free love, free speech, homosexuality, birth control, the labor movement and Isadora Duncan's breakthrough in modern dance One of her famed quotations was, "Marriage is to love as Capitalism is to labor." Emma styled herself as a secular Jew who was in touch with her immigrant past but at home, intellectually and socially, in a heterogeneous milieu. She held forth on such topics as "The Failure of Capitalism," "The Failure of Christianity," "Nietzsche," "Man: Monogamist or Varietist?" and "Sex: The Great Element for Creative Work." Asked about Goldman's favorite lover, Ben Reitman, Margaret Anderson said he was not difficult to like if you could drop all your ideas about how a human being should look, act and smell.

In 1912, textile workers went on strike in Lawrence, Massachusetts against cruel subsistence standards of living. The workers walked out in response to a pay cut that equaled the price of three loaves of bread, an intolerable hardship for families subsisting on bread, molasses and beans. When employers retaliated with a massive show of force, anarchists among the strikers called in the International Workers of the World. The IWW, often called the Wobblies, was a militant, left-wing organization active primarily in western mining and timber camps. They believed in meeting the violence of strikebreakers and owners with violence of their own including sabotage and assassination. Led by Big Bill Haywood, they fought tooth and nail the inequalities of *laissez faire* capitalism.

Because of police violence against families, a committee headed by Margaret Sanger and Dolly Sloan arranged for the children of strikers to be cared for in New York by sympathetic families. They were met at the train station in Lawrence by angry police who attacked the mothers, children, and middle class women who had come by train to help the youngsters. Beating up hardened male workers in remote mining towns in the West was one thing, but clubbing women and children in a town in Massachusetts was another. Sanger timed their arrival in New York before a crowd of reporters. The children, many gaunt and pale from hunger and some bleeding from the blows of law enforcement agents, touched the hardenend hearts of the purveyors of mass media.

What was forged was an alliance between leftist intelligentsia and labor with access to the existing media, a potential collaboration for constructive change for workers caged in subhuman conditions. It resounded out of the American past from when the quintessential colonial generation guided a nation into being and created a functioning government. That remains our shining example of intelligence coupled with political activity, often a rare phenomenon.

In 1912, it was a turn of great significance for artists and intellectuals to collaborate with working people and identify with working class struggles everywhere. They were able to rouse a previously unimaginable kind of outside support, including protest from the middle-class stimulated by extensive newspaper coverage. It was the first strike to attract sympathy from mass-circu-lation magazines and to picture the Wobblies in a positive light for their constructive conduct. After two months, in a stunning victory, the strikers got a full settlement, pay cuts rescind-ed and wage increases across the board. Lawrence was the

Armed troops facing strikers at Lawrence, 1912

most successful strike of the Progressive Era. Of course, labor and leftist causes were anathema to *laissez faire* capitalists. They could not yet see beyond the prerogatives of unlimited rights of private ownership and prof-its to the value of building mass purchasing power into the existing system.

The potential for constructive change in this unique coalition was destroyed by government repression in the drive for all out mobilization in 1917-18 for the "Great War." After the declaration of war in April of 1917, violence escalated against workers, those considered radicals and antiwar opposition. People were beaten, tortured, threatened with death, even shot and hung by fellow citizens, police and soldiers.

The Federal Espionage Act and the Sedition Act set long prison terms for anyone convicted of obstructing the war effort. Any work stop-pages by strikes were construed to be unpatriotic. Radical journals were denied mailing privileges. An attempt to unionize the copper mines in Bisbee, Arizona in 1917 resulted in union activists and strikers being rounded up, locked in boxcars, and shipped to the middle of the New Mexican desert. Volunteer spy catchers coalesced into a network of super patriots dedicated to the surveillance of their neighbors, colleagues and co-workers.

After the war came the Red Scare and the Palmer Raids against sus-pected Bolsheviks. The raids violated constitutional rights. Agents tapped phones and intercepted telegrams without court orders. Liberal writers who had been writing in a sellers' market found their work virtually unprintable.

The government effectively smashed the IWW, sending 100 convicted members in Chicago to prison for up to 20 years.

For the first time protestors encountered physical danger in New York City. During a suffrage demonstration against Wilson who was vacillating on votes for women, angry soldiers attacked marchers of both sexes.

Goldman went on trial in June 1917 on a charge of war obstructionism. War hysteria surged. She wanted to be convicted for it would show what crimes were committed in the name of democracy. Goldman was at her best, stunning, witty and spellbinding. She said, "Gentlemen of the jury, we respect your patriotism. We would not, if we could, have you change its meaning for yourself. But may there not be different kinds of patriotism as there are different kinds of liberty? I for one cannot believe that love of one's country must consist in blindness to its social faults, in deafness to its social discords, in inarticulation of its social wrongs. Neither can I believe that the mere accident of birth in a certain country or the mere scrap of a citizen's paper constitutes the love of country."

Within 39 minutes the jury came back in with a guilty verdict. The judge imposed the maximum sentence of two years in federal prison. Goldman declared, "Nothing better could have happened. From now on no one will dare maintain in any public meeting that we have free speech and free press."

Released in the summer of 1919, Goldman was tailed by agents from the Justice Department. No longer accused of being a German spy, she was considered a Soviet agent and became a prime target for deportation. Emma was a celebrity scapegoat, a symbol of foreign menace in America. Immigration officials ordered her, along with 249 other radicals, to Ellis Island, to be sent on a "Red Ark" to Russia. She thumbed her nose at officials as the ship pulled away on a freezing February morning. A young J. Edgar Hoover was on the pier watching the forced departure.

Eventually, she was exiled from Russia for her denunciation of authoritarian Communist rule. She drifted about Europe on temporary visas, a woman without a home. Her private grief was almost unbearable.

The back of New York City's Bohemia had been broken.

In the "Roaring Twenties," the Village was co-opted by an increasingly leisured, consumerist society into a tourist attraction. Visitors spent money on spicy fare in Gypsy teashops and were led into insiders' hideaways by "authentic" bohemian guides. Former members of the community went underground and charged admission to arty evenings in candlelit garrets frequented by down-and-out women paid to impersonate poets and artists' models. Bohemia was swallowed by the middle class, its potential for change emasculated.

In actuality, the tide of American history ran against such an improbable coalition for change. One of the strongest single themes in our past is that of the predominance of conservative property rights. In the terrible depression of 1893, the Democratic Party President Grover Cleveland, a fiscal moderate, refused aid for the widespread suffering of the unemployed and poor. The United States lagged far behind European nations in social services.

The *Gospel of Success* preached that in America every person, no matter how lowborn, could achieve success. The greatest hero in all of American History was not the Minuteman, the Mountain Man, the Frontiersman, the Dough Boy or G.I. Joe. The most revered and enduing of all American idols was the *self-made man;* the man who started with nothing but a proper upbringing and built a fortune or a successful profession or a brilliant political career or all of them combined. He was a rugged individualist not needing governmental charity and his achievements were the just products of his own effort, ingenuity and sacrifice. He was responsible for his own well-being. Success was most often judged in terms of wealth, accumulation and power. If he crushed people along the way that's the way the game was played. Social Darwinism incorporated the concept of survival of the fittest into American business practices, justifying any means to achieve the desired ends.

In the 1920s, President Calvin Coolidge hit the nail on the head when he said, "The business of America is business." He added, "The man who builds a factory builds a temple. The men who work there, worship there." His portrait hung in Ronald Reagan's office.

In Bruce Barton's best seller of that era, *The Man Nobody Knows*, Jesus was portrayed as a super salesman who created an organization of twelve men who went out and sold salvation to build a vast and encompassing empire. He was one of the greatest business executives in history. Yet, in that same decade, college students voting on the three greatest figures of all time had Christ third following Henry Ford and Napoleon Bonaparte.

In 1933, with Congress rubber-stamping his first 100 days, Franklin D. Roosevelt might have partially socialized the failing bank system by bringing it more fully under national governmental control. Instead, he took steps to regain the peoples' confidence in fiscal institutions and re-opened them on their existent basis. Originally a balanced budget man, he was forced to the left by the exigencies of the massive depression and he backed controversial measures like Social Security, the National Labor Relations Act, the Works Progress Administration and the Tennessee Valley

Authority. This far-reaching social legislation also quieted FDR's critics on the left such as *share the wealth* demagogues Huey Long and Father Francis Townshend.

Despite the cries from the conservatives about socialism, he preserved the basic free enterprise system during its greatest crisis.

The influential Columbia historian Richard Hofstadter's *The American Political Tradition: And the Men Who Made It* presented a brilliant exposition demythologizing key figures of our past and showing the commonality of their beliefs in property rights and the free enterprise system were stronger than their differences. They viewed that system as potentially the most productive and beneficial to all people.

The current rise of the powerful multinational corporations and increasing globalization of the free market economy are logical extensions of Professor Hofstadter's hypothesis. In thinking of how the system would be of benefit to all people, however, it is unlikely that he then envisioned the accelerated growth of the enormous disparity of wealth that is now spiraling out of control and dooming millions to misery and poverty.

A legacy of Margaret Sanger and Emma Goldman

Anasazi Child

Anasazi child
setting seep-willow snares,
cool wings of breath wind
sweeping from the rim,
sung sound of emerald river
sliding over rock,
red eye of Sun Father
sinking along the esplanade.

Brown fingers
of multicolored corn,
mouth suckled on juicy heart
of prickly pear fruit

strewn by Changing Woman
into the maw of the canyon.

Anasazi child
wrapped in rush cry of water,
crouched between shadow and rock,
bathed in the wan sorrow
of the pale moon rising.

Silence

A new sunrise,
corn pollen
sprinkled over lives
and the warmth
of love against love.

The earth
and last cry of light

across the edge of land and sight,
voiceless sigh of wind.

Silence.
Silence ascending.
Silence ascending through
man's soul and woman's soul
into
the universe.

The Times They Are A-Changin'?

I graduated high school in 1949 and came of age in the so-called placid Fifties. Most of us were sold on the American Dream. Its main affirmations were: graduate college; find the girl you will love for the rest of your life; get a job with a large corporation that offers long-term security; and live in your own cozy suburban kingdom with your station wagon, two and a half children and faithful dog, your own Lassie. We lived for that dream. Pop music, songs like "Across a Crowded Room" or "Younger than Springtime," told us of romantic and lasting love. In college, poetry and literature were eschewed for engineering and corporation finance. My best friends and I graduated at the same time,

The American Dream—Frat life in 1950

married at the same time, had our first babies at the same time and bought our homes in God-sent suburban neighborhoods at the same time. We were a synchronized generation believing wholeheartedly in the existing system. The only difference was that I ended up teaching, while 43 of my fraternity brothers became millionaires.

America seemed at the height of civilization and enjoying a prosperous and stable decade. Or was it? During my first year at the University of Wisconsin, 1950, David Riesman published *The Lonely Crowd*. His book was an attempt to relate individual psychology to entire societies. Reisman argued that as social systems develop they go through three stages. In tribal villages and ancient civilizations, people tended to be tradition-directed relying on ritual, routine and religion. In the second stage, populations showed a rapid increase in size. With greater mobility and the rapid accumulation of capital, the almost constant expansion bred character types who lived socially without strict and self-evident traditional direction. Their elders implanted the values that governed their lives and behavior early in life, leading to a distinct individualism and a consistency within the individual from one situation to another. These people tended to be inner-directed. Each person had his own internal gyroscope. The classic inner-directed society was Victorian Britain or America in the age of the self-made man.

In the third stage, populations leveled off at a much higher level and more people lived in cities, there was more abundance and leisure and societies were more centralized and bureaucratized. This society created the *other-directed person*. In particular, Reisman saw a decline in the influence and authority of parents and home life and a rise in the influence of mass media and the peer group in the lives of young people. The children in such a society develop a need for direction from, and the approval of, others. That created a modern form of conformity in which the chief area of sensitivity was the desire to be liked by other people, to be popular. Other-directed people were more interested in their own psychological development than the greater good of all. They did not want to be esteemed but loved. Their most important aim was to get along with others and be part of the in-group. They also became a marketing category; both the manufacturers of children's to young adults' products and the media that advertises and sells those products targeted them.

The year after I graduated college, married and entered the United States Army, 1955, Eric Fromm published *The Sane Society*. Could an entire society be labeled "sick"? America and Protestant countries like Denmark, Norway, and Sweden had higher rates of suicide, murder, violence and drug and alcohol abuse than other areas of the world. The problem with capitalism, for all its strengths, and itself the result of so many freedoms, was that it sometimes had terrible consequences for mankind.

Twentieth century work was, for most people, dehumanizing, boring and meaningless. The assembly line consumed people in constant repetitive tasks; they became machine-like cogs in a greater machine. The constricting experience of modern work was directly related to mental health. Mass society turned man into a commodity; his value as a person lay in his salability, not his human qualities of love, reason or his artistic capacities. Being trapped in alienating work had consequences for friendship, fairness and trust. Fromm worried that people were becoming indifferent to others; and if everyone was a commodity, they were no different than things. The aim was the recovery of not so much man's sanity but his dignity, the major theme of Arthur Miller's 1949 play *Death of a Salesman*.

In 1956, the year I was discharged from the Army and entered teaching, W. H. Whyte came out with *Organization Man*. His was a not overly sympathetic account of the other-directed person in postwar America. Vast organizations both attracted and bred a certain type of individual who possessed a kind of psychology most suited to the corporate or bureaucratic life. The way to climb the ladder in an organization was to be part of the team, part of the group, to be popular and to avoid rocking the boat. The main motives inside corporations were belonging and togetherness. Pleasing your immediate boss was more important than ingenuity. Whyte was concerned with the trend in education where fewer students were enrolling in the humanities and physical science, opting instead for practical courses in engineering, education, business and agriculture. This, to the author, represented a narrowing of human lives. People knew less and usually mixed with fellow students with the same interests, living a more constricted and one-dimensional ethic.

Organization man led his life in a *benign tyranny* in suburban enclaves that were extensions of the office where social life was constricted to bridge parties, cocktail hours and dinner, barbecues and birthday gatherings. People had to be outgoing, by far their most important quality. Dutiful employees sacrificed their privacy and idiosyncrasies and replaced them with an enjoyable, secure and unreflective lifestyle. Materialistically, his cage was gilded, but it was still a cage, the *bourgeoisie box* I spoke of earlier. No one felt more caged than some of the wives tending their suburban homes and families.

Yet, in the face of a large degree of bland conformity, a significant number of restless, creative and alienated individuals protested the established system by deliberately living alternative lifestyles and creating alternative forms of writing, art, music and humor.

In the early 1940s, a French Canadian runner named Jack Kerouac, possibly headed for stardom on Lou Little's Columbia University team, broke his leg, fell out with the coach and lost his scholarship. Dropping out of school, he met an intellectual Jew, Allen Ginsberg, who had been inspired by an epiphany of ecstatic joy in which the dead, mystical William Blake read poetry to him. Following a bust and caught with stolen goods, Ginsberg went into a mental institution as had his mother before him. He was a tortured soul until he met the right psychiatrist who told him it was okay to love men, write poetry and drop out of the materialistic rat race. Disliking the classical and formalistic literature he studied at Columbia, Allen decided to develop an alternative form of writing based on spontaneity and self-expression. His style was eloquently raw and dedicated to subvert what he felt was an almost official culture based on middle-class notions of propriety and success.

The two new friends ran across William Burroughs, the pale, dead-pan, drug-taking and pesticide-shooting master of English prose. They hung out together in the old Bohemian center of New York. Eventually, Burroughs would write to Ginsberg, "I'm getting so far out one day I won't come back at all." Twenty-five years before Timothy Leary, Burroughs tuned in, turned on and dropped out. Later, during a drunken and drugged game of William Tell in Mexico City, William shot and killed his wife, Joan. Instead of knocking a champagne glass off her head, the bullet punc-tured her forehead.

Back in the early days, in New York City in the late 1940s, he took Kerouac and Ginsberg down an alley to a narrow door, knocked, knocked again and it opened to reveal lowlife Herbert Huncke, a pimp, petty thief, junkie, and pusher, banned by the police from Times Square. Huncke guid-ed them into the nether world, the underbelly of junkies, whores, drugs and black jazz. Here, the Beat movement was born. They became, according to Norman Mailer, the white Negroes or hipsters. They went AWOL from white bread, mainstream American life.

Scornful, brilliant, irreverent, acrimonious, deflating mores, flaunt-ing accepted manners, inspired by be-bop jazz in their writing, which Jack called "bop prosody," they attacked conformist, paranoid, McCarthy, gray flannel suit, new suburbia, organization man, Cold War, *I want you to like me,* consumer-driven, WASP America. Instinctively, they felt something had gone cockeyed with the American system triumphant at mid-century. They refused to be boxed in by a dollar-dominated world.

There was an artistic stirring behind the facade of the vanilla *Leave it to Beaver* age. In 1945, Jackson Pollock, a tormented alcoholic abstrac-tionist, was releasing tensions in paintings without preconceived notions, letting spontaneity direct his painting. He created the involuntary rhythms of the trance dance, mirrors of mind, motion out of stillness and patterns out of chaos. In 1947, Tennessee Williams' stage play featured Marlon Brando in *Streetcar Named Desire.* The play trumpeted the birth of both the actors' studio and method acting in American theater.

Theolonius Monk, Charlie Bird Parker and Dizzy Gillespie were blowing improv be-bop jazz right out of their guts, notes that sliced souls. Kerouac believed them to be the American equivalents of Bach, Beethoven and Brahms. Their music shaped his prose. He wanted to blow it onto the page straight out of his gut subconscious and let it lie there without changes. Young writers Neil Simon, Woody Allen and Mel Block helped skyrocket Sid Caesar's *Show of Shows* through existing boundaries of com-edy. Doing so, they paved the way for Lenny Bruce and Lord Buckley to garbage middle class concepts of what was permissible.

Kerouac's writing and Ginsberg's poetry were characteristic of the Beat desire to be, affirming existence as a positive value in a time of apathy. Their quest for experience was as all-consuming as it was for climbers or river runners. Whether jubilant or disastrous was of less importance than seeking intense human contact that would facilitate the exploration of their own humanity, bad and good, without blinking. Their quest was to escape from a reactive, vicarious existence orchestrated by mass media.

Gary Snyder, a West Coast poet, Zen thinker and deep ecologist, argued that to seek the depths of being and to avoid the deadening materialism of Western culture, it was necessary to see wilderness as the unconscious and explore it; to wander the world in a state of attuned mindfulness. He advocated that senators and representatives be added to Congress to represent the forests, mountains, plains and wild places. Temporarily relocated in San Francisco's North Beach, the Beat avant-garde group refused to accept standard American values as permanent.

Allen Ginsberg

The Six Gallery was an automobile repair garage converted by artists into an exhibition space. The upstairs reading held there on October 7, 1955 has been called the first Beat poetry reading. More than 120 artistic renegades crowded the room. It was the first public reading for Ginsberg, Snyder, Michael McClure and Buddhist Phil Whalen. Kerouac took up a collection for wine, went out and bought homemade Italian red for 85 cents a gallon. Ginsberg had drunk a great deal. He was nervous, but the emotional impact of his poem, *Howl*, took over and he swayed to its powerful rhythm, chanting and sustaining his breath like a Jewish cantor, cherishing the provocative language. Led by Kerouac, the audience joined in chanting, "Go, go," at the end of each line as if they were at a jazz club. *Howl* vibrated with energy and action; jumping off bridges, enigmatic subway rides, cross country journeys, slashing wrists and joyous copulations. It was frantically alive:

> I saw the best minds of my
> generation destroyed by madness,
> starving hysterically naked
> dragging themselves through

negro streets at dawn looking for
an angry fix, angelheaded hipsters
burning for the ancient heavenly
connection to the starry dynamo
in the machinery of the night.

The poem carried the crowd back to pre-modern oral traditions in which the performance counted as much as the words themselves. Ginsberg was trying to shift culture from its more rational and civilizing role back to a more communal practice of collective experience. A rebellious impulse was unleashed against men who had too much money, too many houses, controlled too many things and knelt before the idol of security. Allen's poetry opened the gates for other poets, including the itinerant poetic minstrel Bob Dylan, to say in their own way what had been previously banned or considered outrageous.

Instead of submitting to intellectual poetry journals, Ginsberg deliberately publicized the Beat movement by getting interviews and articles in *Time* and *Life* magazines. The rapidly expanding paperback book trade played its part. The publisher of *Howl* was poet Lawrence Ferlinghetti, owner of City Lights, the first paperback bookstore in the United States. He stood by Ginsberg through an obscenity trial over the poem.

The Beat culture came to have three important ingredients: an alternative view of what culture was; an alternative mode of experience through drugs and/or meditation; and its own frontier mentality, epitomized by the road culture or as Gary Snyder termed it, the "rucksack (backpack) revolution."

Jack Kerouac

In 1957, Jack Kerouac's *On the Road* was published. It possessed an incredible energy and a sense of speed, the pace of change, of impermanence mocking the idol of security. Neal Cassady appeared in the book as the character Dean Moriarty. He was a dynamo of pure white id, screaming, gyrating, crazy, alive, screwing three women a day, screeching Hudsons coast to coast in 48 hours, sticking his head right into the horns in jazz spots. Kerouac wrote, "The only people for me are the mad ones, the ones who are mad to live, mad to talk, mad to be saved, desirous of everything at the same time, the ones who never yawn or say commonplace things but burn, burn, burn like fabulous yellow roman candles exploding like spiders across the stars."

As Peter Watson, author of *The American Mind* wrote, "The 'road' became the symbol of an alternative way of life, rootless but not aimless, mobile but with a sense of place, materially poor but generous and spiritually abundant, intellectually and morally adventurous rather than physically so. With Kerouac, travel became part of the new lifestyle."

The Beats were a non-violent culture. Gary Snyder was an expert in preparing oriental teas and helped elderly neighbors plant their flowers down the street from him in Berkeley. Both he and Phil Whalen became Zen monks. There was a strong representation of Eastern thought and spiritualism in Beat writing. Burroughs accidentally shooting his wife and a 1944 murder committed by Lucien Carr were exceptions to the general non-violent norm of those associated with the movement.

The Beats found the Fifties suffocating. They craved a need for affirmation in spite of a deep sense of doom in western culture augmented by the insanity of possible nuclear devastation. They paralleled the cynicism of the intellectuals of the Twenties impacted by the inane sacrifice of life in the trenches and no man's land of World War One.

The invention of the long-playing record by the Columbia Record Company in 1948, and the first "single" introduced by RCA a year later, fueled the take off of pop music culture. It came out strong in 1954 and 1955 when disk jockey Alan Freed at WJW in Cleveland, Ohio began playing Rhythm and Blues, normally termed race music, and now calling it Rock and Roll. He claimed he invented the term but it had been used in the black music scene for years, slang for sexual intercourse. Repackaged, it was no longer black music, and white stations could play it. Some regard "Sh-Boom" by The Chords as the first R&R song. White performers like Bill Haley and Elvis Presley were imitating race music and hitting the pinnacle of commercial success. TV programs like *American Bandstand* further popularized the songs. It was a catalyst in creating a youth culture and eventually the generation gap, putting forth anthems of R&R, drugs and sex.

The Beat breakthrough in writing, poetry, jazz and the right to a lifestyle of their choosing was followed by the rise of the Counter Culture, flower-power, anti-war Sixties. The Beatles had unlocked the youth market as a whole and Bob Dylan seized the power of rock and used it to change consciousness. With his nasal whine, riveting lyrics and figurative language, he transformed folk music—retaining its traditional protest themes and his own eloquence to speak of social injustice.

In 1972, Bob, his wife Sara, and their children lived secretly in Scottsdale, Arizona. Dylan's mother and my mother-in-law had been childhood friends in Minnesota. They brought our two families together. We goofed around, playing basketball and floating the Lower Salt River. One

179

of my students, Paul Montesano, who came up to my house to get in the games, was asked at school how Dylan played basketball. Paul answered, "Kind of like he sings." Bob soaked up everything around him and remained quiet and enigmatic. One weekend we took the Dylans down to the beach at Rocky Point, Mexico on the Gulf of California.

Hanging out with Bobby D.

I rowed Bob out to a shrimp boat where we were welcomed, given coffee, and showed the pulled-up net filled with rays, small sand sharks and trigger fish mixed in the with the variously sized shrimp. Rowing back, we entered a sublime scene. The water, windless, was smooth as glass. Across it mixed the low rays of the setting sun and a rising full moon in undulations of soft and shifting colors. I noticed Bob absorbing the beauty all around us and thought, *He's going to say something about how wonderful this is that will give me an insight into how he processes beauty and where all that poetry comes from.* Our eyes met as Bob looked at me. Then he looked away and I did the same. Once again our eyes met and he said, "Can I row now?" Bobby would forever remain a mystery to me.

In the spring of 1963, when Police Chief Bull Connor's police dogs and firehoses were unleashed on black protesters, Dylan's "Blowing in the Wind" sold 300,000 copies in two weeks after being released by Peter, Paul & Mary. That summer, before it was the thing to do, he sang in Mississippi. The itinerant lyric poet sang "The Times They Are A-Changin'," which became the anthem of the generation gap.

Come mothers and fathers
Throughout the land
And don't criticize
What you can't understand
Your sons and your daughters
Are beyond your command.
Your old road is
Rapidly agin'.
Please get out of the new one

180

If you can't lend your hand
For the times they are a-changin'.

"Mr. Tambourine Man" was pure poetry fused in subconscious fire. It spoke to the present rather than the past or future and possessed a hallucinatory aura:

Then take me disappearin' through the smoke rings of my mind
Down the foggy ruins of time, far past the frozen leaves
The haunted, frightened trees, out on the windy beach
Far from the twisted reach of crazy sorrow.
Yes, to dance beneath the diamond sky with one hand waving free,
Silhouetted by the sea, circled by the circus sands,
With all memory and fate driven deep beneath the waves,
Let me forget about today until tomorrow.

Hey! Mr. Tambourine Man, play a song for me,
I'm not sleepy and there is no place I'm going to.
Hey! Mr. Tambourine Man, play a song for me,
In the jingle jangle morning I'll come followin' you.

The release of energy in the Hydra-headed movement of the Sixties was a two-edged sword. It battled an establishment that was destroying the environment and engaged in an unwise, unnecessary and perhaps unwinnable war. It battled for minority rights. Yet, the lid blew off, releasing a Dionysian ecstasy, the dark pouring out to obscure the light. This was the descent of ideals into the drugs, sex and hedonism that fueled Haight Ashbury and took Joplin, Hendrix, Morrison and nine of my former students in consciousless overdosed nights. And, like Greenwich Village, the turmoil of civil, women's, and gay rights plus the impulse for freedom and change was co-opted by the system. Head shops, tie-dye shirts, tattoos and radical journals all became cogs in the production-consumption cycle.

Young people can now have their belly rings, multiple earrings and pierced tongues; women and men their tattoos; women love women, men love men; kids smoke joints and try to be cool heavy metal, rap, pop, bop wannabes and it *all feeds the system*. Blacks can be doctors or lawyers and it feeds the system. Multi-ethnic restaurants are established in cities and smaller communities and it feeds the system. Even the drug trade and imprisonment of non-violent offenders feeds the privatization of prisons. The "war on drugs" creates jobs. Three hairy hermaphrodites can be married and the cost of the minister, flowers and reception feed the system.

181

Those still on the road, the angry new young Beats, craving intensity, and the West Coast gangsta rappers feed the system. Rebellion today is against meaningless lives growing out of slum ignorance, poverty, and mechanization. *I have tattoos, body piercing, and green spiked hair, therefore I am.* None of the beat eloquence or ensuing anti-war protests or enlarged choice in lifestyles have slowed to any necessary degree the on-going PAC political influence or multinational super corporate juggernaut that is despoiling the planet and effectively buying off needed reform.

A provocative book is *Bobos in Paradise* by David Brooks. His main thesis is that the *flower children of the Sixties* or the Bohemian expression of that era has fused with the *Yuppies* or Bourgeoisie of the Eighties to produce a new elite based on SAT scores and education that combine characteristics of both or have become the Bohemian Bourgeoisie, or "Bobos." These are your CEOs who wear Levis to work, use butcher paper to have their employees brainstorm on, think up great new overpriced connoisseur items to manufacture and trek Tibet on vacation. As Brooks uses one example, "The Rowena company doesn't just try to persuade us that its irons really press out wrinkles. It sends out little catalogues called *The Feng Shui of Ironing*. In feng shui terms the literature informs us, 'A wrinkle is actually tension in the fabric. Releasing the tension by removing the wrinkle improves the flow of ch'i.'" If Brooks's hypothesis is true, it seems like the new elite either has each of their feet on opposite sides of a widening divide or, conversely, might use their talents to retain affluence in new, self-sustainable business endeavors. Or are they merely sporting a hip veneer over an inner core of traditional business practices?

What emerged of value from the Beat and Hippie eras? What is our heritage from the aftermath of the marches, protest, violence, depravity, creativity, uproar and genius?

One is Gary Snyder's deep ecology and ideas about a necessary union with nature and the rise of an environmental consciousness. It is a remarkable phenomenon achieved in a brief period of historic time.

A second, particularly exemplified by Snyder, Alan Watts, Ram Dass, Ginsberg and Whalen, is the importation of Eastern thought, especially the Zen Buddhist concept of the impermanence of material things, a belief in non-attachment and the need for spiritualism in America to mitigate its hunger for possessions.

Third, is a greater freedom and tolerance of individual lifestyles and progress towards minority rights. The latter is a battle far from won.

Fourth, is the rise of a strong feminist movement battling for sexual choice, equal opportunities, important roles to play and equal pay.

Finally, is a more intelligent definition of patriotism, a conviction that the government should be called to task when it thwarts the public will or refuses to enforce its own laws. The Freedom of Information Act and rise of Class Action Suits were a partial answer to stopping secret government and corporate activity harmful to the people, the environment and the ideals of democracy. These *against the grain* protest activities need to be reasserted and strengthened in the 21st century.

Clandestine operations—such as the Contra arms deal, Ollie North's flaunting of Congressional will, President George Bush Jr.'s refusal to let the public know who helped shape his energy policy or corporations hiding the harmful impact of PCBs (poly-chlorinated biphenyls) for 20 years have engendered righteous opposition. The current administration seems to have its share of secret goals and hidden agendas of more long-range import than fellatio in the Oval Office.

Success measured by wealth, power and influence has become the basic foundation of the American way of life. Its entrenchment has enormously rewarded the few at the expense of the many and contributed to the debasement of human life on the planet.

Seeking the discovery of inner peace is vital to mitigate the possessive ethic of Western culture. We need a pathway in order to transform a powerful industrial paradigm fiercely defending its privileges and recalcitrant to change.

The aim of all great spiritual traditions is to offer us relief from the drama of self and history. Its aim is to know who we are and be able to dwell (to whatever extent we are able) in a world inside of ourselves that is peaceful and serene so we don't need so much external, ego-driven reward, recognition or status.

Its aim is to detach us from the suffering of so much desire and personal drama. Its purpose is to submerge our ego in service, a cause like environmentalism, population control or the worship of God that is greater than our individual selves. One possible key to the future, although probably a minor one, is a person-to-person change in individual consciousness towards an enlightened perspective elevating the promise of both the existing and emerging world.

Meditation Is Not What You Think

Pueblo Canyon

Cliffs rise into
inhospitable heights
hiding abandoned shafts
and eroded mining roads.

Morning scrubs rose
on perpendicular walls.
I trudge upward through juniper
and scrub oak. The trail twists
into tunnels of bear brush and
clumps of prickly pear. Lichen
is bound to boulders
where spray grass blooms
and a thrush sings in ascending spirals.
On flat granite stands a grandfather manzanita
brittle and ancient as bristlecone pine.

A land of premonitions and endings.
A land where a man, sated with life,
could go to die.

I climb, sweating, through the scent of fennel
and tangled grass up,up, up
into the curved concourse of Pueblo Canyon,
past ruins and the mouth of a plundered mine;
walk under the rain of waterfall, past mossy seeps,
crunching over scree and shale
to remnants of the pueblos:

> *three story walls still solid;*
> *intricate maze of interlocking rock,*
> *variegated flat stones slotted by articulate*
> *craftsmanship, fingers smudged into mud,*
> *gateway to a bygone world.*

The Decline of Western Civilization?

O swald Spengler was born in 1880 in Blankenberg, 100 miles southwest of Berlin. His undemonstrative parents forced him into an isolation that shaped his later career. He read and thought a great deal. As a teenager, he was greatly influenced by the philosophy of Friedrich Wilhelm Nietzsche. Nietzsche, in the early stages of syphilis when he formulated his ideas, believed history was a struggle between those who express the iron will of a barbaric lifeforce against the civilized masses of effete democracies. The masses, particularly in Britain and the United States, had been deadened by the impact of mechanization and an oozing commercialism. They existed primarily to accumulate materialistic wealth.

All civilization owed its existence to men of prey with an unbroken strength of will who hurled themselves on weaker, more civilized and peaceful races, on societies that were corrupt, decadent and in decline. These men of prey he called Aryans. They became the *Ubermench* or supermen who would form a new ruling caste. They thought with their blood, were beyond good and evil, had more life-energy and were more complete human beings than jaded materialists; these noble warriors created values for themselves and society. This strong aristocratic class formu-

lated its own definition of right and wrong, honor and duty, truth and fantasy, beauty and ugliness. They forced their will and their views on the conquered. Morality negated life. Conventional Western civilization marked the end of humanity.

It is interesting to note that Mencken's *homo boobiens* of the *effete* democracies rose up to decisively defeat the *Ubermench* in two world wars during the twentieth century.

Nietzsche died from the

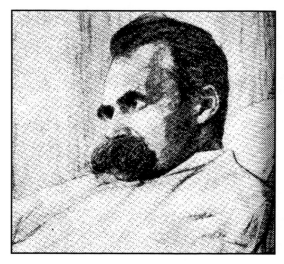

Friedrich Wilhelm Nietzsche

tertiary phase of syphilis in an insane asylum. He insisted he was the Kaiser and Bismarck had ordered his incarceration. He had uncontrollable rages. He died in 1900, the beginning of the century where his philosophy, buttressed by the Social Darwinian concept of survival of the fittest, reaped a terrible harvest in the rise of Hitler's National Socialism. To an extent, the Third Reich misinterpreted both Darwin and Nietzsche, but the philosopher's legacy became a tool leading to mass murder.

In 1903, Oswald Spengler failed his doctoral exams. He passed them the next year but found top-flight teaching positions unattainable and, in 1905, had a nervous breakdown. Forced to teach in schools rather than a university, he quit to become a writer. He became a fierce critic of acquisitive western society. His greatest work, *The Decline of the West*, was published in 1918.

Spengler examined eight major world civilizations and explained how each went through a cycle of growth, maturity and decline. There was no linear historical development, only the rise and fall of individual cultures. The rise of a culture depended on two factors—the race and the *Geist* or spirit, the inwardly lived experience of the *"we."* The West was obsessed with materialistic science, while in Germany there was more feeling of the inner spirit. In the Fatherland, the sense of the *"we"* was stronger. This led men to exchange the practical freedoms of America and England for the inner freedom that comes from serving and being part of an organic whole. Western civilization was dying.

Ironically, his book appeared six months before German defeat in World War I. Yet, it was so successful and made Spengler such a celebrity that people had to wait at least three days before they could get in to see him. Dietrich Eckart, who helped form the German Workers Party, was greatly impressed by his work. The party chose the twisted cross or swastika for its political symbol. Another fan of Spengler, Alfred Rosenberg, joined the GWP and soon after brought in one of his friends just back from the front—Adolf Hitler. Like Nietzsche, the philosophy of Spengler was to be translated into an agonizing reality.

Objectively, no matter how alien his thinking may seem to us, the basic question raised by Spengler is still a viable one. Is our society in a state of decline? If so, to what extent? Professor Morris Berman of John Hopkins University, in his provocative book *The Twilight of American Culture,* believes there are four important criteria found in declining civilizations. They are:

- An accelerating disparity of wealth between the rich and poor.
- Declining efficiency in solving socio-economic problems.
- Rapidly dropping levels of literacy, critical understanding, and general intellectual awareness.
- The emptying out of cultural content and replacing it with kitsch. Kitsch is something phony, clumsy, witless, untalented,

vacant, vapid or boring that people can be persuaded is genuine, graceful, bright or fascinating.

To what extent do these criteria apply to our current society?

● **Inequality of wealth.** The top one percent of the nation saw its income level grow 78 percent between 1977 and 1993. By 1997 this elite one percent owned 47 percent of America's wealth. There has been an ongoing redistribution of income towards the rich. We are in a spiral of inequality. By 1996, the 447 richest people on the planet had assets equal to the poorest 2.5 billion, 42 percent of the world's population. The affluence of the few is purchased by the misery of the multitudes. The continuation of current policies will further accelerate this phenomenon.

In comparison with ancient Rome, during the reign of Nero (A.D. 54-68), roughly 2,000 men owned nearly all the land between the Rhine and the Euphrates. The rich were very, very rich and the poor were very, very poor. The top echelon had pulled up the ladder leaving the masses stranded below.

Now, of the world's 100 largest economies, 51 are corporations rather than countries. The 500 largest corporations account for 70 percent of the world's trade.

Warm by the Fire

Gray-bellied clouds fold over uplifts of land,
escarpments descending to benches
of salt sage terraced like rice paddies.
Rock raised and marked by time,
striped lines of oxidation draining

asymmetrically, plummeting
from pinion pine to cottonwoods
rooted along the river.
Upthrust rims and metamorphic granite
useless to the GNP, land without profit or sale,
whose purpose runs to its own.

Warm by the fire,
I sit and sip coffee,
proud of what I don't own,
of what I did not become.

- **Social problem solving**. More than 139 years ago, President Lincoln issued the Emancipation Proclamation, and two years later the Thirteenth Amendment legally ended slavery, but racism and racial inequality still plague the nation. Random violence, alcoholism, drug use, molestation, child abuse, gang feuds, suicide, mental illness and poverty have proven intractable. When I was in third grade in Cincinnati, I used to ride my bike all over the city and go exploring on my own. Sometimes I met my dad for lunch at the old oyster bar downtown. No one worried about anything happening to me. Even the depression drifters at a nearby hobo camp in the woods in back of our house were men who told me stories and sang me songs. Nowadays, parents have to know where their children are every minute.

The shootings in schools are perhaps the most acute danger flag waving in our faces. The random, unnecessary and unpredictable death of the young leaves a repulsive nausea in the pit of all our stomachs and an ache of helplessness in our hearts. *I kill therefore I am.* Partly at fault is the inequality of wealth and of the government spending. billions of dollars for corporate welfare and weapons, but much less to bolster substandard schools; an ailing war against the dark power of the inner city to mold dysfunctional lives. Given the thrust of the Bush Administration, we may soon be spending more on weapons and warfare than the combined total of the next 14 largest national military budgets.

- **Dumbing down**. In their controversial 1994 book, *The Bell Curve*, authors Richard J. Herrenstein and Charles Murry argue that a cognitive elite was emerging as part of the American social structure. The cognitive elite was getting richer while everyone else was struggling to stay even. This group was increasingly segregated both in the work place and within the social strata where they live. They were increasingly likely to intermarry, augmenting the trend to consolidate wealth.

Conversely, students who drop out of school usually come from the bottom 25 percent of the I.Q. range. Low-I.Q. parents are more likely to be on welfare and have low-birth weight children. Low I.Q. parents are more likely to spend time in prison. Asians outperform whites who outperform blacks on newer, improved I. Q. tests. People with lower I.Q.s are having more children than the rest of the population. Inequality of wealth and opportunity has ghettoized the losers into a pathological combination of broken spirit, drugs, gangs and ignorance. In the opinion of some sociological researchers, there is a declining intelligence level in the United States.

An educational survey of 22,000 high school students in 1995 showed that 50 percent of them were unaware of the Cold War and 60 percent had no idea how the United States came into existence. Some of them thought the Civil War was fought in the 1960s and that we declared our independence from Germany. The pony express ran from Isthmus to Panama. Of the 158 countries in the U.N., the United States ranks 49th in literacy.

In practice, the school system has been dumbed down to meet the needs of average and below average students. If I taught an average American History class in 1989 with the standards I used in 1959, I would have had to fail 85 percent of the class. In 1989, we had finished a session on the Sand Creek Massacre. Colonel John Chivington, a Bible-thumping preacher and Indian-hating military man, led an icy October morning surprise attack against the Cheyenne and Arapaho people *after* they had been given government permission to winter at Sand Creek. His forces slaughtered more women and children than warriors. One student writing an essay on an exam informed me, "Colonel Chivington was not a good Christian. If he was a good Christian he would have realized if God had wanted the Indians exterminated, He would have created them exterminated." I read her answer and felt depleted.

Fortunately, in my last years of teaching, the bright kids were as smart and motivated as ever. I loved working with the Advanced Placement American History classes in which the students gain college credit in high school. My high school AP kids were writing more proficient and profound papers than my senior Methodology class at Arizona State University. Today's computer whiz students from advanced courses are an academic elite with unlimited promise. It remains to be seen what values will shape the course of their illimitable future.

- **A diluted culture.** The level of American mass culture goes hand-in-hand with declining intelligence. Numerous sociologists and educators feel that we are undergoing a steady lobotomizing of our culture. We are becoming Ramboized. They see a world of learning disappearing before their eyes.

Corporate takeover of intellectual property and buying out of independent publishers has lowered the taste in reading. With media control, it feeds tidbits of vapid news into public discourse. Its long-term goal seems to be to turn intelligent citizens into mindless consumers. Most of the publishing in the United States is in the hands of six corporations. Corporate profit mentality is beginning to dictate what goes on in the market.

Thousands of potentially good authors are ignored as publishers push their giant profit-makers like Stephen King, Danielle Steel, Patrica Cornwell, Carol Higgins Clark or John Grisham. Bookstores are filled with "how to" books, especially how to get rich. Television is the epitome of putting buyers in touch with advertising via programs appealing to the lowest common denominator of mass taste. More and more, shows are a string of commercial messages interrupted by bits of programming. There are kaleidoscopes of swirling images to convince the viewers they are changing channels even if they aren't.

We now have four billion square feet of land devoted to shopping malls and the average American is bombarded by phone, mail and mass media to buy, buy, and buy. We celebrate commercial corporate consumerism for its own sake. Political scientist Benjamin Barber refers to it as *McWorld*. With the dizzying flair of special effects advertisements and its prodigious technological growth, America seems vibrant and indomitable. The problem is that its frenzied energy celebrates little that is substantial beyond buying and owning things. The United States is evolving into a corporate oligarchy hiding behind the mask of democracy. Business giants buy out political leaders with campaign contributions. To an extent, mass media has become our imagination, our power to envision, charting the commercial future for us. Life becomes one gigantic movie. Microsoft and AT&T are now creating classroom curricula for five-year olds. Try to get where you want on the Internet without running an irritating gauntlet of special deal ads. *Of course I want to own a $29.99 digital camera. I buy, therefore I am.*

People want simple answers to complex problems. If you send ten copies of this message out to ten people within 72 hours you will have a remarkable stroke of good fortune. This is God's truth. Hype is life. Slogans work. Shopping is entertainment, even a form of therapy. Who ends up with the most toys is an ideology. Many Americans fail to perceive the degree that corporations have taken over our lives. Why should they? In accumulated surveys, 42 percent of American adults cannot locate Japan on a world map. Fifteen percent could not locate the United States. One in ten voters did not know who the Republican or Democratic nominees were in the Election of 1996. When I wait in the check out line in a grocery, I glance over at *The National Enquirer* and its copycat magazines and wonder, *Who in hell reads that garbage? Are people that stupid? That's hard to believe.* Polls show that 70 percent of Americans believe in angels, 50 percent believe in UFOs and 71 percent of them believe the U.S. Government is involved in a cover-up about the subject. Thirty percent believe they have made contact with the dead. And we thought we had transcended the Age of Superstition.

No wonder Jim Rose, one of my former students, could became a millionaire. He put together a freak show with people stabbing long needles through their flesh, blowing up hot water bottles until they explode, having beer and milk and chocolate pumped into their stomachs then pumped out again for members of the audience to drink, eating maggots and worms, eating razor blades and Dr. Lifto swinging a heavy iron attached to a ring in his stretched-out penis. A few years back, I saw their show in Phoenix then the entire crew came over to party at my house. In talking to the cast, I was told that the only thing they all had in common was the fact that none of their mothers had ever seen them perform. *The Wall Street Journal* did an article on the show. Its conclusion was that Mr. Rose's successful venture proved that Americans would pay to see anything.

In lives of material possession that lack intimacy or depth or meaning, constant diversion and entertainment is a must. Among the excellent novels and unread poetry, the intelligent and incisive films or television shows and some superb theater, most Americans settle for swill and garbage at the trough of mass culture.

Are we a declining society? This is, of course, an open-ended question that can be argued up and down across the land. Besides mindless violence, what bothers me the most is political apathy and the lack of accurate information, depth and a broad perspective on crucial issues, especially those dealing with the environment. With mass media sucked into large corporate entities and news provided on a shock value, immediate interest and entertainment basis, bedrock issues are obscured.

To me, the epitome of this was turning to any channel and watching cars driving down the freeway in the coverage of the O. J. Simpson saga. On and on they drove; boring and useless hype. What about the 19,000 babies who starve to death in the world *everyday*? A report on insider profiteering or the revelation of exactly who is profting from our new military build up would have been more valuable. Without a widespread and intelligent consciousness, the changes needed to create a sustainable society will be difficult to achieve.

An Unremembered Father

River, inner pulse of the millennium,
has run all the years of man's frail ascent
from chemical soup of shallow seas
to angiosperm explosion

scattering seeds and wild grasses
that coaxed ferret-like rodents inland,
birthing mammalian creatures,
enlarged brain augmented
by thumb and forefinger,
shade of comprehension
in brute-eyed beasts
fashioning tools and fire,
gatherers and hunters
sacrificing to seminal gods.

Centuries march into
the breakdown
of the bicameral mind,
consciousness crawling from its cave,
spanning centuries to the genius of Mozart
and Beethoven, mad journey of Nietzsche,
man-angel tied to dinosaurian swamp,
instinctual kill of lioness, misshapen dwarf clinging
to the dark side of the psyche.

River flowed before Hiroshima,
Verdun, Chancellorsville;
before Christ, Mohammed and
the birth of Buddha, river flowed.
Before book, poem or love river flowed.

Land, the land;
river, the river
drift down ridges of time.
An unremembered father
calling us home.

192

Ancestral Graves

Tilted fault lines
narrow to swallow sky
as I dare the inner gorge
drawn towards the sea
where waves wash
over the ashes of my father.

Anticlines and esplanades
cramp down
to the knifed edge
where rapids rage
through the mouth
of black-fluted schist.

Ancestral graves in the Ukraine,
marked monuments in Maryland,
father's remains on the ocean floor,
mother's bones and headstone

neighboring her brother and parents.
A new baby born as Aunt Ida's
mottled time runs out.

Rain, river, and current;
rock, water, and wind;
flesh, blood, and breath;
cycles in cycles
run.

A Watershed Era

We stand at a precarious crossroads today. The corporate mind and ongoing corporate structure were formed in an era of resource abundance. They are now confronted with growing resource scarcity and have yet to make necessary crucial adjustments. We bear the weight of *cultural lag* at a critical time in human history. The corporate world continues to operate and influence political decisions towards its fundamental goals of greater profit, increased productivity and a higher standard of living for greater numbers of people. These aims of modern commerce, coupled with an ever increasing population, are approaching a point beyond the natural environment's capability to sustain the existing system and perhaps life itself.

Some centuries are more savage than others. The one that has just ended is one of the most brutal in history. This brief span of time bears witness to the useless sacrifice of life in the trenches of "The Great War," the Great Depression, starvation in the Ukraine, millions dead in World War II, six million butchered in the Holocaust, the power of the sun's one million degrees come to earth at Hiroshima and Nagasaki, birth of the hydrogen bomb, war in Korea, doomsday tension in the Cold War, useless tragedy in Vietnam, extermination in Cambodia, Ruwanda, and the Balkans, the rise of terrorism and biological warfare and the specter of AIDS and other deadly viruses. Man's impact on man and on the planet have been magnified by unparalleled technological progress. The changes underway today are compressed into just a few decades and are global in scope. The question facing our generation is, *Will CEOs and government officials take charge and implement rational shift to sustainable economies or stand by counting profits as env*

Natural Capital

ronmental systems break down?

As futurist Paul Hawken reported in his landmark article "Natural Capital" in *Mother Jones* magazine, ". . . it has also been one of the most disingenuous centuries in the chronicles of man. New technologies have yielded health, luxury, and comfort for a significant minority of the human population, but this paradigm has its dark side. A Faustian bargain has been made in exchange for these gains. Masked behind exciting and impressive technological progress and increased creature comfort, we have reached a watershed in capitalistic enterprise. We are reaching a shortage of natural capital."

Natural capital comprises the resources we use, both nonrenewable —as coal, oil, and metal ore—and renewable such as forests, aquifers, fisheries, and grasslands. We think of natural resources in terms of needed raw materials like lumber, yet now their most important value lies in the services they provide in their natural state. Not pulpwood but forest cover, not depleted food production but topsoil. Living systems feed us, protect us, heal us, clean the planet and let us breathe. They are a form of income and life support in the blessings of clean air and water, climate stabilization, oxygen production, protection against ultraviolet radiation, climate regulation, rainfall, flood prevention, ocean productivity, fertile soil, watersheds and waste processors.

Natural capital is worth trillions of dollars to industry and these subsidies are running out.

Huge political donations, a carbon based energy system, corporate welfare and a culture saturated with shopping malls, consumption for the sake of consumption, accumulation of material wealth and media violence are intrinsic pillars of an archaic paradigm. Television, Nintendo and the Internet are making astute shoppers of two year olds. We have made holy what is destroying us. If we fail to adjust the ongoing system to existing reality, we face a rendezvous not with destiny but disaster.

Over 100,000 synthetic chemicals are on the market and are augmented by 1,000 new ones each year. In 1962, my former wife, Sherri, and I were swept up in an international media blitz over the drug thalidomide, a European tranquilizer used for morning sickness by pregnant women that resulted in the birth of thousands of deformed babies, many with stub fins instead of arms. Sherri had used thalidomide that I brought back from Europe and her gynecologist told us we had a 50 percent chance of having a deformed child. He showed us pictures of the thalidomide babies being born in Europe at that time.

After discussing the situation together, we opted to have an abortion. This was a difficult decision because we loved our existing four chil-

195

Natural capital

dren but we had a strong conviction that we did not want to chance bringing a severely malformed child into the world. Blocked in the United States by the courts and not given a visa to Japan because of the intense publicity, we flew to Sweden.

With its lakes and firs, the part of Stockholm we stayed in reminded Sherri of her home in Duluth, Minnesota. Beset by 4,000 letters, some investigated by the FBI, threatening to cut the arms off our children or castrate me, I was impressed by the rational way the issue was handled by the Swedish government. A woman desiring an abortion underwent a thorough physical, mental and social-economic screening by various experts. She was treated with courtesy and professionalism. The results were used to decide whether the right to an abortion should be granted. Usually, the process took about two weeks without hysterical picketing, bombing of clinics or murders of doctors. Women were allowed the abortion procedure in about 50 percent of the cases. Sherri went through the process like anyone else before being operated on at Karolinksa Hospital in Stockholm. The fetus was deformed. Pope John XIII condemned us. Church leaders in Sweden told the pontiff that, if he didn't mine, they would handle religion in their own country. Because of the enormous publicity incurred, our 15 minutes of fame had historic consequences. It dragged the previously unmentionable topic of abortion into open debate, a step towards *Roe v. Wade, 1972;* it helped tighten the laws about using new drugs; and it was one of two events that punctured the myth that the placenta screened harmful substances from the developing baby. Sherri and I later had two more healthy children. Fittingly, during the thalidomide crisis, Rachel Carson's *Silent Spring* began serialization in *The New Yorker*.

If thalidomide exploded the myth of the inviolable womb, then DES

> *We have made holy what is destroying us*

gutted the notion that birth defects have to be immediate and visible to be important. DES was diethystilestrol, a man-made estrogen.

In 1938, scientist Edward Dodds synthesized DES while, coincidentally, a Swiss chemist, Paul Muller, discovered a powerful new pesticide — DDT. Both were hailed as *wonder substances*. Eventually, Dodds was knighted and Muller won the Nobel Prize. By 1957, DES was given to prevent miscarriages and was said to produce bigger, healthier babies. It was

Sherri and I in the calm rationality of Stockholm

also used to impede milk production after childbirth, treat menopausal symptoms and prostate cancer and to stunt growth of teenage girls becoming unfashionably tall. In April 1971, *The New England Journal of Medicine* linked a rare vaginal cancer appearing in young girls to DES taken by their mothers during pregnancy. One of the first patients died in 1968 at 18 years of age. Others discovered that they could not bear children. While they were still in the womb, their future dreams had been stolen by invisible chemicals passed on from their mothers. DES has also been linked to an increased incidence of breast cancer. One in every seven women in the United States will battle breast cancer during her lifetime.

Scientists discovered that DES disrupted the hormone messages sent at crucial times to the developing fetus. Scientists have stumbled upon other chemicals, both man-made and natural, that act as hormone disrupters and hormone mimics. One of the major results of such disrupters and mimics has been problems with reproduction in the ensuing generation. The key element is timing. If excess estrogen even in relatively low dosages is administered at a critical time in fetal development, it can alter the growing baby.

A second result has been the impact of excess estrogen on developing male babies. In addition to a rise in testicular cancer, there has also been a drop in the average male sperm count. Danish researchers have found the

197

average male sperm count had dropped 45 percent from an average of 113 million per milliliter of semen in 1940 to 66 million per milliliter in 1990. The volume of semen ejaculated had dropped by 25 percent, making the sperm decline equivalent to 50 percent. The number of men with extremely low sperm counts has tripled. The number of men with extremely high sperm counts had decreased. Prostate difficulties have increased.

The 209 compounds classified as PCBs augmented by 75 dioxins and 134 furans have documented disruptive effects. Some linger in the body for years. Dioxin is the most dangerous chemical on earth, a thousand times stronger than strychnine. These toxins often target the thyroid and adrenal glands. Depressed thyroid levels have also been linked to breast cancer.

Chemical engineers have created chemicals that jeopardize fertility and the unborn. They have unknowingly spread them far and wide across the face of the earth. I always had the dream of someday moving out into the desert or a remote place to get away from toxicity of the environment. It's too late for that. Kongsoya, part of Norway's Svalbard Archipelago, is a rocky, treeless island lying east of Greenland at 79 degrees north latitude. It serves as a maternity ward for polar bears. Pregnant females often seek the island's Bogen Calley, digging their nursery dens on its south-facing slopes as winter sets in. In hibernation during the long winter night, they

A chemical toxic environment

give birth to one-pound cubs and nurse them for several months before emerging with 20-pound youngsters in the spring. There has been an alarming drop in bear fertility. Seven of twelve bears emerged without offspring in 1992. Svalbard is remote and pristine, yet research has shown that the bears are highly contaminated with industrial chemicals, including PCBs, DDT and other disrupters. When researchers looked for an uncontaminated population to use as an experimental control group they couldn't find one. Even the Arctic Inuit carried all the disrupters.

The book, *Our Stolen Future* by scientists Theo Colborn, Diane Dumanoski and John Peterson Myers, concludes, "The Twentieth Century is a watershed in the relationship between humans and the earth. The awesome power of science and technology and sheer number of people increase the scale of impact from regional to global. They are beginning to alter fundamental systems that support life. Billions of pounds of man-made chemicals have been released during the past half-century. The systems undermined are among those that make life possible. There is no clean, uncontaminated place or any human being who hasn't acquired a considerable load of persistent hormone disrupting chemicals. We are all guinea pigs."

American productive efficiency is a mirage. From the planned obsolescence of the 1950s to our throwaway mentality of today we are the most wasteful nation on the face of the earth. Eight out of ten of our products are one-time use and throw away items. Until it closed in 2001, New Yorkers dumped 26 million pounds of trash daily into Fresh Kills on Staten Island, the world's largest landfill. Now that staggering mass of garbage is trucked to North Carolina.

The concept of natural capital is not figured into industrial computations. The Freeport-McMoRan gold mine in Irian Jaya dumps tons of waste daily into Indonesian rivers. Only a fraction of the polluted tonnage comes to the U.S. as gold. The rest remains there. The use of arsenic and cyanide in gold production is one of the most toxic processes on earth. The cost of erosion, silting of streams, destruction of fish life and floods is not figured into the price of clear-cut timber.

Total waste equals 250 trillion pounds a year in the U.S. Primarily paper, glass, plastic, aluminum, and steel are recycled—less than 5 percent of the total waste system. For every 100 pounds of product we manufacture in our country we create an average of 2,200 pounds of waste.

Of the $7 trillion spent in the U.S. every year, we waste at least $2 trillion. The World Resources Institute found, among other expenses, that inflated overhead in the current health system costs $250 billion. Fifty-two billion dollars is spent on substance abuse. Sixty-nine billion dollars per year is lavished on obesity treatments. There now are 1.2 billion obese people in the world to match the 1.2 billion who are malnourished. One hundred billion is spent on health problems related to air pollution.

Our unnecessary complex tax code costs $250 billion for audit, bookkeeping, accounting and record keeping.

Crime costs taxpayers $450 billion, lawsuits $350 billion, and disbursement for SuperFund sites is at $500 billion.

Highway accidents cost $358 billion per annum. Road congestion costs $100 billion a year in lost productivity. Hidden costs of auto exhaust in disease and plant damage totals $300 billion. The lack of high standards of home and office energy efficiency costs $300 billion.

Highway accidents cost $358 billion per year

This is a partial list. It does not contain, among other expenses, the loss of fisheries, damage by overgrazing, water pollution, forest depletion, decreasing aguifer levels and topsoil loss. We have also entered the intial stages of another era of mass extinction of species. This will be, if not stopped, the first mass extinction caused by one species, man, harming all the rest.

Economist Herman E. Daly cautions that we are facing a historic juncture, a *watershed*, because the limits to increased prosperity are not the lack of man-made capital, but the lack of natural capital. The limits to increased fish harvests are not boats, but productive fisheries; the limits to pulp and lumber production are not sawmills, but plentiful forests.

Our first necessity is to revise the tax system to stop subsidizing destructive enterprise. Our government currently subsidizes environmental exploitation, gasoline-burning cars and big corporations. We don't like to subsidize clean technologies that will lead to more jobs and innovations. Specifically, we subsidize carbon-based oil and coal extraction. We massively subsidize a transportation network that has led to suburban sprawl and urban decay. We subsidize agricultural production, nonproduction, destruction and restoration. We subsidize cattle grazing on public lands and pay for soil conservation. Extolling a free enterprise and free market economy, we spend billions in corporate welfare each year. European nations are far ahead of us in shifting taxes from income to carbon-based fuels that feed global warming and increasingly destructive weather patterns.

Population size is the *crucial variable* in achieving a sustainable economy. In this sense, *sustainability means the management of environ-*

200

ment and resource systems so their ability to support future generations is *not diminished.* What size population would make this goal attainable? Donald Mann, President of Negative Population Growth, believes that the optimum size of the world population should be between 1.5 and 2 billion. That was the number of people on the planet in the first decade of the twentieth century. He feels that a specific population target is the prerequisite for action.

The alternative would be to continue our aimless drift towards a projected population figure of 9,309,051,539 human beings by 2050, which may be beyond the earth's carrying capacity if we value clean air, clean water, a nontoxic environment and a continuation of the planet's ability to sustain human life. The result will be a rising death rate

"We are all guinea pigs."

and human misery and suffering on a more massive scale than has ever existed.

NPG suggests that a fertility rate of 1.5 children per mother is needed for several decades in order to halt and reverse world population growth. That level of fertility could be reached if no woman had more than two children as many others would voluntarily have only one child or no children at all. A lower fertility ratio than 1.5 is not desirable because of its disrupting effects on age structure. A graying Europe with declining birth rates may soon face this problem. By 2050, Italy's population will have dropped from 57 to 41 million. In the Europe of today there are five people of working age for every retiree—by 2050 there will be only two. Healthy population decline needs to be a slow and orderly process.

By contrast, among the developed nations, the United States is the largest still growing at a pace that would double our population in this century. The immigration of 1,000,000 people per year and

Twice as many cars on the freeway

their subsequent offspring contributes to this predicament. It's hard to imagine another United States, just as large, crammed into our existing boundaries: double the number of houses and paved areas plus twice as many cars on the freeway, twice as many people wanting to use wilderness or run rivers, shop in malls, enjoy affluence. Since each of us puts *20 to 30 times* the amount of carbon in the air than a resident of a developing nation, our failure to limit growth could have a profound impact on continued global warming.

Saguaro Cactus—monarch of the Sonoran Desert

When not on whitewater, I guide convention tourists down the flat section of the Lower Salt River just northeast of Phoenix. I like introducing them to the combination of flowing water, the Sonoran desert and the way life-forms adapt to the heat and low rainfall. Most of the visitors are more interested in the golf courses or the price of houses we pass on the way out to the river than the natural wonders that await them.

What dismays me is the pall of smog and dust hanging over not only the city but even the distant Superstition and Mazatzal mountain ranges. The entire region is drowning in a toxic gray soup. A view looking out over the entire valley is disheartening. By the time they are built, freeways are inadequate for burgeoning traffic.

Every time I drive past an area I haven't been to for awhile there are new subdivisions of unimaginative, identical, expensive houses without yards, a corresponding increase of traffic and new shopping malls each with the same franchised shops I see all over the greater metropolitan area, the country and now a great portion of the world.

Phoenix is sprawling like a drunk on a spree, a Los Angeles wannabe. Two thirds of the entire population of Arizona lives in the metropolitan area, approximately 2.5 million persons. The city covers 2,000 square miles. Twelve million visitors come through Phoenix each year, the average stay being four to five days. Many of these "Snowbirds" often stay the entire winter. Nearby lakes and recreational areas are overcrowded. Floating the Lower Salt River recently, I saw fishermen crowded within ten feet of one another at the good holes trying to hook frequently stocked trout. I now wear a mask to jog. The quality of everyday life has diminished and become more impersonal—all in the name of progress.

Some people say, "If you don't like it here, get the hell out, move away." Yet the idea of involvement with organizations working to improve the situation and my close network of river friends provides a strong lure to stay put. Besides, I get away into wild places for at least four to six months per year.

It is interesting to note that Arizona is one of four states including Maine, Vermont and Massachusetts where state representatives from the governor on down have the option of rejecting all private campaign contributions and qualifying for public financing of their run for office. About a third of Maine's legislature and a quarter of Arizona's got elected running clean—that is, they collected a series of five-dollar donations and then pledge to raise no other money and abide by strict spending limits. This is one way to limit the corruptive power of large corporate donations to candidates. Officials winning clean elections have said they feel more free to express honest viewpoints and decide issues on the objective merit of the proposed legislation.

At this writing, the passage of the Shays-Meehan campaign financing reform bill promises but does not guarantee reform. The bill, although not a panacea, would ban "soft money" and could be a step forward in an attempt to clean up the nation's scandalous and corrupt fund raising system. Ideally, it would be a move to make our government more responsive to the people and less to the giant corporations dominating the past nine administrations. Nevertheless, I will retain my criticsm of corporate influence in government because it takes years to discover how effective any piece of legislation will be. Will loopholes or ways be found to circumvent it? Will it accomplish what it is designed to do? Will new means be found for corporations to exert their influence?

Although its enforcement teeth were pulled by conservative interests, the Meat Inspection Act of 1906 worked because the huge meat packing companies needed to regain public trust so they complied with its provisions. Conversely, we have clean air and water laws that have been consistently circumvented because of corporate duplicity and a lack of vigorous executive enforcement. In the case of the EPA, George Bush's budget cuts and appointment of corporate officials and lobbyists to key jobs shows how a watchdog agency can be rendered less effective if not impotent.

Campaign financial reform will need an effective independent supervisory agency and free access to public television to be viable. How effective it functions over time will tell if it proves to be an instrument in regenerating representative democracy more responsive to the needs of our citizens.

Weight of Spring

Growl, grumble, roll on river
pour, quarry, gouge the earth
into crevices, crevasses,
and cragged heights.

Fed from far mountains
where the undecipherable
weight of spring
melts winter into water,

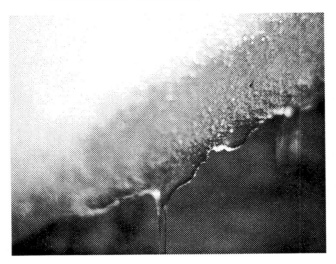

torrent carrying silt,
laying down soil as it swells
past spear-tipped yucca
and under ledges

of

disheveled

symmetry.

The Shape of the Future

Fortunately, there are technological trends that will flower into new lifestyles and possess the potential to build a sane economic paradigm. If successful, it will follow the rules of nature, use less material energy, stop environmental destruction and witness new investment in natural capital.

William McDonough, the head of the University of Virginia's School of Architecture, advocates basic principles that mimic nature. The first is that waste equals food. The concept of waste must be eliminated in industrial design. Every process must be shaped so that the products themselves, as well as leftover chemicals, materials and effluents become *food* for other processes.

The second basic principle is to rely on current solar and wind income and diminish our reliance on hydrocarbon fuels. In short, design systems that "sip" energy rather than gulp it down.

Finally, a new criterion for evaluating production is needed. This is to respect diversity by evaluating every design for its impact on plant, animal and human life. Will the product, in the long run, enhance people's identity, independence, and integrity? Will it enhance sustainability?

We see this future already taking shape as new urban architects such as Peter Calthorpe, Andres Duany, and Elizabeth Plater-Zyberk are designing communities that could eliminate

Population control plus sustainable production equals the preservation of wilderness.

40 to 60 percent of transportation needs. Internet-based transactions could render shopping malls obsolete. Future products will include diodes that emit light for 20 years and ultrasound washing machines that clean clothes

without water. Automobile manufacturers will be responsible for the disposal of their brand of used cars. The impetus will be to build cars that can be deconstructed easily and recycled into newer models. The Herman Miller Company currently designs furniture that can be reused and remanufactured a number of times.

Ray Anderson, CEO of Interface, a billion-dollar multinational carpet and flooring company, conceives a product to be a *service* to the customer rather than thinking of it as a *thing*. He has developed the "Evergreen Lease" to turn his flooring into a service. Modern carpeting remains on the floor up to 12 years after which it remains in landfills for as long as 20,000 years. This constitutes less than .06 percent efficiency. Americans throw away 3.5 billion pounds, 920 million square yards of carpeting each year. At Interface, as carpet tiles wear out and are replaced, old ones are recycled and made into new units. The customer does not pay an installation cost, only a monthly fee for constantly new-looking and functional carpeting.

Chemists William McDonough and Michael Braungart helped design a line of upholstery fabric rendering the manufacturing process and final product free of hazardous chemicals. Design Tex out of New York surveyed 7,500 chemicals and only 34 survived the screening process. The fabric, now produced in Switzerland, is a mixture of wool and the plant fiber ramie that comes in a normal range of colors, sells for a competitive price, and can be torn up and recycled into new material.

The main task at the Rocky Mountain Institute's Hypercar Center is to increase car efficiency. It is designing an ultra-light, ultra-tough carbon-fiber body powered by a scooter-size hybrid electric motor with a gas turbine or fuel cell providing a constant source of electricity. It would be 90 percent less polluting than a conventional car and get between 100 to 200 miles to the gallon. Modular plug-in components will make it easier to repair or recycle than a regular automobile. In attacking the traditional manufacturing of automobiles it tackles head on perhaps the most wasteful product ever created by human engineering.

The Toyota Prius, Honda Insight, and Honda Civic Hybrid are now available. They are hybrid electric-gasoline vehicles that get from 42 to 61 miles to the gallon and are less polluting than normal cars. During the Recession of 2002, they sold well in spite of offers on domestic vehicles for zero financing and no payments until 2003 to boost sagging sales.

The kenaf plant is considered one of the most promising alternatives to virgin soft and hard woods for paper production. A herbaceous annual related to cotton and okra, kenaf is a member of the mallow family indigenous to West Africa. On Earth Day 1995, conservationist David Brower's latest book, *Let the Mountains Talk, Let the Rivers Run*

(HarperCollins), became the first hardcover book to be published on 100 percent kenaf paper. It is an excellent alternative for pulping wood because of its rapid growth. Kenaf reaches 12-18 feet in 150 days while southern pine must grow 14 to 17 years before it can be harvested. It also has a high yield of fiber, three to five times more per acre than traditionally used trees. To cap its advantages, is takes less chemicals, heat and time to pulp kenaf fibers because they are not as tough as wood pulp and contain less lignin. Lignin is a resin that binds the cellulose fibers in plants and trees together. Kenaf can be processed with hydrogen peroxide, a less damaging agent than the chlorine used on wood pulp. It is as yet an underdeveloped industry because of high startup costs, smaller economies of scale and *government subsidies* to the traditional pulp, paper, and timber industries.

Virgin wood paper is cheaper but its prices do not reflect environmental or natural capital costs such as destruction of forest ecosystems, fragmentation of wildlife habitat, erosion of topsoil, flooding and the pollution of water systems. Kenaf is totally renewable on a yearly basis and would eliminate cutting down 20-year-old forests. In addition, kenaf combined with soybean oil substituted for plastic resins is being used by auto manufacturers for compressed panels on doors and as a substitute for fiberglass. The new composite panels are just as strong and use few or no toxic chemicals in the manufacturing process.

My youngest daughter, Kristi, was the associate producer of a documentary film about the planning going into the construction of a new Health Science Center at the University of Texas at Houston. It is designed in such a manner to make better long-term sustainable choices for the future. It emphasizes the use of solar energy over fossil fuels, a reduced use of power and the utilization of as much daylight as possible for indoor illumination. The concrete to be used will be made of fly ash from coal-fired power plants. It has three times the strength of normal cement and creates less carbon dioxide in production. The building will be, to the degree that is possible, polyvinyl chloride (PVC) free. When PVC burns it unleashes toxins, carbon dioxide and chlorine; it is the asbestos of the new century. Flooring requirements will be supplied as a service not a product, tile that can be replaced and recycled rather than ending up in a landfill. Rainwater will be trapped on the roof to use for all purposes except human consumption. Great numbers of trees are being planted on the grounds to absorb the reduced level of carbon dioxide emitted.

The building will be utilized 20 hours a day, every day of the week. Cool air will be pumped into raised floors, keeping the workers comfortable without the need to air condition the entire building space. It will be a structure utilizing the best of future planning and compatible with the needs of the planet. The eventual goal will be to produce a net energy producing building.

Patrick Henry cried, "Give me liberty or give me death." Petitions and speeches inspired Colonial resistance to George III and British tax policies. But instead of the undying glory of triumphant pronouncements, what drew British attention to the problem was not the cries of patriots but the non-importation agreements that boycotted the buying of British-made goods. It became patriotic to wear homespun and use local products manufactured in defiance of the laws of the Empire. This struck British merchants in a mortal place—their pocketbooks. Parliament was inundated by protests from their local businesses and the agitation in the distant colonies was brought home where it could not be ignored.

Against the buttressed power of gargantuan business mergers and takeovers and their political influence, the most decisive weapons we possess as individuals are our choices as consumers. *How and what we buy* is a bottom line power in the hands of the masses. The trend towards *buying green* is a potential catalyst for constructive change. For example, Co-op America facilitates the individual's access to products and services from thousands of businesses that care about the environment, respect workers and support their communities.

Exploring the Internet, one can discover numerous environmentally dedicated businesses that enables you to *buy, go and grow green.*

Speaking of the Internet, globalization is a two-edged sword. The democratization of technology, finance and information allows individuals access to invest or shop throughout nearly the entire world. It has created vast markets and accelerated the flow of capital, geographically diversified manufacturing and it has speeded the pace of change. This cyberspace battleground gives the opportunity for like-minded individuals to unite in worldwide coalitions for sane environmental practices. It will

> *Buy, go and grow green*

play an increasingly immense role in protecting the viability of our Earth Mother. As consciousness is raised, corporations disregarding sound environmental processes may lose investment capital as well as sales.

One example of constructive consumerism was the Campaign for Corporate Accountability that mounted a boycott late in 1999 against Kraft, a subsidiary of Philip Morris. From universities to churches, high schools and supermarkets, students and community activists built a boycott of Kraft Foods. Students at the University of Wisconsin, Stanford and the University of North Carolina organized counter-recruitment actions at job fairs where Kraft hoped to recruit from among the nation's most talented graduates. Bumper stickers, leaflets and committed individuals decried being part of a corporation that is pushing addictive and deadly tobacco on young people around the world. The San Francisco Unified School District adopted a selective purchasing policy to keep Kraft out of school lunch-rooms and vending machines. In Fact, a non-profit, non-partisan, national membership organization, is mobilizing people around the world in grass-roots campaigns. Its most recent impact has been the production of a doc-umentary film, *Making a Killing,* that exposes Philip Morris's deadly abus-es around the world and the ways people are organizing to stop them. It shows the $62 billion global corporation handing out free Marlboros to boys in Vietnam to spread addiction.

Efforts to coordinate the con-cept of renewable energy with farming are encouraging. Energy from the wind, plants and sun can be harvest-ed forever. Wind developers are installing large tur-bines on farms and ranches in a number of states. As report-ed in *Nucleus: The Magazine of the Union of Concerned Scientists,* by 2020 wind energy could provide farmers and rural landowners

A new dawning

with $1.2 billion in new income and 80,000 new jobs. A wind turbine uses only a quarter acre of land and can earn up to $2,000 in royalties per year.

An Iowa co-op in Chariton Valley has planted 5,500 acres in switch-grass to be burned with coal in a giant power plant. If successful, the project will scale up to 50,000 acres and supply five percent of the plant's fuel.

Roger Decker, a dairy farmer, is generating power from cow manure. A methane digester heats manure to 100 degrees F. This produces methane, which powers a turbine and generates enough electricity for his farm and 50 houses. The operation also eliminates carbon dioxide emissions that contribute to global warming.

Fighting to protect necessary life systems

All these new options are just the tip of a technological iceberg that can retain free market global enterprise and, simultaneously, create a healthier environment.

Ironically, denigrated organizations accused of radicalism, tree hugging, spotted owl lovingand spiking trees for Jesus—organizations like Earth First, Rainforest Action Network, the Nature Conservancy, the Sierra Club, Greenpeace and others, have now become the *real capitalists.* By facing such issues as greenhouse gases, chemical contamination, the loss of fisheries, wildlife corridors and primary forests, they are doing more to preserve a viable business future than all of the chambers of commerce put together. They are fighting to protect necessary life systems when the world's population and the demand for services are exploding.

Doing more with less is compassionate, prosperous, and enduring—thus more intelligent. Ending conspicuous consumption, practicing conservation in energy expenditure and living more simply will be the tenets of a new age.

Restoring the environment will be good business in the 21st century. It will not only be creative but profitable. Can we in essence divorce the sanctity of life from the quality of life? How sacred is life on a battlefield or during famine or pestilence? Life can be cheapened or uplifted. Nine billion human beings who outstrip the planet's capacity to sustain life are not as sacred as 1.5 billion who have a clean and healthy habitat and have again gained the value of rareness, community and individual dignity.

It appears our belief system and existing economic-political-multi-national establishment is at odds with what the cutting edge of science is telling us about the condition of our earth and the nature of the universe, creating the most classic and dangerous incidence of *cultural lag* in human history. The key question is, *Can we recognize our interdependence with all life and the planet that sustains it?* As the marvelous poet Octavio Paz wrote:

> the invisible
> barriers, the mad and decaying masks

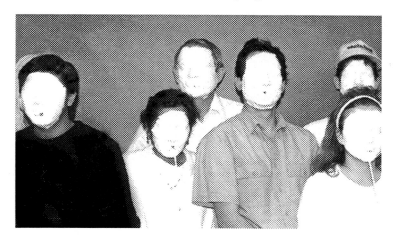

> that used to separate us, man from man,
> and man from his own self,
> they are thrown down
> for an enormous instant and we see darkly
> our own lost unity, how vulnerable it is
> to be women and men
> the glory it is to be man
> and share our bread and share our sun
>   and our death
> and dark forgotten marvel
>   of being alive.

Mrs. Mertyl Getz

Swatting mosquitoes, sweaty
Mrs. Mertyl Getz of Cincinnati, Ohio
huffs and puffs, drags her cellulite
up into the mouth of a side canyon
where wind and rain winnow
intractable cliffs.

Spade-foot toads slumber
beneath sand, wildflowers
splay in the decaying
remains of a deer.
The niched rock
of an Anasazi granary
harbors pictographs,

trilobite fossils,
and night feeding bats;
all prelude
to the arrival of Mrs. Getz
still swatting mosquitoes,
complaining of the heat,
missing Wheel of Fortune
and Wednesday night mah-jongg,
wishing Mr. Getz was still alive
to listen to her complain.

The Attack on America

The horror of seeing jets crash and fireball into the World Trade Towers, the wreckage and gap at the twisted Pentagon, and the towers imploding, tons of debris crumbling down crushing the thousands trapped inside, both shocked and unified Americans. The instantaneous grief rending thousands of families was palpable to all. Attempts to show tolerance towards the Muslim faith and the countless acts of sacrifice, bravery and kindness, known and unknown, are tributes to the resiliency of the United States of America and to our democratic heritage.

Our resolve to find and punish the perpetrators has been backed by forming a coalition of nations who know that this type of sudden violence cannot go unchecked in the world and the blind hate that produced it cannot be condoned.

When violence is overt and dramatic as it was at Pearl Harbor or in the September 11, 2001 attacks, the nation is galvanized and its citizens wholeheartedly back the administration's retaliatory measures.

Yet, Americans have been under attack for generations without the nationwide resolve and

President George W. Bush

reaction witnessed to terrorism. The long-run use of violence has been more stealth-like, and, in the long run, potentially more dangerous to the USA and all the nations of the earth.

From the previous century on, it is the violence done to human lungs digging in the dust of the coal mines of Pennsylvania, West Virginia and Kentucky; the lingering coughing away of life from silicosis in the dismal shacks and shanties of the region. In the Thirties, it was sending men to work on the Gauley diversion tunnel, digging into pure silica before the dust has settled from blasting. Their choice was to go in and dig for 25 cents an hour or to watch their families starve. They doggedly shuffled into the tunnel and died like flies.

In the Fifties, it was the violence to Navajo miners in the uranium mines from radiation. They were told they were safe. Those reassurances rang hollow when the miners later wasted away from cancer. More recently, it is the violence of dioxins, furans, DDT, PCBs and mercury used in manufacturing processes; pesticides or herbicides sprayed over the vast fields of agribusiness; and toxic wastes dumped illegally. It is DES and other synthetic chemicals and their negative impact on the reproductive process. It is the violence of the Love Canal, the leukemia clusters in St. George, Utah from atomic testing on the Nevada flats, and the inversions and chemical smog increasing the incidence of emphysema and bronchitis. It

> *America has been under attack for generations.*

is hydrofluocarbons attacking the ozone layer or the hothouse gases like carbon dioxide affecting global warming and weather patterns. It is warmer water eating at healthy coral reefs. We have mounted a more devastating, complete and long-range attack upon ourselves than could all the terrorist organizations in the world. We have expoentially increased the magnitude of the attack with runaway population growth.

Our government found worldwide support for a war on terrorism. But we need to include in our lexicon a new definition of violence, one that recognizes and criminalizes this widespread and ongoing toxic sabotage of America and other nations and the current attempts to obstruct the war on environmental degradation in trade for corporate profit.

In 2,000, at a crucial time in history when far-seeing leadership and long-range environmental action was necessary, we stumbled through a controversial and convoluted election to elect a president influenced by exceedingly powerful business interests. According to the Center for Responsive Politics, for his 1999-2000 election campaign, George W. Bush received $2.6 million from agribusiness, $4 million from real estate interests, $1.2 million from the automotive industry, $2.8 million from energy companies and $1.8 million from oil and gas interests. That totals $12.4 million from gigantic firms who want business, profits and pollution as usual. Their mandate, not that of the people, seems to be the base he's working from.

The Presidency, the Congress and power-laden interests are interwoven at a time when bold new programs are needed in the name of humanity and the world at large. Instead of diminishing the gap between environmental reality and the impact of multinational capitalism, the over-all course of American government in recent decades has enlarged the current dangers of *cultural lag.* This trend goes far beyond partisan policies. To say it is a Republican Party problem would overlook Democratic Party ties to powerful interests and the snail's pace progress on the problems besetting the environment during President Clinton's eight years in office. Also subservient to corporate interests, the Democratics no longer offer a viable alternative to Republican policies. The prestige and power of the United States of America catalyzes the acceleration towards crisis by failing to provide leadership in an era when average men in public office could become great and competent men could become giants, founding fathers of the future.

With his submission to the corporate will, his dedication to carbon-based industry, his return to the voodoo economics and the Cold War imperatives of the Reagan Administration, President Bush is actively increasing the gap between solving the accumulated threats to human life on the planet and the ongoing, insider influenced, multinational, pollute-as-usual, current economic-political paradigm. The President sees the environment as a subset of the economy. In doing so, he has inverted reality. The economies of all nations are based on the continuing health and viability of the environment. They are the subsets.

The bottom line—over population

The imperative question is, *What kind of social and physical environment will our grandchildren and great grandchildren and their children inherit if we fail to act?*

The American corporate answer seems to be, *A wonderful society as long as our grandchildren and great grandchildren and their children are in the top quintile, the one percent of the population who controlled 40 percent of the nation's wealth in 1989 before inequality accelerated.*

As much as we need to support the President's strategy against terrorist organizations and the groups who harbor them, it still doesn't make his current environmental policies wise nor good for the long-term benefit of the nation. In addition, it is disingenuous to push anti-environmental legislation by wrapping it in the flag and passing it off as a wartime necessity. This tactic is politics of the lowest denominator and smears the honest dissent necessary in a democracy by planting innuendos of treason. Since September 11, 2001, there has been an outpouring of patriotism and display of American flags. The flag is a symbol. What about the land itself—the mountains, forests, rivers, and deserts the flag also represents? A look at some of the issues:

● **Overpopulation:** On his first day in office, President Bush imposed the "gag rule" of the Reagan Era and his father's administration. This placed strict restrictions on U.S. funds to international family groups involved in abortion, even those not performing operations but only counseling people or lobbying governments on the issue. This act imposes the individual religious beliefs of a minority of American citizens upon other nations and their burgeoning populations. It was political maneuvering that appealed to a segment of the President's constituents but is blind to the single most important issue threatening the well-being of future generations, overpopulation.

President Bush also proposed dropping a requirement that all health insurance programs for federal employees cover a broad range of birth control. This angered women's groups and lawmakers from both parties who favor contraceptive benefits not only for federal workers but also for all employees.

● **New appointees and environmental laws:** The selection of Spencer Abraham, a champion of the auto industry, as Secretary of Energy and Gale Norton as Secretary of the Interior was a

The specter of a polluted planet

dueling glove slap in the face of environmentalists. As the first woman Secretary of the Interior, Norton is responsible for managing nearly half a million acres of federal lands including the entire National Parks System. She is responsible for enforcing laws that protect threatened and endangered species and govern the management of national wildlife refuges.

Norton previously worked for the Mountain States Legal Foundation which lobbied for increased logging and mining on public lands. Rather than protecting our public lands and wildlife, she endorsed drilling for oil in the Arctic National Wildlife Refuge and weakening the Endangered Species Act. She helped found the Council of Republicans for Environmental Advocacy or CREA, which sounds like a Green group but really was an empty public relations ploy designed to polish the images of elected officials and companies that had controversial environmental records. Their sponsors have included the National Coal Council, the Chemical Manufacturers Association and the National Mining Association. Many appointees to key positions throughout the Administration are former lobbyists or employees of powerful timber, oil and gas, coal mining and energy companies.

The highest patriotism is to protest unfair and unwise governmental policies

The President ordered suspension of a rule that strengthened the government's ability to deny contracts to companies that have violated workplace safety, environmental and other federal laws. It gives our government *less* power to withhold contracts from companies who pollute and break the law.

- **Clean air and pure water:** To debilitate the Environmental Protection Agency in 2001, the president asked for cuts of $158 million from the agency's core efforts to enforce laws that keep polluters from corrupting the air we breathe and the water we drink. He talked about the need for research but cut $56 million intended to study ways to improve family health. Overall, he is cutting $500 million from the EPA annual budget.

Meanwhile, the EPA rescinded a law that safeguarded public access to information about the potential consequences of chemical plant accidents.

The Yucca Mountain nuclear waste site in Nevada sits above an aquifer that is a critical source of water for irrigation, dairy farming and drinking water. The government set new radiation protection standards for operating, implying it will go ahead as planned to develop the site against the resistance of environmental organizations. The new standards may violate the Safe Drinking Water Act by possibly allowing radioactive pollution to seep into underground fresh water within the mountain. Members of an independent science advisory panel concluded there are enormous gaps in what the Energy Department knows about the site, a volcanic structure, and the safety of high-tech canisters full of nuclear waste that it is proposing to put in the storage area. In a hurry to start using the site, the government position was that if research turns up a problem later on the engineers will fix it. Is this a gamble worth taking?

The chemical, beef, and poultry industries are waging an intense campaign to further delay an EPA study showing that consumption of animal fat and dairy products containing traces of dioxin can cause cancer in humans. Under the current administration, the study could be held up for years.

God's children need space and a healthy environment in which to grow

● **Global warming:** In a bombshell late in March of 2001, President Bush announced he was unilaterally pulling the United States out of the 1997 Kyoto Protocol on climate change. His explanation indicated it would not be in the best economic interest of the United States. With four percent of the world's population, our country releases 25 percent of the world's greenhouse gases. The move engendered harsh commentary across Europe that the USA is behaving like an arrogant superpower, a rogue nation that places itself above the need to make economic sacrifices for the benefit of the rest of the world. Bush's decision to reverse his campaign promise came after intense lobbying by coal and oil lobbies and con-

218

gressional conservatives. Without the cooperation of the world's greatest polluter, efforts to contain global warming will be debilitated.

A broad coalition of U.S. religious groups petitioned Bush to reconsider his approach or risk alienating a growing faith-based movement committed to protecting the environment. They maintain, "If credible evidence exists to indicate our present course could threaten the quality of life for God's creation and God's children, this becomes an issue of paramount moral concern." The addition of religious-moral arguments for environmental preservation is a belated recognition that the fate of mankind is interwoven with that of the land and stimulates the rise of a spirituality recognizing that man cannot be separated from his environment. It is Moses casting his rod into a snake at the edge of a future clear-cut site, or Jesus bringing Lazarus back from his greed-driven attempts to open wilderness to drilling and mining.

- **Energy policy:** On May 15, 2001, Bush unveiled his Energy Plan for the American people. It relied heavily on building power plants plus exploration, drilling and digging for coal, gas and oil. It threatened our public lands, promised to make our air dirtier and to accelerate global warming. In addition to cutting funds for research into alternative fuel processes, it proposed weakening environmental standards endangering the air we breathe, the water we drink and the lands we use.

The United States is the largest producer of carbon dioxide, the primary gas that causes global warming. In the face of the findings of 2,000 scientists working to document global warming, the United States' president questioned their conclusions and wrote, "I do not believe . . . that the government should impose on power plants mandatory emissions for carbon dioxide."

This may halt lawsuits against 51 power plants to make them add pollution controls as established by the Clean Air Act. Instead, the President would favor voluntary cleanup programs that have previously proven to be ineffective.

Bush signed two executive orders. The first should make it easier for the voices of coal, oil, and nuclear industries to be heard in decisions relating to energy production.

The second establishes an Energy Task Force that may bypass critical environment and public health standards to increase production. This is designed to ease the permit process—including environmental considerations—for refinery, nuclear and hydroelectric dam construction. The Bush Administration budget cuts energy efficiency research by more than 50 percent in some areas.

In addition, the President has moved to weaken energy efficiency standards in other ways. The final goals devised over six years of planning would have made new air conditioners 30 percent more effective by 2006. The President has moved to weaken this goal.

The administration declared backing for the so-called "Clean Coal" Program. The program is funded in the budget at $150 million for the first year with plans to spend $2 billion over ten years. The term "Clean Coal" is an oxymoron. There is no way to clean it up. As a preferred fuel, generating more than half the nation's electricity, the billion-plus tons burned every year create 60 percent of the nation's sulfur dioxide emissions, a quarter of its nitrogen oxide, a third of its mercury and nearly a third of its greenhouse carbon dioxide. Bush would like to burn even more coal in the future. "We've got to understand that we need to work on the supply side," the president said, "and coal is in abundant supply here in America." BTU for BTU, coal emits twice as much carbon dioxide as natural gas. The $2 billion in corporate welfare funds planned on "clean coal" would be better spent on researching and developing clean, renewable resources of energy like solar, hydrogen and wind power.

● **Protecting wildlife and wilderness:** One of the President's pet projects is to drill for oil in the Arctic National Wildlife Refuge. He has already earmarked $1.2 billion for the acquisition of leases in that region. The proposed drilling would do little to meet our energy needs and would ensure that this wondrous landscape—home to polar bears, wolves, caribou and hundreds of thousands of migratory birds—would be invaded. Much of the intrusion would violate the breeding and calving areas of the prime species. It is a volatile and unnecessary move.

In May of 2001, the Bush Administration canceled a 2004 deadline for automakers to develop prototype cars that would get up to 80 miles per gallon and could be put into production in a few years. It also cut funding by 28 percent to encourage cleaner, more fuel-efficient cars and trucks. Energy Secretary Spencer Abraham told Congress his department was switching to "longer-termed technologies" without indicating the details or advantages of his plan. Fuel economy is a sound national energy, economic and foreign policy all rolled into one. Every increase of one mile per gallon in auto fuel efficiency saves more oil than would be gained by drilling the Arctic National Wildlife Refuge. An improvement of 3.7 miles per gallon would eliminate all our need for Persian Gulf oil.

Contained in Bush's budget proposal is the elimination of all federal funding to enforce court orders stemming from citizen suits. Citizen suits have been critical to ensuring that the government protects endangered species. The President's actions would weaken the Endangered Species

Act, our nation's premiere wildlife protection law. In April 2001, Bush cut funding for popular farm conservation programs, like the Wetlands Reserve Program. Currently, there are 1,300 farmers waiting to protect 570,000 acres of wetlands. The program acts as a tool for curbing urban sprawl which swallows two million acres of open land a year.

Breaking a campaign promise on the environment, Bush abandoned a pledge to invest $100 million a year in a program for rainforest conservation. During his campaign he said, "We will link debt reduction and the conservation of tropical forest because these forests affect the air we breathe, the food we eat, medicines that cure disease and are home to more than half of the earth's animal and plant species."

A wasteful society

What or who changed his mind?

The Bush budget has made decided cuts in Interior Department funds. Sixty million has been stricken from the land acquisition program under the Land and Water Conservation Fund, defying a bipartisan agreement reached last year. $168 million will be cut from the U.S. Fish and Wildlife Service, slashing money dedicated to protecting wildlife habitat, wetlands restoration and endangered species. The budget adds $15 million for oil drilling and mining exploration and cuts money for conservation by the same amount.

In Quebec, President Bush signed a declaration promising to expand AFTA rules throughout the Western Hemisphere. These rules have been previously used to attack and weaken environmental protection and have favored investors over labor rights and safety in the work place.

Despite overwhelming public support for protecting our wild forests, President Bush is letting the state of Idaho and the timber industry pursue further exploitation. In testimony to Congress, Bush officials gave notice they would seek to increase logging in federal public forests and will attempt to reverse regulations protecting 58 million acres of national forest from logging and road building. Eager to start logging 41,000 acres in the

Bitterroot National Forest, they are trying to evade the laws that require public comment. The only voices the administration listens to are those pushing for exploitation of our natural resources.

● **The Military Budget:** The proposed military build up seems to have little to do with the threat to America unless you think that Al Qaeda's next move will be an invasion by several armored divisions. Ordinary citizens are puzzled why fighting fanatical attacks by small cells of individuals justifies spending billions on archaic Cold War weapons like the 70-ton Crusader howitzer and three new fighter planes including the F-22 jet and resurrecting Reagan's Star Wars Program. Those excessive portions, the "heavy pork" of the military budget seem to say, "Leave no defense contractor behind," including the Carlyle Group in which his father reputably has a managerial position and investments. Could not some of those funds be cut and other portions of the money better serve us in an attempt to control or buy up fissionable material surpluses in Europe that might fall into the hands of terrorists?

● **Cognitive Dissonance:** One of the ways in which leaders often end up working against the best interests of their country is a phenomenon termed *cognitive dissonance.* This is a process where individuals tend to block out and not hear opinions that differ from their already set views of reality. George Bush, Jr. has been an oil man and has been deeply influenced by the twelve years of Reagan's and his father's administrations. It is nearly impossible for him to get outside that frame of reference and acknowledge the work of 2,000 qualified and objective scientists. He dismisses a view foreign to his thought processes by referring to their conclusions as *fuzzy science.* His relatively narrow focus is illustrated by the president's move to abolish the White House Council on Environmental Quality.

A key asset of many great politicians has been their ability to compromise and to learn in office. John Kennedy was led into the Bay of Pigs fiasco by information from primarily the military and the CIA. In the Cuban Missile Crisis, he assembled a broader base of imput. When will our current leader rise above a narrow mind set and a restricted group of corporate advisors?

While firemen and police were dying in downtown New York and service men and women were risking their lives on the line in Afghanistan, the Administration and its cronies were allowing multinational companies to mount their most concerted effort in 20 years to roll back clean-air measures, exploit public lands and stuff the pockets of themselves and their shareholders with undeserved wealth. They make it a fitting time to bring back the nineteenth century term *Robber Barons.* Proposals to cut capital

222

gains taxes for the wealthy and to eliminate the corporate alternative minimum tax were offered to fight recession. This tax was enacted 15 years ago to prevent corporations from taking so many credits and deductions that they owed little if any taxes. Bush not only wanted to repeal the minimum tax, but to refund to those corporations all the minimum tax they have ever been assessed.

Being cloaked in the mantle of a wartime president only increased his intransigence. This trait bodes ill for any concessions on the part of the administration to a sane environmental policy. The Administration invoked "national security" to justify massive oil development, including drilling in the Arctic National Wildlife Range. But homeland security also includes wildland protection. The clean air and water, biological diversity and inspiration of our national parks and wilderness areas are of vital importance. To plunder the most inpirational lands we have inherited is not patriotism. The courageous action is to protect them. Each generation serves as trustees of these natural treasures and this Administration is trading their obligations to the future for current profit and power.

> *"We have gotten past the stage, my fellow citizens, when we are to be pardoned if we treat any part of our country as something to be skinned for two or three years for the use of the present generation, whether it be the forest, the water, the scenery."*
> *. . . Theodore Roosevelt*

I Have Wanted

I have wanted to be understood
by those not yet born,
to be known where feather clouds fly

and maidens chase barefoot boys
into madness.

I have wanted to unbutton the skin of self
and love unwombed by
the weightless currency of song.

When death stalks down my limbs
lay me unembalmed
into the hollow eyes of earth
where rot will have its way;
back to the mother
maggoted and wormed,
burst of silence mouthed by lambs.

Send me not to angels or absolution
but set my flesh to work,
make rich the blood
in the mouth of tomorrow.

Against the Grain

number of my former students have resisted the material inducements of our culture and have dedicated their careers towards meaningful change. I call them my *against the grain people*. We have already detailed the contributions of the Gillenwater brothers. Another example is John Scudder, a teacher and political activist. When I moved to Coronado High School in Scottsdale, Arizona in the 1980s, John was a member of one of my Advanced Placement courses.

I would start with 35 students in my two accelerated classes and grind them hard the first nine weeks. By the end of "history boot camp," I had about 15 kids left in each period, just what I wanted—those who could carry a heavy load, work hard, were highly motivated, the best of the best and a group small enough to hold meaningful discussions. During the crunch, I walked into class one day and saw one of the boys in the front row looking glum. He was an intensely bright lad, Mark Riebert, who was academically gifted yet a cartoon illiterate. I used to put Gary Larson cartoons on my exams before he was popular and well known. When we reviewed the results of exams, we had to explain the cartoons to Mark. Anyway, he was glum, giving off bad vibes. I had nicknamed him Repo Man and asked, "Repo, what's the matter with you today?"

Mark exploded, blurting out, "Goddamn you, Finkbine, and Goddamn this class. You are working us to death. I don't have a social life anymore, Goddamn you." The class sat there shocked and hushed. No one moved. No one spoke. The tension was palpable. He was AP dead meat.

After an interminable silence, I said, "Hey, Repo."

"Yeah, what?"

"Feel better?"

He thought for a moment and said, ""Yeah, some."

"Hey, Repo."

"What?"

"Okay if I lecture a bit now?"

"Yeah, all right, go ahead."

Scudder got a group together and the nights before big exams they would meet at Denny's at midnight and study through the rest of the night. They called themselves *The Dead Historians Society*. I felt proud. I was another Robin Williams. They would die for me. Five years later they told me they only did that once and on the way to school early in the morning, John said, "You know if we really wanted to honor Finkbine, we would cut school and go float the river."

"I think you have something there," Lance Huffman agreed. They drove to the campus, enlisted a few girls in their adventure and were off to the Lower Salt River, kissing off school and the big exam as well. The part of my ego that was Robin Williams deflated fatally.

"Did you have to tell me?" I complained. "I was happier the way I was."

Lance Huffman

John and Lance both have an embarrassment of intellectual riches and could have forged successful business careers. Instead they both decided to teach. Huffman returned to his alma mater, Coronado High School, and was able to enthuse a freshman history class with an attempt to change the status of the Student Council. They wanted to transform it from being a rubber stamp for the administration and engaged in trivial affairs to a body concerned with the real-life concerns of the students. Lance was called in by the principal and told to turn off his freshman burner. He told her, "No way. I've got those kids interested in class and politically active for the first time in their lives and I'm not going to cop out on them. They are actually enthused about school."

"You had better listen to me, Mr. Huffman. You work for me."

"No I don't. I work for those kids. That's what teaching's all about. They come before you, the school board, and the whole state of Arizona for that matter." At the time, he was married with three children and to put his job on the line for his ideals took enormous courage. For his stand, Lance was denied tenure and not rehired. Fortunately, he got a job in a new high school in west Phoenix and talks rapturously about the two advanced freshman English classes he has acquired there. Watching television commercials, his seven-year-old daughter asks, "What are they lying about in this commercial, Daddy? I know they are lying but I'm not sure what about."

John Scudder handles 7th grade English at Palo Verde Middle School during the day. Two nights a week, he teaches recent Mexican immigrants how to speak, read and write English. Scudder lives in a small house downtown in a multiracial neighborhood. Realizing that neither of

226

the major political parties offered a way out of the corporate morass, he led a local campaign to back Ralph Nader's bid for the presidency. He is consistently published in the letters to the editor section of *The Arizona Republic*. He is battling against current legislation to impose standardized AIMS tests in Arizona schools and against using those test scores to put teachers on a performance pay scale. In a recent letter, John used the example of the eighteenth century prodigy Jedediah Buxton and his visit to a London theater to see Shakespeare's **Richard III**. When asked what he thought about the performance, Buxton responded by saying there were 5,202 dance steps performed and 12,445 words spoken by the actors. He had absolutely nothing to say about the substance or meaning of the play. He had been completely caught up in so-called objective evidence. John argues, and my 31 years of teaching supports the contention, that the most important things that happen in a classroom cannot be measured. A child is more than a test score.

I had a psychology class at Arcadia where we had no textbook and did an entire semester of interactive exercises built around various themes like anxiety, relationships, stress, depression, integrity, death and self-respect. We worked hard to build a trust level so the students could feel free to express themselves. One day a senior girl, Nancy, stood with tears running down her face. She said, "I'm going to tell you something I haven't been able to tell my parents or my boyfriend." She hesitated and blurted out, "A year and a half ago I was raped." In a flash, the entire class was crying and hugging Nancy and each other.

Then one of my boys said, "I better not hear anything about this on campus. Either we have a trust level in this class or we don't." I ran into Nancy two years later and she told me that she was speaking about the subject at student meetings at the University of Arizona and counseling girls who had also been violated. Measure that on a standardized test!

Naturally, if they are going to be evaluated and paid on the basis of test results, teachers will teach the test and possibly miss the heart and soul of their subject matter. As Governor of Texas, George Bush, Jr. crowed about the improvement he had brought to education. But, Mr. Scudder writes, "There was a mysterious coincidence. On the test which was considered the most important by the politicians and the media, their TAAS exam, there was an amazing jump in test scores. Meanwhile, on another standardized test there was no similar improvement in scores. The explanation was simple: the teachers taught exactly what was on the test and nothing more. Some "Higher Standards." And this is not unique to Texas. This kind of drill-and-kill, memorize-the-answer form of anti-learning that ignores creativity and critical thinking is forcing children to become one-dimensional, test-taking automatons."

John also fights against the elimination of bilingual education, for the establishment of a livable wage for teachers and for universal health care. He explains, "One in four children in the United States has no health care provider." He battles for public financing of all political campaigns that would remove the Big Money warp of our government.

Bridging the isolation of a modern metropolis, John has created the *Philosopher Café,* inviting an informed cross-section of teachers, environ-

John Scudder

mentalists, poets, writers, social workers and intellectuals to nibble on tasteful treats and sip wine as they discuss crucial issues. In his small flat filled with spirited conversation and the airing of creative views, these sessions recreate a sense of Greenwich Village and the Bohemians of an earlier era. It is an *against the grain* gathering of people convinced they cannot buy their way to happiness and who value clean air and water and ghetto literacy above driving a $60,000 car or a Caribbean cruise.

A dangerous under consumer, John works with inner city kids, organizes groups, works to further his political views and sees through the chimera and glitter of our media-driven society. He is a prototype of the critical citizenship needed for constructive change in a world begging for change.

Although I believe in my mystical connection to wilderness, and that we would be better off as a nation and a portion of the earth's population if we lived more simply and consumed less, I don't expect it to happen. I know how much my raft means to me both as a source of identity and adventure. It is also a petroleum product. Why should not someone else's Ferrari or Lexus mean just as much to them? As for living more simply, material abundance and overconsumption *are* the American way of life. I, too, am embedded in the system and my Mazda truck contributes its share to Phoenix smog. So where does all this leave me?

For one, I treasure the fact that I have experienced wild places and worked on and run whitewater rivers. These experiences have added a dimension to my life that has given me pleasure, meaning, satisfaction and changed my values and lifestyle. I would not want everybody to do this, for then the wilderness would

Thank God for rivers left to run

be trampled and so crowded it would lose its capacity to inspire reverence. On the other hand, I realize that the buying and owning of things is the chief way people achieve meaning in their lives.

We swim in a sea of commercialism. Two-to five-year-olds average more than 28 hours of television a week. Current teenagers have spent years of their lives watching and listening to commercials. The average adult sees at least 500 ads each day. The greatest salesman in the world, our TV box, is filled with a kaleidoscope of swirling and fast hammering images and viewers tune into the message that the shining, safe, fast turning, cling-to-the-road Mercedes, or a Giorgio Armani suit, new Rolex or Viagra will resurrect their lives and guarantee them fulfillment, or at least getting laid.

One morning, on

The lure of wilderness—13,341 feet up

229

Internet news, next to an article about U.S. Forces continuing to pound Kaliban positions in Afghanistan, was one about the Fashion Police commentary on who wore what at The Women in Film luncheon. In spite of her lace-sleeved, off-the-shoulder Tstanaka sweater, Jane Mayle designer jeans, and Manolo Blahnick pumps, Cameron Diaz was derided for baby bangs. Jennie Garth was chastised for her change from blonde to new dark tresses even though clothed appropriately in a sleeveless Tahari dress. Doesn't anyone ever learn from Madonna's hair color mistakes?

In his provocative book, *Lead Us Into Temptation: The Triumph of American Materialism*, professor and author James B. Twitchell maintains, "People are dispirited with materialism because they have too little, not because they have too much . . . Matters such as branding, packaging, fashion and the act of shopping itself are now the central meaning-making acts in our postmodern world . . . If Greece gave us philosophy, Britain gave us drama, Austria gave us music, Germany gave us politics, Italy gave us art, then America has recently contributed mass-produced and mass-consumed objects."

Democracy is the right to buy anything you want.

You are what you eat. You are also what you wear, drive, where you go on vacation, where you live and even that on which you decide to video-munch. One market analyst said, "Tell me what you buy and I'll tell you who you are and who you want to be." Materialism is the driving force of popular culture and popular culture is shaping just about everything else.

Freedom's just another word for lots of things to buy. Or perhaps that should be, *Freedom's just another word for nothing left to buy.*

Advertising and religion are part of the same meaning-making process. Pagan religions had dryads, nymphs, mythic personages like Zeus or Jupiter—they became the saints, cherubs and seraphim of the Christian heavens. Now we have the Three Arches, Michelin man, Aunt Jemima, the White Knight, Gatorade, and the Energizer Bunny—great grandchildren of earlier deities. Fasting, prayer, ritual and penance called forth the older gods. Their modern counterparts are summoned by the anticipation of purchase. Holy relics once gave magical power from on high. Now Nike endows Michael Jordan-like power to wannabe athletes.

Formerly, what was sold (besides indulgences) was salvation. Now we have the modern salvation of knowing how to meet and defeat the demons and devils of body odor, iron poor blood, ring around the collar, vaginal odor, dishpan hands or that affliction of all afflictions, split ends on wrong-colored hair. The Holy Grail today is to have a closet full of all upscale brands or, if you've had a spill on an expensive rug, maybe it's a spot remover.

The family that pays together stays together.

Although I have sold or given away most of my possessions to lighten the load and become a 70-year old pseudo Jack Kerouac, spending time out on the road and doing river trips part of each year, the point is that we are not going to lessen American materialism. Attempts to convince people to simplify their lives will help but will not solve attempts to preserve the environment or lessen environmental despoliation.

Secondly, we cannot slow the process and progress of global free market capitalism. The multinationals are here to stay. Nation after nation is inexorably moving towards making the private sector its primary instrument of economic growth. Cold War walls have been torn down and tariffs have followed. Deregulation, opening domestic markets to foreign investment and ownership, and opening telecommunications systems to private ownership and funds mark the transition that is underway and will not, in the long run, be turned back.

A pervasive democratization of finance, technology and information is driving the pace of globalization. When isolated villages have access to the Internet, no restrictive government will be able to hide the truth from its people. Corporations will find it more difficult to cover up destructive polluting practices. There is an army of investors out there everywhere, nameless, faceless, sitting at their computers and moving money around. In addition, there are the larger players, the multinationals. They are not interested in brands, just the facts, ma'am. Where's the best place to put our money? What companies and nations are good investments, which ones are not?

A future dinosaur

We, the environmentally concerned, cannot turn back materialism nor halt globalization but we can become a significant player in the new game.

In spite of President Bush's retrograde and reactionary "burn carbon fossil fuels until we drop" ideology, worldwide environmental consciousness is growing. The new chief officer of the Ford Motor Company, William Clay Ford, Jr., admits that his business harms the environment and wants to make real progress on issues like global warming. Formerly, as chairman, he took off the company's blinders by quitting the Global Climate Coalition, a conspiracy of polluting companies that denied scientific research proving global warming. Within four months, General Motors and Daimler-Chrysler also pulled out. He was the force behind the company's "corporate citizenship" reports, admitting that Ford's vehicles and factories annually emit 400 million metric tons of carbon dioxide. His goal is to achieve an average fuel economy of 40 miles per gallon for the company's cars, pickups, and SUVs, saving the United States almost one million barrels of oil per day. That's more than half as much as our nation imports from Saudi Arabia. It's more than we will ever get by drilling the Arctic National Wildlife Refuge. As previously mentioned, both Toyota and Honda are putting cleaner, gasoline-electric hybrid cars on the road. The waiting list to buy a 41-miles-per-gallon Toyota Prius is three months at this point in time when traditional car sales are sagging.

I still trumpet the virtues of wilderness adventure, buying green, meditating, being satisfied with less and giving the land back its mystic and sacred identity—but, at the same time, I know that won't be enough. We will need millions of environmentally conscious individuals all over the world united into one cohesive web to protest unwise legislation in any nation of the world, to take investment money out of any corporations damaging the earth and put it into green firms working for sustainability. We will have to invest in alternative fuels, to limit population growth and to weave our concerns into the ongoing and evolving values that will drive the ever-growing global system. Here's to the day that billions of dollars will flow out of any nation unless it practices sustainable capitalism and becomes responsive to the needs of the ordinary people of its land.

Our future battleground

The Mothering Earth

Immersed in the Grand Canyon, I am kin to towering walls and impervious stone, to wild arms of ocotillo and juicy hearts of tuna fruit ripening on prickly pear buds. The miracle of being overwhelms me, the inexplicable combinations of factors and events that permits life to exist on our tiny planet, a speck in the spinning dimensions of the universe.

Immersed in the Grand Canyon

If the bonding force between hydrogen and helium were a shade stronger, hydrogen would be unstable and stars like our sun could not exist. If the Newtonian gravitational force constant was slightly different, all stars would become either blue giants or red dwarfs, either too hot or too cold to sustain life.

Quantum physicists speculate that the elements we need for life were not created in the big bang. Bringing them to being required the death of a giant star, a supernova. After approximately 10 percent of the hydrogen of such a star has been converted into helium, it becomes unstable and collapses into a relatively small, dense ball of matter, its temperature so intense that hot helium nuclei collide and fuse to make carbon, oxygen and the other heavier elements. The oxygen we breathe is born in the collapse of a supernova; stars have died so we might live. We are stardust.

Even the great mass extinctions, about nine of them in the last 250 million years, are a pruning of the tree of life. The end of the Permian Age, about 240 million years ago, halved the family of marine invertebrates. More dramatic and widely known is the disappearance of the dinosaurs in Cretaceous times 65 million years ago. In addition to the giant reptiles, 90 percent of the zooplankton died out. Such extinctions paved the way for the development of new species; in this case the spawning of the age of mammals and rise of man. Harvard's prolific paleontologist Stephen Jay Gould believed that the impartial and indifferent facts of the evolutionary process show no provable evidence of a grand design. Man's climb to comprehension happened, but was not foreordained. It was Gould's belief that if the evolutionary process could be started over 1,000 different times you would get 1,000 different results, perhaps 999 without *homo sapiens*. Yet, against all odds, here we are.

Our earth is in a perfect orbit around the sun. A bit closer and our

atmosphere would consist of dense clouds of carbon dioxide, a runaway Greenhouse Effect raising surface temperatures to 900 degrees C., like those on Venus. A bit further from the sun and our oceans would have frozen solid 1.7 billion years ago. The earth is not only the right distance from the sun but it's the right size. If smaller, its atmosphere would be pulled away by the

Dense clouds of carbon dioxide

gravitational force of the moon.

Regardless of movies and science fiction books about aliens, to our current provable knowledge, Earth is the only spot in the light-yeared immensity of space where such an interdependent web of life exists; where beings stand upright, question their origins and worship the miracle of existence. The most recent astrological discoveries indicate that solar systems like ours are rare among the countless stars of countless galaxies.

The lowly trilobite, a primitive sort of crustacean divided into three lobes, was the dominant life species for 200 million years. At only four million years, man is an infant species. Insects have more diversity, greater numbers and a longer reign on the planet. Bacteria are older, more persistent and weigh more collectively than human beings. Scientists believe that the earliest form of physical life was a single-cell that first appeared 3.8 billion years ago, although new research may push that date back even farther. Single-celled organisms lived alone on the planet for more than 2 billion years before any other lifeforms emerged, and these single celled beings are still alive today. Indeed, they are the most successful lifeform.

During their first 2 billion years, bacteria invented all the essential chemical systems that sustain us today—photosynthesis, fermentation, oxygen breathing and the fixing of nitrogen into proteins. Without bacteria our planet would be as lifeless as the moon. These single-celled organisms prepared our world for us and prepared us for our world.

We carry around inside of us trillions and trillions of single-celled beings. The number of bacteria inside your mouth at this moment is greater than the number of people who have ever lived. Our concept of the individual is warped. All of us are walking communities. Bacteria have the unique ability to join themselves together to create new life forms in a process called symbiogenesis. It created microscopic beings called protoctists—one of the first and most important forms of complex life. They invented locomotion, our form of digestion, visual and other sensory systems, chromosomal DNA, the ability to create bones and the first gendered system of reproduction. Their struggles for survival have made us what we are today.

Cells first became mobile by merging with whiplashing spirochetes. Their bodies pulse in a wave-like motion. We contain the DNA of those spirochetes and our lives are built around their legacy. Look at human spermatozoa with their whip-like tails and then at the long axon and dendrite tentacles extending from our brain and nerve cells and recognize the close similarities between these structures and the spirochetes. Our ability to procreate and communicate is based on the shape of one-celled beings, a refinement of basic microbial design. We have an inseparable connection to all that's gone before.

A new generation of sportsmen are rising who need wild, free, and healthy streams.

Basic facts do not support the contention that the entire universe exists for the advent and culmination of man. Yet, against all universal odds, the fact that we do have life, consciousness and aesthetic-ethical judgment is so rare a phenomenon that it is inestimable. It is a celebratory fact, a miracle generating a joy of living, of just being. The facts of science are reason enough to be reverent and worship the sacredness of existence. Religion adds certainty, inspiration, and solace to the uncertainties we inherit. Yet it also narrows minds, divides people and drives believers to the futility of *my way is the only way* and bloodshed of jihadic wars. A yearning towards the spiritual is inherent in the human species. It has no quarrel with science and the complexities, oddities and sanctity of the evolutionary process.

I picture the Colorado River grinding into earth, sucking down the sky into a consecrated maze where new gods germinate; gods indigenous to earth, kiva gods of torn Levi's, gods hiking, working in soil, making music, making love, revering the miracle of life in endless space; gods who will drive the more-is-better, you-can-never-be-too-rich, corporate greed, and consumption-is-happiness mystique out of the temple; gods who already eat peaches and have blown up their television sets; gods who refuse to see a small planet burdened with nine billion people who all want credit cards and boom boxes; gods who will turn the seat of values from shopping malls to open spaces and wild places. I want brand new gods, not the old ones in new clothes like the Reformation dressing Jesus in a business suit, making him the super salesman, and selling accumulation of wealth on earth as a way of piling up T-notes in heaven. That was quite a contrivance considering his earthly lifestyle.

I want a god out of Kanzantzakis except he doesn't crawl back up on the cross but stays, falls in love, has children of his own, changes washable diapers, protests the use of pesticides, gets off the grid, plants an organic garden, uses solar panels and starts a green self-sustainable business, products biodegradable and recycled. This god dwells in the greatest of all sanctuaries, the holy of holies—the sacred earth.

DOWN FROM THE CROSS

Snakes twisting in their talons,
eagles circle the cliffs of Cocha Bamba.
Below, a dirt road winds
past haciendas with broken glass
on tops of adobe walls.

Battered trucks blaring Latin music
rut through Mayo villages
where Indian and Spanish bones
rot in common soil
and women finger rosaries
fearful of masked-faced beasts
hungry for sacrifice.

The Virgin rises in Guadalupe,
Madonna with a Yaqui face,
crosses entwined by snaky vines.
Indian ways hulk in churches,
slink by altars, slip snake-like
out doors where blood-faced bats

feed on blossoms
that open only
at night.

Legends retold,
passed from father to son,
worn leather of words,
tales of peyote, corn, deer gods
and the Christ—

Christ, my children,
was a surveyor who came to
measure the land and count
sacred mountains and streams.

With a cry Jesus tears
himself free.

Down off the cross he climbs.
They bathe his wounds;
the shaman hands him
a piece of boiled dog
smeared with ground
> *pitahaya seeds*
> *and they eat together*
> *taking turns telling stories*
> *around the pulse of fire.*

Making do with less and doing more on our own might facilitate an attitude shift towards valuing long-term preservation over short-term resource exploitation and profit. Battles rage but there is now an area of common interest between the combatants. Both conservationists and loggers, in perspective, have a stake in healthy forests and sustainable yield selective cutting. Both rangers and ranchers need healthy and nourishing grazing land. Tourism created by preserving wilderness areas and fishing spots is creating a rising tide of jobs and income. It is time to scale back environmentally destructive corporate operations for the larger, general good.

Cleaning up the planet, developing alternative sources of energy, preventing further pollution, curbing population and investigating scientific solutions to ecological problems will be the preeminent humane challenge of the 21st century. When I think that the Colorado and Green rivers have not been converted into a series of lakes, and remember that there is wild water left to run, I feel there is hope for our joined future. The sacred is alive not just in us, but everywhere. Nature can serve as the text of our religion—that which is holy can be seen inscribed in the veins of leaves and in the vessels of our blood, in the fluidity of a diamondback over rock or the ripple of our biceps on the oars. Towering cliffs are our churches and the grandeur of the Canyon our cathedral.

Jesus saves—
Buddha recycles

From one waterfall to the next

Gazing at canyon walls, climbing from one waterfall to the next, swimming in azure pools fed by underground springs, marveling at cactus in bloom growing out of volcanic rock, watching a baby diamondback ssrattle its warning, amazed at frogs an inch in diameter with spider-like legs climbing vertical rock and losing my thoughts in the gleam of twilight on the water, I sense I am a part, a portion, a bit of a coherent whole, rising out of the mothering earth to love, strive, fail, write and die, sinking back, the miracle reborn again and again. The Canyon never loses its inspiration for me.

Although conditioned not to perceive it, we have the capacity to establish a relationship with the earth in all her myriad beauty that is as nourishing as a love affair. Children of concrete, dedicated to possessions, we are wary of bonding in life-sustaining intimacy with wild places, yet that sustenance belongs to us all. It is nothing less than our own lost heritage and its roots reach deep within us.

Old Tom, who died at Crystal Rapid, is an example. He dealt with

238

increasing loneliness and social isolation by turning to the land. As far as I could see, his accumulation of time on rivers, mountain trails, high desert and deep canyons came to mean as much to him as people. He was becoming part of a greater truth and, there, beyond philosophy or religion, found an abiding presence to ease the pain of aging and social disintegration.

Bonding to the land

I have a number of close river friends who live in Idaho, Colorado, Washington and Oregon. Instead of climbing the ladder of financial success, they looked carefully at their lifestyle. It involves skiing, mountain biking, fishing, hunting, camping, horseback riding, river running, mountain climbing, participation in softball, hardball, soccer, ice hockey leagues and having good friends. They are surrounded by magnificent scenery.

One of their boys was two years old when he reeled in his first trout. He thought he had caught a pet. He wanted to take a bath with it, play with it, and sleep with it. Finally, his parents colored a fish on cardboard, cut it out and put it in bed with him for his nap. On his fourth birthday, with his dad's help, he skied the big mountain. To me, their lifestyle is successful regardless of how much money they do or don't make, what possessions they have or don't have. Kids there fish, hunt, play soccer, baseball, football, hockey, ski and snowboard. It's a terrific way for youngsters to grow up,

Our supreme loyalty is to the earth that nourishes and supports all life

especially with clean air to breathe and surrounded by majestic mountains.

To think lifestyle is a definite starting point, not wanting too much, not working for firms who despoil the environment, being active and outdoors rather than spectators and over consumers. Wilderness and wild water challenge the authenticity of our lives. Is there enough that is fully alive in suburban life to develop and realize our potential? Do half-dead classrooms, fast-food chains, day-to-day routine, visiting malls, vicarious electronic excitement augmented by the artificial thrills of Disneyland offer young people enough genuine experience to develop into competent and resourceful adults? Are we sapped by jammed commuter traffic in sprawling cities and the burden of too many possessions? Is there enough adventure in our hurry up lives? The goals we worry and fret about, the tensions we endure to achieve them, the effort to climb the ladder of gold—are those the things that life is all about? As Kenneth Patchen wrote in his magnificent poem, "American Rhapsody:"

> *Or do you feel?*
> *What is one more night in a lifetime of nights?*
> *What is one more death, or friendship, or divorce*
> *out of two, or three? Of four? Or five?*
> *One more face among so many, many faces, one*
> *more life among so many million lives?*
>
> *But first, baby, as you climb and count the stairs*
> *(and they total the same)*
> *did you, sometime or somewhere*
> *have a different idea?*
> *Is this, baby, what you were born to feel, and do, and be?*

Many trails lead to the mountaintop and there are numerous sources of authentic experience. Athletics, skiing, dance, learning and intimacy offer opportunity for self-exploration. The creative life of the mind is as crucial as that of the spirit.

As *one* path of discovery, the land challenges us and forces us to confront ourselves—to feel the fear of an unleashed force like Crystal Rapid at 44,000 cfs. and search for the courage to run it, is to delve into our frailties and potential. It is a precarious but precious chance to learn more about who we are and what we are capable of achieving. Most important, at such moments we are fully alive. Months of city living can blur together, but I remember vividly every trip I've taken into the solitude and majesty of nature. Wild places give us a chance to claim a life we know as our own rather than dwell in vicarious thrills shaped by the imagination and genius of others.

Jochen Hemmleb, a member of the team that discovered the frozen body of George Mallory on Mount Everest, said, "I don't think climbers climb to risk death. I think they climb to prove to themselves that they are not already dead."

This is what the Grand Canyon is to me—a confrontational force that drags me from my culture back to ancient roots and a birthright long denied. It is a return to a home structured long before my existence in human form.

Reverence

Smoke That Roars

Unraveled rivers
running off the backs of mountains,
Mosi-oa-Tunya, Smoke-that-Roars
plunging past pine,
sluiced down side canyons,
calling to our blood;
marrowed sisters,
brothers of blue water
riding the drop
into the rage of Crystal,

body slams of Sockdolager,
Granite's hard rock punches,
guttural growl of Lava Falls.

Drifting in quiet places,
circled in the belly of time,
carried by Paleozoic beaches
where roots womb
into entrails of silence
more profound than scripture.

They eat meals, patch rafts
and settle down for nights
under star-filled configurations
and blue moons.

Beneath a western sun
they ride quicksilver rivers

that bring them face-to-face
with themselves, with things
they may or may not want to see.

Returning home,
they hug husbands or wives,
kids clinging to their legs,
pack and repair gear.

It's good to be back,
to get on with making a living
or beating the system.
But, deep down,
they are restless,
hungry for the next trip.

Downstream sons and daughters
drifting through their own lives
towards the muffled roar
of the next rapid.

Bibliography

Abram, David. _The Spell of the Sensuous_. New York: Vintage Books, 1996.

Ackerman, Diane. _A Natural History of the Senses_. New York: Vintage Books, 1990.

Armstrong, Karen. _A History of God: The 4,000-Year Quest of Judaism, Christianity, and Islam_. New York: Alfred A. Knopf, 1994.

Baars, Donald L. _Red Rock Country: A Geologic History of the Colorado Plateau_. New York: The Natural History Press, 1972.

Babbitt, Charles. "Who Does the Forest Service Work For?" _Sierra Club Canyon Echo_, Vol. 31, (March, 1995), 1.

Balf, Todd. _The Last River: The Tragic Race for Shangri-la_. New York: Crown Publishers, 2000.

Bangs, Richard and Kallen, Christian. _Rivergods: Exploring the World's Great Wild Rivers_. San Francisco: Sierra Club Books, 1985.

Bangs, Richard and Kallen, Christian, Editors. _Paths Less Traveled: Dispatches from the Front Lines of Exploration_. New York: Atheneum, 1988.

Barlett, Donald L. and Steele, James B. "Corporate Welfare: Paying a Price for Polluters," _Time Magazine_, (November 23, 1998), 72-82.

Batchelor, Stephen. _Buddhism Without Beliefs: A Contemporary Guide to Awakening_. New York: Riverhead Books, 1997.

Berman, Morris. _The Twilight of American Culture_. New York: W. W. Norton, 2000.

Bordewich, Fergus M. _Killing the White Man's Indian_. New York: Doubleday, 1996.

Breashears, David. _High Exposure_. New York: Simon & Schuster, 1999.

Brown, Kenneth A. _Four Corners: History, Land, and People of the Desert Southwest_. New York: arperCollinsPublishers, 1995.

Bryce, Robert M. _Cook and Perry: A Controversy Resolved_. Mechanicksburg, Pennsylvania: Stackpole Books, 1997.

Bullard, Robert D., Editor. _Unequal Protection: Environmental Justice & Communities of Color_. San Francisco: Sierra Club Books, 1994.

Byrd, Richard E. _Alone_. Covelo, California: Island Press, 1938.

Cahill, Tim. "A Darkness on the River," _Outside Magazine_ (November, 1995), 85-96, 168-69.

Calvin, William H. _The River that Flows Uphill: A Journey from the Big Bang to the Big Brain_. San Francisco: Sierra Club Books, 1986.

Campbell, Joseph. _The Power of Myth_. New York: Doubleday, 1998.

Chase, Alston. _Playing God in Yellowstone_. San Diego: A Harvest/HBJ Book, 1987.

Childs, Greg. _The Secret Knowledge of Water_. New York: Little, Brown and Company, 2000.

Christianson, Gale E. _Fox at the River's Edge: A Biography of Loren Eiseley_. New York: Henry Holt and Company, 1990.

Colborn, Theo; Dumanoski, Dianne; and Myers, John Peterson. _Our Stolen Future_. New York: Plume of the Penguin Group, 1996.

Crease, Robert P. and Mann, Charles C. _The Second Creation: Makers of the Revolution in 20th-Century Physics_. New York: Macmillan Publishing Company, 1986.

Curran, Jim. _K-2: Triumph and Tradegy_. Boston: Houghton Mifflin Company, 1987.

Dalai Lama, His Holiness, and Cutler, Howard C. _The Art of Happiness: A Handbook for Living_. New York: Riverhead Books, 1998.

_____. _The World of Tibetan Buddhism: An Overview of Its Philosophy and Practice_. Boston: Wisdom Publications, 1995.

Deloria, Vine, Jr. _God is Red: A Native View of Religion_. Golden, Colorado: Fulcrum Publishing, 1994.

Dillard, Annie. _Pilgrim at Tinker Creek_. New York: Quality Paperback Book Club, 1974.

Dimock, Brad, Conley, Cort, and Welch, Vince. _The Doing of the Thing: The Brief Brilliant Whitewater Career of Buzz Holmstrom_. Flagstaff, Arizona: Fretwater Press, 1998.

Epstein, Daniel Mark. _What My Lips Have Kissed: The Loves and Love Poems of Edna St. Vincent Millay_. New York: Henry Holt & Company, 2001.

Farrer-Halls, Gill. _The Illustrated Encyclopedia of Buddhist Wisdom_. Wheaton, Illinois: Theosophical Publishing House, 2000.

Ferris, Timothy. _The Whole Shebang: A State-of-the-Universe Report_. New York: Simon & Schuster, 1997.

Forsyth, Adrian and Miyata, Ken. _Tropical Nature: Life and Death in the Rain Forests of Central and South America_. New York: A Touchstone Book, 1984.

Fortey, Richard. _Life: A Natural History of the First Four Billion Years of Life on Earth_. New York: Alfred A, Knopf, Inc., 1998.

Foster, Steven and Little, Meredith. _The Book of the Vision Quest: Personal Transformation in the Wilderness_. New York: Simon & Schuster, 1992.

Friedman, Thomas L. _The Lexus and the Olive Tree_. New York: Anchor Books, a division of Random House, Inc., 1999.

Gedicks, Al. _The New Resource Wars: Native and Environmental Struggle Against Multinational Corporations_. Boston: South End Press, 1993.

Ghiglieri, Michael P. *Canyon: The Ultimate Book on Whitewater Rafting in Grand Canyon!* Tucson, Arizona: The University of Arizona Press, 1992.

Goldstein, Joseph. *Insight Meditation: The Practice of Freedom.* Boston: Shambhala Dragon Edition, 1994.

Grunfeld, Tom A. *The Making of Modern Tibet.* Armonk, New York: An East Gate Book, 1996.

Harris, David. *The Last Stand: The War Between Wall Street and Main Street Over California's Ancient Redwoods.* New York: Random House, 1995.

Hawken, Paul. "Natural Capitalism," *Mother Jones Magazine,* (March/April 1997), 40-54.

Hoerner, Andrew J. "Life and Taxes: Green Tax Measures Work." *The Amicus Journal,* (Summer, 1995), 14-17.

Gould, Stephen Jay. *Wonderful Life: The Burgess Shale and the Nature of History.* New York: W.W. Norton & Company, 1989.

_____. *Dinosaur in a Haystack: Reflections in Natural History.* New York: Harmony Books, 1995.

Harrer, Heinrich. *Seven Year's in Tibet.* New York: Penguin Putnam Inc., 1953.

Herzog, Maurice. *Anapurna.* New York: The Lyons Press, 1952.

Kaye, Les. *Zen at Work.* New York: Crown Trade Paperbacks, 1996.

Karliner, Joshua. *The Corporate Planet: Ecology and Politics in the Age of Globalization.* San Francisco: Sierra Club Books, 1997.

Krutch, Joseph Wood. *Grand Canyon: Today and All Its Yesterdays.* Tucson: The University of Arizona Press, 1957.

Lamm, Richard and McCarthy, Michael. *The Angry West: A Vulnerable Land and Its Future.* Boston: Houghton Mifflin Company, 1982.

Levi, Jan Heller, Editor. *A Muriel Rukeyser Reader.* New York: W. W. Norton & Company, 1994.

Lopez, Barry. *Arctic Dreams: Imagination and Desire in a Northern Landscape.* New York: Bantam Books, 1986.

Krakauer, Jon. *Into Thin Air.* New York: Villard, 1997.

Margolis, Jon. "Waaaaaaaaaaaaaaaaahhh! The West Refuses to be Weaned," *High Country News,* (February 20, 1995), 16.

Marston, Ed. "Bush Faces a Reborn Interior," *High Country News.* Paonia, Colorado: Vol. 33, No. 1, p. 16, 2001.

Martin, Russell. *A Story that Stands Like a Dam: Glen Canyon and the Struggle for the Soul of the West.* New York: Henry Holt and Company, 1989.

Maxtone-Graham, John. *Safe Return Doubtful: The Heroic Age of Polar Exploration.* New York: Barnes & Noble, 1988.

May, Rollo. *The Cry for Myth.* New York: W. W. Norton & Company, 1991.

Messner, Reinhold. *Free Spirit: A Climber's Life.* London: Hoder & Stoughton, 1989.

MacMahon, James A., Editor. *Deserts.* New York: Alfred A. Knopf, 1985.

Morris, Richard. *Cosmic Questions.* New York: John Wiley & Sons, Inc., 1993.

Nabhan, Gary Paul. *Gathering the Desert.* Tucson: The University of Arizona Press, 1985.

Nash, Madeleine J. "When Life Exploded," *Time Magazine,* (December 4, 1995), 66-74.

Nash, Roderick. *The Big Drops: Ten Legendary Rapids of the American West.* Boulder, Colorado: Johnson Books, 1989.

Nisker, Wes. *Buddha Nature: A Practical Guide to Enlightenment Through Evolution.* New York: Bantam Books, 1998.

Pope, Carl; McKibben, Bill; Hawken, Paul; Ehrlich, Anne; Ejrlich, Paul; Williams, Terry Tempestl Aridjis; and Sweeny, John. "Getting It Right: How to Insure a Better Future? Prepare for Victory Today," *Sierra Club Magazine,* Vol. 85 (January/February 2000), 40-47, 117.

Reisner, Marc. *Cadillac Desert: The American West and its Disappearing Water.* New York: Viking Penguin, Inc., 1986.

Rinpoche, Khenpo Karthar. *Dharma Paths.* Ithaca, New York: Snow Lion Publications, 1992.

Rudner, Ruth. "Sacred Geographies," *Wilderness Magazine,* (Fall, 1994), 12-28.

Richo, David. *Shadow Dance: Liberating the Power & Creativity of Your Dark Side.* Boston: Shambala, 1999.

Rusho, W. L. *Everett Ruess: A Vagabond for Beauty.* Salt Lake City: Peregrine Smith Books, 1983.

Sagan, Carl. *Billions & Billions: Thoughts on Life and Death at the Brink of the Millennium.* New York: Random House, 1997.

Shaw, Anna Moore. *A Pima Past.* Tucson: The University of Arizona Press, 1974.

Shepard, Paul. *Nature and Madness.* San Francisco: Sierra Club Books, 1982.

Short, Vaughn. *Raging River, Lonely Trail.* Tucson: Two Horses Press, 1978.

Silver, Brian L. *The Ascent of Science.* Oxford: Oxford University Press, 1998.

Silverman, Amy and Kiefer, Michael. "An Environment for Business," *Phoenix New Times,* Vol. 26, March 2-8, 1995, 8-15.

Sobel, Dava. *Gailileo's Daughter: A Historical Memoir of Science, Faith, and Love.* New York: Walker & Company, 1999.

Stansell, Christine. *American Moderns: Bohemian New York and the Creation of a New Century.* New York: Metropolitan Books, Henry Holt and Company, 2000.

Snyder, Gary. *Left Out in the Rain: New Poems 1947-1985.* San Francisco: North Point Press, 1986.

_____. *The Practice of the Wild: Essays by Gary Snyder.* San Francisco: North Point Press, 1990.

Stegner, Wallace. *Beyond the Hundredth Meridian: John Wesley Powell and the Second Opening of the West.* Boston: Houghton Mifflin Company, 1953.

Stevens, Larry. *The Colorado River in Grand Canyon: A Guide.* Flagstaff, Arizona: Red Lake Books, 1983.

Tedlock, Dennis and Tedlock, Barbara, Editors. *Teachings from the American Earth.* New York: Liveright Publishing Corporation, 1975.

Thurman, Robert. *Inner Revolution.* New York: Riverhead Books, 1998.

Tuchman, Barbara W. *The Guns of August.* New York: The MacMillan Company, 1962.

Tudge, Colin. *The Time Before History: 5 Million Years of Human Impact.* New York: Simon & Schuster, 1996.

Twitchell, James B. *Lead Us Into TemptationL The Triumph of American Materialism.* New York: Columbia University Press, 1999.

Volk, Tyler. *Metapatters: Across Space, Time and Mind.* New York: Columbia University Press, 1995.

Wagner, Janet S. "Double Exposure." *Nucleus: The Magazine of the Union of Concerned Scientists.* XVII (Winter 1995-96), 1-3, 12.

Ward, Peter D. and Brownlee, Donald. *Rare Earth: Why Complex Life is so Rare in the Universe.* New York: Copernicus: An Imprint of Springer-Verlag, 2000.

Waters, Frank. *Book of the Hopi.* New York: Penguin Books, 1972.

Waters, Ron. *Never Turn Back: The Life of Whitewater Pioneer Walt Blackadar.* Pocatello, Idaho: The Great Rift Press, 1994.

Watson, Peter. *The Modern Mind: An Intellectual History of the 20th Century.* New York: HarperCollinsPublishers, 2001.

Westwood, Richard E. *Rough Water Man: Elwyn Blake's Colorado River Expeditions.* Las Vegas: University of Nevada Press, 1992.

White, Richard. *"It's Your Misfortune and None of My Own": A New History of the American West.* Norman: University of Oklahoma Press, 1991.

Wickwire, Jim and Bullitt, Dorothy. *Addicted to Danger.* New York: Pocket Books of Simon & Schuster Inc., 1998.

Willis, Clint, Editor. *Epic: Stories of Survival from the World's Highest Peaks.* New York: Thunder's Mouth Press, 1997.

_____. *High: Stories of Survival from Everest and K2.* New York: Thunder's Mouth Press, 1999

_____. *Rough Water: Stories of Survival from the Sea.* New York: Thunder's Mouth Press, 1999.

Wilson, Edward O. *The Diversity of Life.* Cambridge, Massachusetts: The Belknap Press of Harvard University, 1992.

_____. *Consilience: The Unity of Knowledge.* New York: Alfred A. Knopf, 1998.

Zwinger, Ann Haymond. *Downcanyon: A Naturalist Explores the Colorado River through the Grand Canyon.* Tucson: The University of Arizona Press, 1995.

Index

246

254

Yuppies, 182

Z

TO ORDER MORE COPIES OF:

Smoke That Roars

AS GIFTS OR
TO SHARE WITH FRIENDS:

Special Offer: Only Two Cents for Shipping and Handling

Copies of *Smoke That Roars* @ $15.98	Plus **two cents** each for shipping and handling	Total Cost $16.00 each
☐	☐	☐

☐ *Payment Enclosed*   ☐ *Bill Me*

Please bill my   ☐ **Visa**   ☐ **Master Card**

*Signature*_____

*Card Number*_____*Expiration Date*_____

*Name*_____

*Address*_____

_____

Mail To: *Atwell Publishing*, 3737 East
Meadowbrook Avenue, Phoenix, AZ, 85018-3532
E-Mail: robertatwell1034@msn.com